CULTURAL CAPITALS

CULTURAL CAPITALS

Early Modern London and Paris

Karen Newman

PRINCETON UNIVERSITY PRESS

PRINCETON AND OXFORD

Copyright © 2007 by Princeton University Press
Published by Princeton University Press, 41 William Street,
Princeton, New Jersey 08540
In the United Kingdom: Princeton University Press, 6 Oxford Street,
Woodstock, Oxfordshire OX20 1TW

Requests for permission to reproduce material from this work
should be sent to Permissions, Princeton University Press.

Second printing, and first paperback printing, 2009
Paperback ISBN: 978-0-691-14110-7

The Library of Congress has cataloged the cloth edition of this book as follows

Newman, Karen, 1949–
Cultural capitals : early modern London and Paris / Karen Newman.
        p.   cm.
Includes bibliographical references (p.) and index.
ISBN-13: 978-0-691-12754-5 (acid-free paper)
ISBN-10: 0-691-12754-9 (acid-free paper)

1. London (England)—Civilization. 2. Paris (France)—Civilization. 3. London
(England)—History. 4. Paris (France)—History. 5. Sociology, Urban—England—London.
6. Sociology, Urban—France—Paris. 7. Spatial behavior—England—London. 8. Spatial
behavior—France—Paris. I. Title.

DA688.N49 2007
942.1'05—dc22   2006017753

British Library Cataloging-in-Publication Data is available

This book has been composed in Adobe Garamond

Printed on acid-free paper. ∞

press.princeton.edu

Printed in the United States of America

3   5   7   9   10   8   6   4   2

For my mother

KAY NEWMAN

1922–2006

CONTENTS

LIST OF FIGURES

ACKNOWLEDGMENTS

Cultural Capitals has accumulated many debts since I began work on it too many years ago. Other books, projects, and responsibilities have intervened during its writing, and therefore those debts have multiplied. Persons, places, and institutions have offered support and sustained this project over several years, and I am pleased to thank them here: the National Endowment for the Humanities, which supported the earliest research for this book through a Fellowship for University Teachers in 1997–98, and which enabled me to work with faculty in summer seminars I have directed over the last decade; the Folger Library, where I have benefited from its great collections and twice had the opportunity to lead seminars and work with colleagues from whom I have learned much; the many libraries and archives in London and Paris, including the Bibliothèque nationale, the Arsenal, the Bibliothèque historique de la ville de Paris, the Archives nationales, the Archives de la Seine, the Musée Carnavalet, the British Library, the Middle Temple Library, and the Guildhall Library, where I have gathered materials, stumbled across unexpected texts and images, or fallen into stimulating conversations that took me in new directions. I am grateful to Brown University for support during the research and writing of this book, and to Richard Foley, Anne and Joel Ehrenkranz Dean of the Faculty of Arts and Science, and to New York University for supporting the leave that enabled me to complete final revisions.

This book draws on work across several disciplines, not only in early modern literature in which I received my own training but also in history, cultural geography, urban studies, art history, and cultural studies. I wish to acknowledge my obligations to work in those several fields and my gratitude to colleagues in many different institutions, periods, and disciplines for their collaboration and invitations to present and discuss my work, especially Margaret Ferguson, Marjorie Garber, Jonathan Goldberg, Laura Gowing, Roland Greene, John Guillory, Vanessa Harding, Sharon Marcus, Christopher Pye, Peter Stallybrass, and audiences at the Humanities Center of the West at the University of California, Davis, at the Humanities Center at Harvard, and at Stanford, Johns Hopkins, the University of London, the University of California, Berkeley, Williams College, the University of Pennsylvania, and at various conferences over the last several years organized by Celeste Schenck, Henry Turner, Carla Mazzio, Douglas Trevor, and others in the United States, France, and England. Thanks are due as well to Hanne Winarsky at Princeton University Press for her interest and commitment to this project, to the Press's anonymous readers for commentary and suggestions, and to my students in several seminars, particularly Denise Davis, Helga Duncan, Kristi Eastin, Christopher Gaggero, Lauren Shohet, and Zachary Sng.

Research for this book has enabled me to spend time in the two cities that are my subject, London and Paris; there I have benefited from the support and generosity of many colleagues and friends. Their knowledge and love of both cities, and their willingness to share their learning in countless ways, from walking city streets and visiting urban landmarks and monuments, to the pleasures of reading and conversation, often over good food and wine, have contributed to this book in ways I cannot begin to detail. My thanks to Bernard and Noëlle Bismuth, Vivian and Roger Cruise, Vanessa Harding, Lynn and Russell Kelley, Templeton Peck, Roland Pichon, Celeste Schenck, Carol Shapiro, and others too numerous to name but no less appreciated.

Many colleagues and friends at Brown have offered support and sustained me in different ways over the years of working on this project, including Susan Bernstein, Michel-André Bossy, Kevin McLaughlin, Pierre Saint-Amand, Lewis Seifert, Arnold and Ann Weinstein, and Brown's former provost, Robert J. Zimmer, whose commitment to research, for administrators as well as faculty, enabled me to take time to finish this book in the midst of my duties as Dean of the Graduate School. For being my interlocutor over many years, once again I thank Tom Brooks and this time as well, our daughter, Frances Brooks.

Finally, I should like to acknowledge my mother, Kay Newman, who instilled in me a love for cities and their cultural life. Long ago she had the courage to send me off to Paris at seventeen to make my way. That year started me on the intellectual trajectory that made me a comparatist and led to this book. It is dedicated to her with love.

CULTURAL CAPITALS

Introduction

Extension is the essential property of the [physical] world,
just as thinking is the essential property of the mental world.
—DESCARTES

Sir William D'Avenant's *The First Dayes Entertainment at Rutland House*, performed in 1656 in London, as its title page precisely records, "at the back of Rutland House at the upper end of Aldersgate Street in Charter House yard," is sometimes said to herald the revival of the regular drama in England. Often mistakenly termed an opera, D'Avenant's strange theatrical presents Diogenes and Aristophanes seated on two gilded rostra or platforms, declaiming against and for public entertainment, but it ends oddly with a debate between "a bourgeois of Paris" and his "opponent of London," each of whom surveys the capital of the other, enumerating urban ills, pointing out shortcomings in urban planning, and ridiculing metropolitan manners.[1]

As a Royalist who spent four years in Paris with Hobbes, Cowley, Waller, and the exiled English court, D'Avenant was ideally positioned to debate the relative merits of London and Paris. His Parisian bourgeois and his London citizen opponent trumpet each city's imperfections and retail widely repeated censure of each capital: London's narrow crooked tunnel-like streets, sooty, smoky skies, and tobacco-loving populace, its avaricious watermen and the notorious Parisian mud or *la boue de Paris,* overnice Parisian manners, food, and dress, and the disorderly conduct of Parisian servingmen and pages. D'Avenant's two citizens survey customs, diet, dress, child rearing, architecture and housing, traffic, even air quality. Inhabitants and visitors to early modern London and Paris alike suffered, complained, and represented verbally and visually urban ills with which we are all too familiar—noise, filth, disease, starvation, immigration and crowding, violence, crime, traffic, the incongruous and unseemly juxtaposition of the very rich with exploited labor power and the very poor. City dwellers and visitors also enjoyed the myriad pleasures of metropolitan life and the cultural capital capital cities afforded: theater and the book trade, shopping and collecting, walking the streets, seeing and being seen.[2]

Urban historians and geographers as well as cultural critics have studied, written and speculated about the extraordinary impact of urbanization on the modern world, described by Kingsley Davis in his famous article, "The

Urbanization of the Human Population."[3] "The large and dense agglomerations comprising the urban populations," Davis observes, "involve a degree of human contact and of social complexity never before known."[4] By all counts, the late sixteenth and seventeenth centuries saw remarkable urbanization in western Europe.[5] Whereas Venice and Antwerp dominated the urban landscape of Europe in the sixteenth century, by the 1590s both were in decline.[6] Both London and Paris grow prodigiously in the period: London may have quadrupled its population between 1550 and 1650, from more than 80,000 to some 400,000 or more; by 1700 its population was well over half a million.[7] Though Paris did not grow at the same rate, and though a smaller proportion of the overall population of France lived in Paris—2.5 percent as compared with about 7 percent in England—Paris was larger earlier, and its population increased despite the wars of religion and later the Fronde, from roughly 250,000 in 1564 to some 500,000 by 1645.[8] Though London and Paris both saw a remarkable demographic explosion during the late sixteenth and seventeenth centuries, England and France saw a slowdown in both economic and demographic growth in this period. Stagnation and recession precipitated what some historians have called a "crisis" that ultimately cleared the way for new concentrations of capital and the settled prosperity of the Enlightenment.[9] Others have criticized the "crisis" argument, claiming instead that the 150 years from 1500 until the mid–seventeenth century saw extraordinary changes: centralization, internationalization, the Reformation, an increase in population, trade and price hikes, social mobility, and cultural skepticism. Such changes produced first boom, then bust, anxiety and disorder that subsequently provoked the political disturbances that swept Europe in the seventeenth century: the English civil war, the Fronde, the Catalan revolt, the Thirty Years' War. These problems and changes, so the argument goes, were not finally resolved; instead governments sought to mitigate their effects, to enforce settlement in various arenas that dissipated anxiety, uncertainty, unrest, and disorder.[10] But for our purposes, "crisis" or not, both boom and bust precipitated flight to the cities. Not since antiquity had urban populations approached the half-million mark with their attendant demands: reliable food supplies, fresh water, schemes for managing traffic, for firefighting, street lighting, and cleaning, and a host of other issues.

Demographic urbanization represents an important material definition of cities, but scholars of urbanization also study the diversity of nonagricultural occupations and what is sometimes called the *urbanization of society*.[11] While medieval towns and the smaller urban settlements of the early modern period were pervaded by the countryside, during the late sixteenth and seventeenth centuries European societies became increasingly urbanized.[12] Scholars of urbanization describe what they term *structural urbanization*, or the concentration not only of populations but also of activities such as the operation of a centralized state, the production and exchange of goods via large-scale markets, the organization and delivery of resources, especially water and services such as trash collection, and coordinated movement through space.[13] Such rapid growth, population concentration, and the development of large-scale, coordinated activities fostered an unprecedented concentration of both financial and cultural capital and promoted distinctive urban behaviors, social geographies, and new forms of sociability in the early modern city.[14] Though Amsterdam, like London and Paris, grew at a rapid rate and became arguably the urban economic capital of Europe, it never achieved cultural dominance.[15] As Simon Schama has shown, though the Dutch resisted the growing military power of France in the seventeenth century, Amsterdam capitulated "to its cultural tone."[16] So while I recognize the economic importance of the early modern Dutch cities of Antwerp in the sixteenth century and subsequently Amsterdam, my focus will be on London and Paris, which became, as my title indicates, cultural capitals. Both extended across overlapping, sometimes disorderly, communities; their inhabitants were drawn from throughout both countries and abroad, and that variety produced complex societies with multiple identities and loyalties; increasingly, the means of production and distribution were concentrated in London and Paris, audiences grew, and contact with various forms of literacy spread literacies. Cultural producers and consumers were drawn to urban centers that proffered the social knowledge that was one of the principal axes of stratification in early modern Europe; at the same time, cities offered more sites for social exchange across those very boundaries.

Despite the extraordinary pace and extent of urbanization in early modern Europe, urban historians once largely ignored the early modern city, often termed "failed," in favor of the medieval town or the nineteenth-century industrial city.[17] Raymond Williams observed almost thirty years ago that the city as a "distinctive order of settlement, implying a whole different way of life," dates from the seventeenth-century predominance of London and Paris,[18] yet cultural historians of the West have persisted in claiming the nineteenth century as the preeminent metropolitan moment. Dickens's London and the Paris of Baudelaire, Haussmann, and Zola have been the primary focus of scholars of the city as both trope and place. The great metropolitan themes—speculation and capital, the commodity, the crowd, the street, and *flânerie*—have been read as historically specific to nineteenth-century urban culture.[19] "Paris, capital of the nineteenth century," in Walter Benjamin's often-cited phrase, has been read as a production in time, an effect of the proverbial march of "modernity." Despite Benjamin's own sustained assault on the "ideology of progress" and his aim, as announced from the earliest entries in the *Passagen-Werke*, "to drive out any trace of 'development' from the image of history," critics and commentators ascribe Paris's metropolitan preeminence to various forms of political, social, and technological revolution, to "advances" in architecture and engineering, in manufacturing and market-ing, brought about by industrialization.[20]

Though I recognize the significance of time as a determining condition of social life as well as the specificities of nineteenth-century urban culture and its symbolic forms, this book challenges such teleological narratives of the city. Instead it focuses on space and place as determining conditions of economic, social, cultural, psychic, and affective life and on the constitutive relations of time and space. Its purpose is not merely to look backward to point out the significance or resonance of particular urban themes, for the stakes of this attention to space and time are not merely thematic: the nineteenth-century city and its arcades and commodity culture are said to entail hegemonic posi-tions of enunciation and thereby to produce a particular mode of "metropoli-tan" or bourgeois subjectivity. Metropolitan subjectivity was theorized by Georg Simmel in his essay "The Metropolis and Mental Life" as a problem of the individual attempting to assert autonomy in the face of metropolitan stimulation and distraction: noise, traffic, a market economy, the crowd.[21] Yet already in early modern Europe, new configurations of time and urban space produced discursive figures of address and modes of subjectivity that have been claimed exclusively for modernity.

Modernity has been variously defined, periodized, and theorized. It has sometimes been understood "simply as the 'new,' the contemporary, marking a separation from the past and offering reimaginings of the future," but such a reductive view fails to address how institutions, spaces, and processes "re-make time and give content to understandings of what is historically new."[22] Social theories of modernity have frequently posited a distinct rupture or break between premodern and modern societies, a "Big Ditch" produced, it is argued, either by changing modes of production and consumption or by a newly instrumentalized rationality traced to the scientific revolutions of the seventeenth century.[23] Bruno Latour has perhaps most forcefully questioned the notion of a great divide between presumed rational modern societies and allegedly irrational premodern ones. What he terms "the Great Divide" is a ruse that hides continuities with the past and generates repression or erasure, ordering and reordering, sorting and dividing, in order to produce "the im-pression of a modernization that goes in step with time."[24]

Rather than argue for an earlier, originary moment at which metropolitan modernity is imagined to begin, *Cultural Capitals* considers how urban space and its local geographies, newly configured in part by demographics, in part by early forms of capital accumulation, and in part by technological transfor-mation—all features of temporal change—produced forms of cultural capital and articulated certain discursive figures, modes of subjectivity, and enuncia-tion usually claimed solely for modernity. The printing press, the expansion of the known world through the so-called voyages of discovery, and of the unknown world through new scientific hypotheses, new artistic and linguistic

modes of representing and interpreting the world, state formation, new bureaucratic forms, changing modes of production and consumption—all
worked to produce different ways of thinking, believing, and acting that we
have come to call *modern*.[25] My argument is not that seventeenth-century
figures, topoi, and subjects are the same, identical with those of the more
recent past, but that productive relations among city, subject, and text often
claimed for the nineteenth century, and more recently the eighteenth century,
are already at work in the verbal and visual cultures of early modern London
and Paris. By shifting the analytic to space *in* time, this book demonstrates
relations and continuities rather than rupture and break; in doing so, it seeks
to debunk the penchant to understand the present as radically cut off from
the past and thus contributes to Latour's critique of the great divide. The
book also exposes the tendency to pastoralize the past that has characterized
work by cultural critics of both modernity and postmodernity.[26]

The modern concept of space as unlimited extension, as in my epigraph
from Descartes, is arguably historically specific to the early modern period in
Europe: no medieval Germanic or Romance language possessed a word for
our modern idea of space.[27] The Latin word *spatium* is first found in French
before passing into other European languages, but until the sixteenth and
seventeenth centuries it designated simply a topographic interval or, as Paul
Zumthor points out, more often a chronological space or gap.[28] The advent
of this new notion of space and the technologies for representing it is linked
in early modern Europe both to the developing nation-state and to colonial
expansion.[29] Social theory, particularly those traditions that derive from Marx,
Weber, and Adam Smith, has often privileged the category of time over that of
space by focusing on processes of social change, modernization, and technical,
social, and political revolutions. As David Harvey describes this process in his
work on postmodernism, which has turned frequently to space as an analytic
category, "progress is the theoretical object [of social theory], and historical
time its primary dimension. . . . progress entails the conquest of space . . . the
annihilation of space through time."[30] In "Questions on Geography," Foucault
speaks as well of "the devaluation of space that has prevailed for generations."
"Space," he observes, "was treated as the dead, the fixed, the undialectical, the
immobile." In his study of seventeenth-century classicism, *The Order of
Things*, Foucault opposes temporal and spatial epistemological strategies to
analyze not the "progress of knowledge" (xxii) through historical time but
what he terms "configurations within the *space* of knowledge." Spatial metaphors abound: within "what space of order" was knowledge constituted? he
writes of bringing to light an "epistemological field" and, in a well-known
distinction, dubs his enterprise "not so much a history" as an "archaeology,"
a disciplinary practice that entails the compression of time in space.[31] Foucault's text is rife with spatial language: *fields, domains, sites, landmarks, foun-*

dations, grounds, propinquities. And not only nouns, but verbal forms of the spatial as well, including *extend, delimit, ground, mark, constitute, configure.*[32]

Foucault himself was profoundly influenced by the philosophy of Henri Lefebvre and the so-called situationists, by Lefebvre's critique of the myriad metaphoric uses of space—we speak and write of the space of ideology, of the nation-state, of literary space, the space of dreams, the topologies of psycho-analysis, of mental space, to name only a few. In *The Production of Space* Lefebvre insists on the materiality of space and the work of space in social reproduction. He criticizes the geographer's traditional descriptive models, whether empirical or marxist, for their failure to express the variety of urban experience: space as experienced, as perceived, and as imagined. Not only Foucault's preoccupation with an epistemological "espace du savoir" but also his analysis of material space, including Bentham's panopticon, his critique of topography and surveillance, and his analysis of various systems of classifi-cation as forms of spatial ordering owe a debt to Lefebvre's work. These analy-ses of and reflections on space have in turn profoundly influenced the theoreti-cal assumptions, substantive preoccupations, and practices of cultural critics in various disciplines, from Fredric Jameson's work on the Bonaventure Hotel and Edward Soja and Mike Davis on Los Angeles, to urban geographers like David Harvey and Saskia Sassen, to postcolonial theorists, anthropologists, ethnographers, and architectural historians.[33]

But urban and cultural geographers have recently begun to criticize the dominant ways in which space has come to be analyzed. In an important essay entitled "Representing Space," John Agnew argues that two models of space have dominated work in both the social sciences and literary and cultural studies: space has been defined, on the one hand, in relation to the nation-state, its territories, boundaries, and imperialist ambitions and extension; and, on the other, in terms of the core-periphery model, what he terms the *struc-tural representation of space* represented by Wallerstein's *Modern World Sys-tem.*[34] Culture, Agnew claims, has become a function of the structural position of a given unit—core or periphery—or, alternatively, the product of a domi-nant scale, a given nation-state: "Modern social science suffers from a sort of 'agnosia' (or disorder of perception) in which representations of space set boundaries for non-spatial processes rather than provide an understanding of space and society as inextricably intertwined" (261). Agnew argues instead for a "changing matrix of practices that actively mediates scale relationships," for attention to place and what he terms the "contextuality of action and prac-tices." In both philosophy and the social sciences, space and time have often been imagined as a priori universals, with place as the particular. Recently cultural geographers have criticized that distinction and argued that both space and time can only be perceived phenomenologically, as historically expe-rienced and constituted patterns.[35] Space is "culturalized" through the projection or "reproduction of determinate social actions and structures" that transform space into place.[36]

Traditional models of urban space emanating from the Chicago school have recently given way to visions of the postindustrial, postmodern metropolis, a polarized city in which all the enticements of city culture are juxtaposed to urban enclaves of poverty and misery. Revitalized city centers of office towers and high-end shopping malls are surrounded by fragmented neighborhoods and "edge" cities.[37] These changes have affected the way cities are managed and are producing a new urban politics characterized less by the local provision of services and welfare than by what is sometimes termed *entrepreneurialism*.[38] The entrepreneurial city has as "its centerpiece the notion of public-private partnership" and a revival of "traditional local boosterism."[39] These changes and developments in urban spatiality, governance, and self-promotion are useful and provocative for thinking about the early modern city, as we shall see.

This book seeks to show how London and Paris become the overdetermined cultural capitals they became by the eighteenth century and, to some degree, remain today. What material and social actions and structures, from bridge building to theater, to reading and print culture, to the commemoration of and perception of death, produced and registered that transformation? How were London and Paris constituted through images and representations? How did antiquarians and travel writers engage in what today is termed "place marketing"? How did inhabitants, both high and low, and travelers to these two cities perceive urban space and not only represent it, but constitute the new metropolis?

In what follows I will be looking in some detail at the interaction of temporal change with space, place, and cultural production. My inquiry begins in the late sixteenth century, when antiquarians, writers, engravers, and the like first responded to the population explosion in London and Paris; it ends in the 1660s, when London suffered both the plague and the Great Fire, and in Paris with the initial construction of Versailles in 1668 following Louis XIV's determination, in the aftermath of the Fronde, to move political power out of Paris, away from the disorder of the urban street. The aim is not "coverage" or the encyclopedic, which would be impossible in any case; instead, my approach recognizes that what we seek in the past is always an object that cannot be found, that grand narratives and causes are provisional and partial.[40] Yet by reading a range of cultural texts—both texts specific to a given culture, and cultural formations read as texts—I seek to demonstrate what has been termed their "cultural exemplarity."[41] If what we term *modernity* is to be found in the early modern city and its cultural remains, perhaps, as I have suggested earlier, how *modernity* is conceptualized needs to be rethought. The readings that follow offer arguments and raise questions that should provoke readers to further reflection and intellectual work.

Introductions conventionally include a rundown of chapters in which their contents are presented in outline form, an aid to the reader who seeks to know what is to come, particularly when book and chapter titles have become increasingly elliptical and often indicate less and less of what is in store. Before laying out what the reader can expect in the chapters to follow, let me offer some further indications of this book's theoretical questions and assumptions. Like my earlier books *Fashioning Femininity and English Renaissance Drama* and *Fetal Positions: Individualism, Science, Visuality, Cultural Capitals* is concerned with the uneasy relations between history and cultural production; with the status of the archive in literary studies; with the constitution and practice of cultural studies and its objects of study; and with the marginalization of the early modern or "old stuff." These broader, theoretical issues are addressed via readings of early modern visual and verbal texts: the work of the French neoclassical poet and essayist Nicolas Boileau; of the English doctor, essayist, and prose stylist, Sir Thomas Browne; of the French playwright Corneille; of Descartes, Donne, Thomas Nashe, and Isabella Whitney; of the French engravers Abraham Bosse, Adam Pérelle, and Israël Sylvestre; the bourgeois romance writer Madeleine de Scudéry and the urban parodist of the romance, Antoine Furetière; the plays of Dekker, Middleton, Shakespeare, and Jonson; the writings of the antiquarian and topographer John Stow and other French and English writers of antiquities and guidebooks; visual representations of the criers of both London and Paris; and anonymous popular pamphlets, ballads, and street poetry from both sides of the Channel.

Chapter 1 considers the new generic forms invented and developed to help inhabitants and visitors navigate the burgeoning cities of Europe and to aid merchants in their commercial travels. It begins in 1665, at the very end of the period this study considers, with the Italian sculptor Bernini's visit to Paris at Louis XIV's behest and considers the topographic surveys, guidebooks, and pamphlets written about Paris and London in the sixteenth and seventeenth centuries. The account of Bernini's sojourn illustrates the movement of cultural capital in early modern Europe as well as epitomizing two important topoi that characterize the early modern city: the prospect and the promenade. The *Journal du voyage en France du Cavalier Bernin*, written by a Frenchman about an Italian, exemplifies one series of displacements that mediate the notion of travel and the eyewitness account that comes into prominence in the course of the century. But the prospect and the promenade are topoi that characterize the relation of the elite to the urban environment. This chapter also considers those who walk the city's streets through the cheap print, particularly ballads, that traced their steps. Chapter 2 argues for what I call in this study the *topographic imaginary* by considering one of the most prominent images of modernity in early modern Paris, the Pont Neuf. The chapter shows how the changes wrought by urbanization come to be represented in both verbal and visual materials that illustrate what is now the oldest bridge in Paris.

It demonstrates the importance of the bridge itself as a place of dissemination and of the mix of persons that increasingly characterized urban life in the early modern period; the chapter ends with a comparison of the Pont Neuf to London Bridge and a brief consideration of *topophobia* and the Jack Cade episode in Shakespeare's *2 Henry VI*. Chapter 3 is about movement through city space, about walking London, Donne's first satire, and Isabella Whitney's "Wyll and Testament." This chapter ends by considering the impact of new forms of traffic, particularly the coach, on urban subjects. Chapter 4 considers sense and the city, the new sensory dangers presented in metropolitan streets, from the fabled *boue de Paris* to urban noise pollution, by looking at Antoine Furetière's *Le roman bourgeois* and Jonson's *Epicoene, or the Silent Woman*. Chapter 5 is about urban commercial places and practices and their representation in the rarely read French city comedies of Corneille that present such a marked contrast to the more widely read and studied English city comedy. Chapter 6 considers metropolitan reading; it focuses on the seventeenth-century romance and the unequal relation of women to culturally valued, educational travel by reading the work of the bourgeois *salonnière* Madeleine de Scudéry. Chapter 7 is about numeracy and the dead; it considers the relation of death and the memorial, at once an account book and a form of commemoration of the dead, in the early modern city. Chapter 8 considers prostitution and crime in early modern London, and briefly in Paris, and the representation of such urban underworld activities for the pleasure and delectation of an educated, urban elite. I allude only briefly to the cony-catching pamphlets and rogue literature about which so much has recently been written, but look instead at prostitution and Thomas Nashe's *Choise of Valentines*. The chapter and the book end with a consideration of history and the archive's relation to literary and cultural criticism and interpretation. As my title *Cultural Capitals* indicates, and as is appropriate to my literary training, my focus is on cultural and literary texts, not urban or social history. Finally, I do not attempt to give equal time and attention in each chapter to both cities and their texts, a procedure that would produce stilted, artificial comparisons. Instead I have chosen those texts and documents that best represent or invoke a particular feature or problem in early modern London or Paris.

Though sections of some of the chapters to follow have appeared in journals and collections over the last several years, those essays are substantively changed—augmented, placed in a comparative context (my essay on Boileau and the Pont Neuf, for example, now juxtaposes his Satire VI with popular French street poetry about Paris and considers London Bridge, *2 Henry VI*, and the topographic imaginary across the channel; chapter 6, which when it appeared in *Renaissance Drama* considered only Corneille's *La galerie du palais*, now considers as well his *Le menteur* and draws comparisons with *The Roaring Girl*.) *Cultural Capitals: Early Modern London and Paris* is a sustained attempt at the practice of comparative literature in the face of disciplinary conventions in early modern studies that have tended increasingly to encourage work limited by the nation-state and that have moved away from the comparative practice of Renaissance studies.[42] It therefore posits a reader with what have become increasingly devalued forms of cultural capital—knowledge of western languages, and particularly French, and with interests in formal as well as historical questions. For those readers whose training has deprived them of the rich cultural traditions represented by the Romance languages and Latin, translations are provided for those texts not in English.

CHAPTER ONE

Early Modern London and Paris

On April 29, 1665, the architect and sculptor Bernini left Rome for Paris, where he spent several months at the invitation of Louis XIV.[1] Summoned to complete the Palais du Louvre, Bernini was escorted throughout his stay by Paul Fréart, Seigneur de Chantelou, the younger son of a minor French nobleman. An admirer of Italian art and a speaker of the language who had known Bernini during a sojourn in Rome, Chantelou was appointed Bernini's cicerone by the king and wrote an account of the artist's visit to France, supposedly at the request of his elder brother, as this dedicatory note recounts:

> Le désir que vous avez eu d'être instruit de tout ce qui regarde M. le Cavalier Bernin, que le roi a appelé de Rome en France pour le bâtiment du Louvre, a fait que j'ai taché de me souvenir de ce qui s'est passé aux premiers jours de son arrivée, que je ne pensais pas encore à noter ces sortes de particularités, comme j'ai fait depuis. J'en ai donc dressé, suivant votre avis, une espèce de journal que vous recevrez avec cette lettre.

> Knowing how much you wish to learn everything about the Cavalier Bernini, who was summoned by the King to France from Rome to design the new palace of the Louvre, I have tried to remember what happened during the first days of his visit, before I thought of noting down the events of his daily life. On your advice I have arranged it as a sort of journal, which I am sending with this letter.[2]

Chantelou's text presents a double displacement. As its title indicates, it purports to be a journal of Bernini's visit to Paris, but it is written not by Bernini himself but by his royally appointed guide and courier; next, Chantelou himself claims his account was *dressé*—advanced, set right, built, erected, made, fashioned—to please his elder brother's desire to know. Yet the excess of detail in setting forth the circumstances of Bernini's visit ("le roi a appelé de Rome . . .") makes plain that the elder Chantelou's announced desire is itself a pretext, a self-protective aristocratic disclaimer to mitigate the scandal of writing.[3] The *Journal*, heretofore read primarily by art historians interested in Bernini and his bust of Louis XIV, in architectural style, in patronage and clientage systems, and in seventeenth-century aesthetic debates, also demonstrates the movement and fortunes of cultural capital across early modern Europe and provides a snapshot of the cultural life of a seventeenth-century urban elite.

Chantelou's *Journal* in fact exemplifies what I will argue are three topoi of the urban. Two are urban spatial practices that I suggest are heuristically powerful for reading the literature and culture of seventeenth-century Paris and London: the prospect or survey and the promenade; the third is a cultural practice linked to urban exchange and sociability, collecting: the practice of acquiring, displaying, and visiting the great collections being amassed in Europe and particularly, in this case, London and Paris, in the course of the seventeenth century.

Some two months after the artist's arrival in Paris, Chantelou describes a dinner he and Bernini attend in the suburb of Meudon, a village near Saint-Cloud. Meudon's situation presented the visitor with a view of Paris and was a popular place of resort from which to survey the city. Chantelou recounts Bernini's response at the view of Paris presented from Meudon: the artist complains that he could see only a mass of chimneys that made the Parisian skyline resemble a carding comb ("un amas de chéminées [et que cela paraissait comme un peigne à carder]" [102]). He proceeds to compare Paris and its crowded urban prospect with Rome, whose monuments—Saint Peter's, the Coliseum, the palaces of Saint Mark, Farnese, and the Colonna, the Campidoglio—present a magnificent aspect. Chantelou counters that Paris's buildings and monuments, though as beautiful, are pressed one against the other and therefore obscured from view.[4]

This deceptively simple anecdote epitomizes the representational history of the city in the early modern period. Skylines, as architectural historians point out, are urban signatures that trace a distinctive urban identity.[5] Urban landmarks symbolize the collective life of a city, its religious and governmental hierarchies, civic priorities, and technological progress.[6] Until the early modern period, depictions of cities in the West were conventional, even formulaic, often based on the scriptural model of the heavenly Jerusalem. Early images of Jerusalem, for example, often depicted an out-of-scale Dome of the Rock, Florence was represented with a highlighted Santa Maria del Fiore, and medieval Parisian city scenes show Notre Dame looming extravagantly large. During the Renaissance, representations of cities were similarly contrived, but to conform instead to the increasingly secular expectations and military aspirations of a patron or prince or to the mercantile interests of travelers and merchants.[7]

As early as the *Nuremberg Chronicle* we find illustrations of cities, but in the early modern period the most famous collection of city images is Braun and Hogenberg's monumental folio, *Civitates orbis terrarum*, published in five volumes between 1572 and 1618 and produced both for travelers and for those wishing to travel "at home" (figs. 1 and 2).[8] It allowed its owner to view the various cities of Europe from several perspectives: the stereographic—from the ground or from not far above, but at some distance; the aerial—from above; and a combination of the two—maps with elevations. Such perspec-

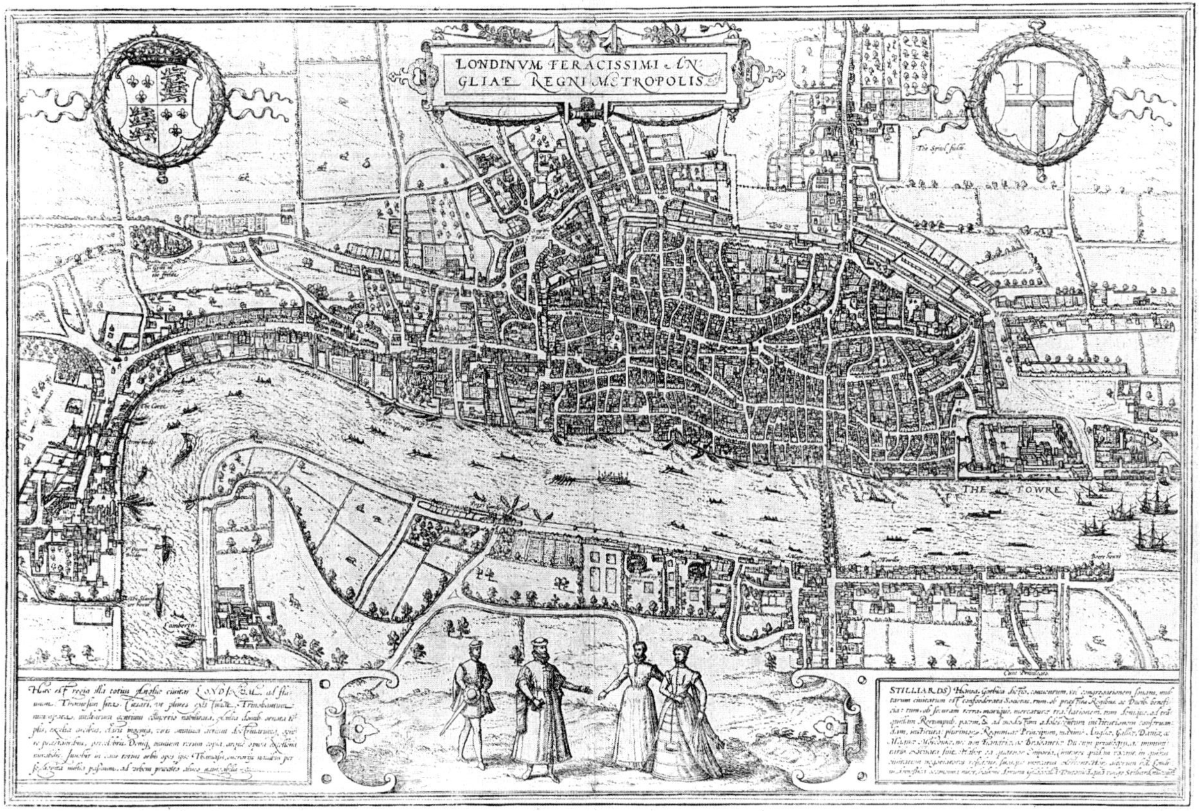

Figure 1. London, 1572, Georg Braun. Folger Library

Figure 2. Paris, 1572, Georg Braun. Bibliothèque nationale

tives helped to produce a totalizing eye/I, a unitary subjectivity organized around a fictive knowledge based on scopic mastery that fosters what Michel de Certeau has called an "erotics of knowledge."[9] Many visual and verbal early modern cityscapes represent their objects from the perspective of a "voyeur-god," from impossible, bird's-eye heights. The affective power and pleasure of such perspectives were already recognized in the seventeenth century. Here is Burton in *The Anatomy of Melancholy.* "A good prospect alone will ease melancholy. . . . What greater pleasure can there now be than to view those elaborate Maps of Ortelius, Mercator, Hondius, &c. To peruse those books of Cities put out by Braunus and Hogenbergius?"[10] Though Burton initially claims that "a good prospect *alone*" will ease melancholy, he goes on to extend that power to the viewing and perusing of maps and urban topographies, that is, to reading. His "now" insists on the novelty of these newly developing technologies and extends the mastery of space they enable from prince and palace to the humanist in his library perusing maps and "books of Cities."

On one hand, Bernini's boast about the prospect of Rome and its skyline emphasizes its social and civic order by foregrounding its public buildings and institutions, its glorious Roman past, and its contemporary artistic achievement. On the other hand, his description of Paris's mass of chimneys like a carding comb implies disorder, helter-skelter growth, and the city's teeming urban populace and its daily work that are mostly missing from Chantelou's account and ordinarily suppressed in the idealizing depictions of the conventional cityscape below the threshold at which visibility begins.[11] Bernini's comparison of Parisian roofs and chimneys to a carding comb also works to pastoralize Paris and undermine its status as a city and cultural center by linking it to the countryside and its homely occupations. Ironically, the very possibility of distinguishing Rome's monuments and palaces marks its difference from Paris—in Bernini's day, Rome was a small city, its palaces and monuments set off by fields and undeveloped green space.[12]

The entry ends with the two men's return to Paris and Bernini's demand that Chantelou and his brother find the artist "quelqu'un intelligent en lunettes," someone skilled in the grinding of lenses. In a parable that continues the comparison of Paris and Rome begun earlier in the evening, Bernini explains that a certain Stefano in Rome had presented him with eyeglasses so well ground they enabled the artist "voir les objets justes et sans alterations, ce qui n'est pas nécessaire pour ceux qui ne demandent des lunettes que pour lire" (to see objects precisely and without distortion, which isn't required by those who need glasses merely for reading [103]). In this fable on the artist's eye, the new technology of lens grinding is appropriated on behalf of the artist's privileged vision. "Lunettes bien taillés" enable him not merely to read, but to see, and what he sees are cities—a spacious, ordered Rome, a crowded, commonplace Paris. But, significantly, that privileged artist's sight is mediated by the narrator Chantelou. Writing disallows presence and the privilege accorded the gaze of the eyewitness. We see not what Bernini's eye/I sees but what Chantelou says he sees. In that displacement is recorded all the complexities of Bernini's position as a foreigner and an artist of the baroque in a culture committed to an increasingly classicizing aesthetic. The seamless constitution of subjectivity around the gaze is disrupted. However exceptional the artist Bernini and his aristocratic handler, Chantelou, the displacements enacted in Chantelou's memorial account of Bernini's visit to Paris, putatively produced for his brother, stage the constitution of a metropolitan subjectivity that pretends to the presence of the gaze and yet is only an effect of writing. In that sense, this book is also concerned with the spatialization of the written word—with maps, prospects, engravings, graphs, paintings, books and pamphlets, epigraphs, typography—in short, with myriad forms of notation.[13]

Chantelou's *Journal* also instances another significant urban spatial practice, the "promenade." Traversing urban space—the streets and gardens, quais and squares, public buildings, fairs, markets, and exchanges of the city—was perhaps the chief pastime of the early modern city dweller regardless of social rank.[14] Organizing urban space to allow for such movement was a significant obligation of the early modern monarch; some of those spaces were open only to the court, some to the elite, still others to *honnêtes gens*, and a few to a broader public.[15] Pedestrian movement and, increasingly in the course of the seventeenth century, vehicular movement shaped urban space to form "systems whose existence in fact makes up the city."[16] The "promenade" is an elite spatial acting out of place that denoted moving to and fro, without a necessary goal or end point, and which begins to be used in the late sixteenth century. Within Chantelou's text, the promenade is a space of enunciation witnessed by the myriad verbs of motion that record the comings and goings of the narrator as he squires his celebrated guest around the city and its environs: *aller, promener, mener, arriver, revenir, retourner, repartir, ramener.* Bernini and his French host pass to and fro, seeing and being seen, sometimes in the coach of the king, through urban spaces. They visit palace and cathedral, *hôtel* and chapel, riding academy and theater, and the grand urban gardens of Paris, often called "promenades," acting out their status. In the course of their daily outings, promenades, and visits, Chantelou takes Bernini to see the collections of the Parisian elite—books, engravings, painting, sculpture, tapestry—and Bernini offers his judgments. There are allusions to the practice of extemporaneous poetic composition, to the technical and aesthetic aspects of theater, to clothing and music, to riding academies and gardens, in short, to the pastimes of an urban elite. Bernini and Chantelou skip over other spaces and practices outside the aristocratic loop, places to which the text alludes only in Bernini's cavalier demand that numerous houses and shops obstructing his grand, never-initiated design for the Louvre be demolished.[17]

Walking the City

If the promenade was a chief pastime of the early modern urban elite, walking was that of the middling sort and the poor.[18] The people of Paris who inhabited the houses and shops Bernini planned to demolish, though excluded from prospect and promenade, experienced the city through walking its streets. In his well-known essay "Walking the City," Michel de Certeau contrasts the view from the top with the everyday practices of city dwellers "down below" who, in traversing the city on foot, produce their own itineraries and maps. They walk, de Certeau says, and thus escape the "imaginary totalizations produced by the eye" from above, in paths and networks "foreign to the 'geometrical' or 'geographical' space of visual, panoptic, or theoretical constructions."[19] The middling sort and the poor experienced the city not from the perspective of de Certeau's voyeur-god or, like Bernini and Chantelou, comfortably ensconced in a coach, but on the ground, often plying—and crying—their trades. The streets of both Paris and London were filled with criers and hawkers, tradesmen, servants, apprentices, thieves, vagabonds, masterless men and women, and the teeming multitudes of immigrants that enabled extraordinary demographic growth despite crime, disease, and infant and child mortality.[20] This mix of persons walked below the prospect city, through what de Certeau terms "an urban 'text' they write without being able to read it" (93), producing "spatial stories" made up of intersecting networks, "fragments of trajectories," altered spaces, paths that intertwine.

Yet there is evidence that those below did sometimes "read" the texts they wrote in moving through the city, and such "spatial stories" were produced and recorded in a variety of literary and visual forms.[21] Street ballads and broadsides in England, *feuilles volantes* in France, pamphlets and chapbooks, almanacs, news-sheets, city comedies, and a host of other texts record the changes brought about by urbanization and the mobile practices that characterize the bustling city from quite a different perspective from either prospect or promenade. Sung and peddled in the streets by colporteurs, sold out of shops and stalls, affixed to alehouse walls, or performed in the public theaters, alehouses, and other venues, they record everyday urban life as it moves through and around the city, past city landmarks, through commercial districts and activities, intersecting with all manner of persons, encountering neighbors, suffering accidents, experiencing or committing crimes.[22] These texts both represent urban life and/or were popular with urban and provincial readers and audiences across social divisions.[23] They tell the stories of upwardly mobile apprentices and servants like Dick Whittington, the gastronomic and sententious escapades of Gros Guillaume, and the Parisian encounters of the charlatan Tabarin. They tour London taverns and the various degrees of persons and trades that frequent them, offer advice to London dames to "kepe virtue in store," or thank the city fathers for constructing a new fountain. News-sheets offer intelligence of the Thirty Years' War, *mazarinades* satirize Cardinal Mazarin and his party throughout the Fronde years, and various groups, including women and apprentices, petition parliament in print during the English Civil War. Ballads lament cruel love, floods, strange births, executions, murders, papists, and foreigners; pamphlets present religious controversies, record the escapades of cony-catchers, and recount fantasies of the underworld as a society turned upside down; they provide guides to London and Paris for the unsuspecting provincial and dramatize the exploits of rogues and shape changers like Moll Frith. Some are set in London or Paris and record each city's places and activities; others are popular reading or hearing for both elite and nonelite readers and audiences.[24] The most popular ballads and chapbooks seem to have been printed over and over again, though the size of editions is unknown. We need to be skeptical about what kind of access to the middling sort and the poor such materials provide, since they may well offer largely "forms of downward mediation by educational or literate elites."[25] Nevertheless, we should also bear in mind, as a privileged contemporary opined, "More solid Things do not show the complexion of the Times so well as Ballads and Libells."[26]

It is estimated that some 3,750 immigrants were needed annually to fuel the extraordinary demographic growth of London in the later sixteenth and seventeenth centuries. Paris similarly depended on an influx of immigrants to regain and sustain its growth following the precipitous decline in its population during the wars of religion.[27] Immigrants were attracted to both cities by their perceived opportunities for employment and by what in the English context is sometimes termed "'betterment' migration as children from middling provincial backgrounds sought their fortunes in the expanding commercial and manufacturing opportunities of the metropolis."[28] Street literature frequently recounted the fortunes of such immigrants in their move to the city and their struggle to succeed. Conversely, these texts played an important role in promoting and idealizing commercial success and a "mercantile cultural ideal."[29] In England, perhaps no story of this kind was more popular than that of Dick Whittington, whose rise from servant to Lord Mayor of London admirably represents the genre. Though the historical Dick Whittington lived in the late fourteenth and early fifteenth centuries, the popularity of his story dates from the period of London's extraordinary demographic growth under consideration here.[30] A lost play, *The History of Richard Whittington, of his lowe byrth [and] his great Fortune*, "as plaied by princes servants," was entered in the Stationer's Register in 1605; five months later a popular ballad about him was registered; the earliest surviving text is Richard Johnson's "Song of Sir *Richard Whittington* who by strange fortune, came to bee thrice Lord Maior of London, with his bountifull guifts and liberallity given to this honorable Citty," published in a collection of songs and ballads in 1612. Whittington's story was retold in countless genres throughout the seventeenth and succeeding centuries. In the nineteenth century his life was the source for pantomime and a popular subject for children's stories, plays, and the like. His legend is presented as part of the City's history at the Museum of London and as a source of city walks for tourists even today. Though there are many versions of Whittington's legendary life, its outlines are the same. As a young boy, Whittington walks to London from Gloucestershire to seek his fortune. Taken in by a wealthy merchant, Whittington works hard and is well treated by his master but suffers at the hands of an "imperious Cook-maid" who treats him so badly that he determines to run away. As he makes his way out of London, he hears "the bells of Bow-Church in Cheap-side," which seemed to be saying to him:

Turn again Whittington
Thrice Lord Mayor of London
Turn again Whittington
Thrice Lord Mayor of London.[31]

The message makes such an impression on him that he determines to return to service and bear patiently the cook's ill-treatment. When his master sets sail to the Indies, he offers to let his servants send any goods they might have to trade. Whittington has nothing to trade but his cat. When the ship lands on a wealthy island overrun with rats, Dick's cat saves the day, he becomes a wealthy wool exporter and marries his master's daughter, and the prophecy of his becoming thrice Lord Mayor is fulfilled.[32] At his death, now Sir Richard Whittington, he makes a number of charitable bequests that better the lives of Londoners, including the rebuilding of Newgate.

Though in fact many aspects of Dick Whittington's story do not correspond to what we know about gaining the freedom of London (apprenticeship, not capital, patronage, or marriage to a wealthy Londoner's daughter, seems to have provided such access), it did, however, epitomize fantasies of possibility for sixteenth-century urban readers and audiences. Whittington's story is one of "'betterment' migration" that undoubtedly appealed to persons of the lower and middling sort who saw opportunity in London. In some versions of the tale, before striking out for London, Dick hears that the streets of the city are paved with gold. His story of upward mobility has it all: an impoverished youth, a benevolent master, a cruel superior, prophecy, a ship to the exotic Indies, extraordinary wealth and commercial success, marriage to the boss's daughter, a title, high public office and power, and good works and philanthropy. And Whittington's success is made possible by the city itself: the bells of Bow Church in London's major market area, Cheapside, ring to solicit him back to London. The title page of Pepys's chapbook version shows four episodes from Whittington's story (fig. 3): a small panel showing his presentation of his cat to his master, with a table filled with plate and goods presumably proffered by other servants in the household; a small panel showing the ship itself at sea; a third showing him alone with only his cat that dramatizes Whittington's poverty; and finally, to the right, a large panel showing the Lord Mayor's pageant with Whittington now on horseback riding through the streets to popular acclaim, with fireworks exploding and well-wishers throwing their hats in the air.[33] It adumbrates the civic ideology of the Lord Mayor's shows in which the city was allegorized and its history rehearsed.[34] Yet like Dekker's *Shoemaker's Holiday*, in which Simon Eyre's fortune is built not on his craft, shoemaking, but by trade in foreign commodities, so Whittington's success is based on a similar contradiction. His success comes about not through his hard work and loyalty but by fabulous wealth built on "the labor of unseen workmen in foreign lands" that provides the capital with which Whittington builds his fortune as a wool merchant, a fortune so vast he lends money to kings.[35]

Whittington's legend presents a view from the streets of the city, from everyday commerce to civic ceremony and ritual, a view of possibility and triumph that appealed to generations of Londoners and aspiring citizens seeking to make their fortunes there. But many migrants to the city were not so fortunate. There are also countless tales of young men and women driven out of the city by poverty and circumstance, of others led into crime and prostitution in the city's streets, prodigal tales that produced a literature of warning and titillation in the cony-catching pamphlets that retail the city's dangers and cons. A few texts eschew the sensational to recount stories of grinding work, unfair dismissal, seduction, and betrayal.[36] The city and its exploding growth generated pamphlets, broadsides, and books for various audiences both high and low seeking to negotiate the city, a literature in which London itself becomes both subject and commodity.

Surveys and Guidebooks

Inhabitants of early modern London and Paris recognized the profound changes wrought by urbanization and produced, as I have argued, a host of new representational forms to explore them. In the wake of those changes, London and Paris came to be perceived as terra incognita, unknown land to which it was inconceivable for the foreigner, the visitor, or the immigrant from the country to go unaided by guidebook or atlas. Although there are medieval texts recounting the origins and history of cities such as William Fitz Stephen's *Libellum de situ et nobilitate Londini*, the late sixteenth and early seventeenth centuries saw the proliferation of a new mode of writing to record urban topography that can appropriately be called, following the English antiquarian and topographer John Stow, the survey.[37] Stow's great *Survey of Lon-*

The Excellent and Renowned

HISTORY

Of the Famous

Sir *Richard Whittington*,

Three times Lord-Mayor of the Honoura-
ble City of *LONDON.*

*Giving an Account of all the Remarkable and noted
Paſſages of his Life.*

This may be Printed, *R. P.*

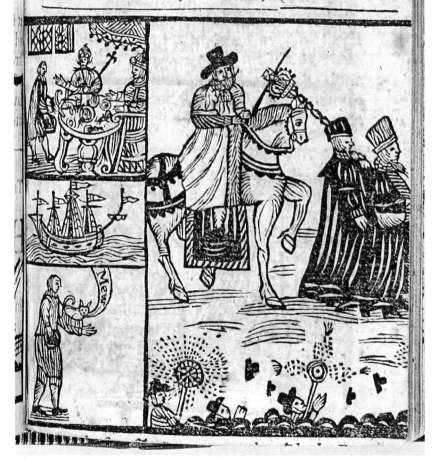

Figure 3. Title page, *The Excellent and Renowned History of the Famous Sir Richard Whittington.* Magdalene College, Cambridge

Figure 4. Visscher's long view of London, ca. 1625. Folger Library

don, first published at the fin de siècle in 1598 and then again in 1603, witnesses the sixteenth-century consolidation of the nation-state through the development and practice of topography.[38] As much recent work in cartography, cultural geography, and cultural studies has demonstrated, the topographic survey is not only a form of geographic description but also a language of power, even of domination.[39] Topographic or chorographic description allowed for the visual and conceptual possession of the physical kingdom just as the work of Sidney, Spenser, and Shakespeare has been said to take possession of the "kingdom" of the English language.[40] *Topography* is defined as "the science or practice of describing a particular place, city, town, manor, parish, or tract of land." Topography is a system of description that rationalizes property relations, that treats the use and organization of space, land, and the built environment as unquestioned facts rather than conventions or the products of ideology or power relations.[41] The omnipresent figure of geographic or topographic discourse is the list, catalog, or inventory that enables both writer and reader to reduce "the abundant, disparate and changing facts of urban life to telling and economical schemes."[42] Such representations of space allow material processes to be not only talked about and understood but also comprehended and mastered. The etymology of *topography* suggests its role in defining norms, since *topo* comes from the Greek τόπος, which means both place and commonplace, that is, both a particular portion of space of definite or indefinite extent and that which is generally understood or commonly agreed upon. *Survey* is defined as "the act of looking at something as a whole, or from a commanding position," as in Visscher's long view (fig. 4), and readers of early modern maps have often remarked on the inscription of observers on maps, surveys, and prospects who are represented from a commanding position with the city below. As can be seen in figure 1, these are not common observers but members of the elite apparently at their leisure whose

EMPORIUMQUE TOTO ORBE CELEBERRIMUM

status is marked by both their clothing and their attitudes.[43] In surveying a particular place or city through a map or prospect, the viewer shares that proprietary position. Not only visual representations but also guidebooks and verbal descriptions allowed for the conceptual possession of urban space.

John Stow is perhaps the best known of the early modern English topographers, and his *Survay* the most widely read example, but there were many other English practitioners and topographies. Saxton's county maps, William Camden's *Britannia* (1586), Norden's *Speculum Britanniae* (1593), and Speed's aptly named *Theatre of the Empire of Great Britain* (1611) all produce "England" and map an expanding Britain as it encompasses and dominates Wales, Ireland, and Scotland. Though only Stow devotes his entire text to London, early modern topographers and antiquarians recognized and marked the city's status as metropolis. Already in the sixteenth century, the anonymous *A Breefe Discourse* (1584) declares London a metropolis and notes its role as the emporium of England.[44] Camden calls it "the Epitome and Breviary of Britain"; Norden begins with the county of "Myddlesex" that is "graced with that chiefe and head Citie LONDON"; in 1611, Speed dubs London "the mart of the world," a trope that is repeated throughout the seventeenth and eighteenth centuries. "Thither," he boasts, "are brought the silk of Asia, the spices from Africa, the balms from Grecia, and the riches of both the Indies East and West";[45] by 1676, Speed's editor dedicates his *Theatre of the Empire* not to the king, as in the 1611 edition, but to the city of London itself. In 1615, Anthony Munday, one of Stow's continuators, personifies the city as "the ancient mother of the whole land," an oft-repeated trope (fig. 5).[46] London was the seat of government, of trade, and of capital. As H. J. Dyos observes, there converged all the nation's major institutions: the Crown, Parliament, government, law, commerce, industry, finance, fashion.[47] Its phenomenal growth was so pronounced that James I famously complained, "With time, England will only be London, and the whole country be laide waste."[48]

Figure 5. London and Westminster personified.
Michael Drayton's *Poly-Olbion*, 1622. Huntington Library

In 1657, the traveler James Howell published his *Londinopolis; an Historicall Discourse or Perlustration of the City of London, The Imperial Chamber, and Chief Emporium of Great Britain whereunto is added another of the City of Westminster, with the Courts of Justice, Antiquities, and new Buildings thereunto belonging.* Even its title threatens urban encroachment; in fact, much of Howell's text is borrowed from Stow.[49] Howell's book is dedicated to the city itself, recounts its history and monuments (it begins with a dedicatory poem to London Bridge in Latin and in English), and quotes Tacitus on London's reputation as a "Mart for multitude of Merchants and Commerce." If the city deserved its reputation for commerce then, asks Howell rhetorically, what must it be now?

Stow's book is curious; it straddles the generic space of social history, humanist etiological folktale, and guidebook.[50] Recent commentary on the *Survay* emphasizes Stow's nostalgic antiquarianism and his efforts to preserve London's past by his re-creation of the ceremonial city of the queen's progresses, of a London "informed by a hierarchical sense of space and its significance," but that emphasis obscures both the formal novelty of the survey and its powerful representation of a burgeoning city for which the nostalgic epithet "Elizabethan" is no longer apt.[51] Though he begins with a conventional set piece on the Roman origins of the city, its founders, and antiquity, he moves quickly away from legend to the description of London's "walles, gates, ditches, and fresh waters, the bridges, towers and castles, the schooles of learning and houses of law, the orders and customes, sportes and pastimes, watchings and martiall exercises."[52] Having traced the "honor and worthines of the Cittizens," Stow is ready "to set downe the distribution of this Citty into parts" (117).[53] London's walls, once fortifications, by Stow's time were useless for protection but continued to mark off ritual boundaries, from those that determined the wine tax, to the location of the theaters, to the itinerary of royal progresses and the place of civic pageants and ceremonial occasions. London's civic elite provided Stow with his social model, and London's city spaces, particularly within its walls, are defined as theirs. The *Survay* and the genre itself witness the power of printing and the book to enable mastery of vast public, urban spaces with their teeming and seemingly unmanageable populations whom Lawrence Manley claims Stow himself neither names nor describes.[54]

Formally, the *Survay* is filled with lists, series, tabulations, epitomes, all rhetorical modes "by which large things are contained and written small" and thereby mastered.[55] Stow's *Survay* and the spate of histories, guidebooks, annals, chronicles, and catalogs that crowd the lists of seventeenth-century printers in both London and Paris graphically enact the ways in which the production of knowledge is power and how anxieties about and around urbanization were managed and subdued. Stow, as many have noted, was a conservative. He lamented the loss of greensward within the city precincts and sprinkles the *Survay* with his memories.[56] Where once there was a farm at which as a child he bought milk, now there are large storehouses for grain and commodities. Stow regrets the past, and that regret gives the *Survay* an elegiac quality; he continually revisits the sites of his childhood and finds them changed, thereby measuring urban temporality spatially and affectively. Lawrence Manley, quoting Foucault, writes of the way urban temporality is measured by a human observer/narrator who masters the disparate and chaotic experience of urban life. In "Questions of Geography," discussed in the introduction, Foucault writes of the danger of "metaphorising the transformations of discourse in a vocabulary of time [which] necessarily leads to the utilization of the model of individual consciousness with its intrinsic temporality."[57] By recounting and re-creating the urban through the observing/narrating I, the subject seems to control the ungovernable masses and material disorder of city life. The circuitous routes of Stow's personal itinerary remain only in these memory traces, for the most part sublimated by method and the developing scientific and totalizing discourses of topography and the modern map. Similarly, Stow's

lists of London's civic elite—its Lord Mayors, its guild leaders and household-
ers, borough by borough, hierarchize and define urban space as the property
of an elite. Missing from Stow's account, as from so much urban boosterism,
are the small craftsmen and laborers, the foreigners and transients, vagabonds,
and the poor that made up more than half of London's urban population.[58]

As many readers have noted, Stow's *Survay of London* is organized as a walk:
"I will beginne at the East, and so proceede thorough the high and most
principall streete of the cittie to the west. . . . by the conduite to the West
corner against the Stockes . . . then by the said Stockes (a market place both
of fish and flesh standing in the midst of the cittie) through the Poultrie (a
streete so called) to the great conduite in west Cheape, and so through Cheape
to the Standarde. . . . Then by the Standard to the great crosse. . . . And then
to the little Conduit by Paules gate" (118–19). Stow's is a walking tour, not
a landscape, a human endeavor that traces his pedestrian's way through London from east to west.[59] The hurly-burly of city life is subjugated to the ocular
control of the viewing subject as he moves through urban space seeing and
being seen.[60]

London's growth is reproduced in the growth of Stow's text itself, which
was extended, augmented, and reprinted throughout the seventeenth century
and into the eighteenth century.[61] As Vanessa Harding observes, "Stow's com-
pact, structured account—though itself a historical palimpsest—and Strype's
more prolix, discursive work, infilled, interpolated, and asymmetric, [reflect]
the changed shape and appearance of the cities they describe."[62] The early
editions of Stow's *Survay* are folios, destined for an elite buyer and reader, but
there were also portable, less expensive guides for travelers and merchants such
as *The Post of the World wherein is contayned the antiquities and originall of the
most famous Cities in Europe*, published in London in 1576, that announced
on its title page its usefulness to "Gentlemen, Marchants, Factors, or any
other Persons disposed to travaile."[63] This cheap, practical, pocket-size book
included descriptions of cities, distances, and the most practical and frequently used ways of getting from one city to the next. It provided lists of
holidays, values and denominations of coin, and a table of equivalents for
miles—in short, it is an early version of a business traveler's guide. *The Post*
begins with the German cities and Antwerp, then still the primary trade city
of Europe, before moving to Italy and on to London (with a dedication to
Sir Thomas Gresham and that "sumptuous monument . . . called the Royall
Exchange"), then to Paris, and finally to Spanish and Portuguese cities. This
little book ends with a list of principal fairs and markets, organized by city
and date, and finally, in a fit of patriotic convention, an inventory of England's
kings since William the Conqueror. It demonstrates the importance of geographic knowledge to merchant capitalism and its practices.[64]

There were also popular London "guides" such as Donald Lupton's *London
and the countrey carbonadoed and quartered into several characters* (1632) that

lays out the city for new arrivals from the country and records contemporary attitudes toward London's extraordinary growth.[65] Comic allegory replaces urban description: London is a woman, by turns glutton, expectant mother, mother of many daughters, her beauty said to be diminished by her size. Lupton begins, "She is growne so Great, I am almost affraide to meddle with Her; she's certainly a great world, there are so many little worlds in Her." The narrator goes on to enumerate those "many little worlds" that are "the country-mans Laborinth, he can find many things in it, but many times looseth himselfe." Lupton then guides the reader through the maze that is London beginning with the Tower, then Saint Paul's, on to London Bridge, the Exchanges, Cheapside, the Inns of Court, Smithfield, Bridewell, Ludgate, Paris Garden, fencing and dancing schools, criers and hawkers, and so on, retailing to newcomers what they can expect from each. Each place, like London itself, is allegorized as a London character: the bridge, "He bears much"; the Exchanges, "They are strange politicians, for they bring *Turkey* and *Spaine* into *London*, and carry London thither"; Cheapside will sell anything, including, he warns, what is not its own; Paris Garden is a "foul Denne" filled with the unemployed, swaggering roarers, cunning cheaters, rotten bawds, swearing drunkards; in the streets are fishwives and criers: "You must heare them cry before you know what they are furnished withal." Lupton presents all the places of the city and its suburbs, its inhabitants, its commodities, its dangers and pleasures (play-houses, "when I please I'll come to see them"), outlining for newcomers what to expect.[66] But his is also a knowing picture of the city for its inhabitants who appreciate his characterizations and in-jokes about London's various well-known places. It relies on both the newcomer/reader's desire to know more of the town, and the Londoner's pleasure of recognition, of his or her superior knowledge. The second part of *London and the countrey carbonadoed* tells of changes in the country that parallel changes in the city: the decline in hospitality, enclosure, and more. Lupton ends his little book with a final section on the news-sheets that reported on the Thirty Years' War. Lupton's is only one example of the many texts that marketed knowledge of the growing city by describing its places.

Numerous French examples preceded Stow and his generation of topographers and antiquarians. The printer and writer Gilles Corrozet is perhaps the earliest French practitioner of the form. He straddles the older genre of the history or praise of cities and the new form of survey or guidebook. His *La fleur des antiquitez, singularitez et excellences de la plus que noble et triumphante ville et cité de Paris, capitalle du royaulme de France* (1532) is, properly speaking, a praise or history of Paris. But in the second edition, printed the following year in 1533, Corrozet adds a series of lists useful to any literate visitor or inhabitant of the capital: of streets organized by quarters, and of churches and schools.[67] *La fleur* was reprinted several times, and in 1543 with additions on shopping in Paris, on the everyday expenses of its inhabitants, and on the

Paris criers. A new list of streets included both where they begin and end and the topographic whereabouts of churches and schools.[68] In 1550 Corrozet published *Les antiquitez, histoires et singularitez de Paris*, which was even more complete and which he offers to Claude Guiot, counselor to the king and "prévôt" of merchants. It was subsequently printed in Lyon, where it must have been useful to the numerous merchants and commercial travelers who made their way between Lyon, the main trade center on the route to Italy, and Paris. Many Parisian editions with augmentations by others appeared, as did other guides by French and non-Frenchmen alike.[69] There is even a curious verse description by Michel de Marolles entitled *Paris ou description de cette ville* (1677). But perhaps the most widely known, at least until the appearance of Germain Brice's *Description nouvelle de ce qu'il y a de plus remarquable dans la ville de Paris* (1684), and the only early guide that merits comparison with Stow's *Survay,* is Jacques Du Breul's *Le théâtre des antiquitez de Paris* (1612), the first guide to be organized by districts.[70]

Like Stow's *Survay,* Du Breul's work was enlarged by subsequent compilers and went through numerous editions in the course of the seventeenth century. On his title page appears the proud epithet "Parisien." Like Stow, Du Breul begins conventionally with the city's founding—by Hercules—but the bulk of his text records the principal buildings and inhabitants of the city in four books organized by quarters: the city (Cité), the university (Left Bank), the *ville* (Right Bank), and the suburbs. Paris is an idealized cityscape, a panorama of churches, palaces, public buildings, bridges, fountains, and "their" principle persons, in other words, the ideological and material panorama of the elite. Movement through space rather than time is the survey's organizing principle of textual development. Just as in Stow's *Survay,* the small craftsmen and urban poor that similarly made up the majority of the Parisan population are missing from Du Breul's record.

Du Breul and Stow are peripatetics, pedestrians who traverse their cities' streets tracing the ways in which power operates and social knowledge is produced and acquired. *Peripatetic,* as seventeenth-century writers well knew, was the term used to describe Aristotle's philosophical school, so named for the walk in the Lyceum where Aristotle taught. As the English traveler and Parisian visitor James Howell puts it in his *Instructions for forreine travell* (1642), "*Peregrination . . .* may be not improperly called a *moving Academy,* or the true *Peripatetique Schoole.*"[71] Howell's defense of travel as philosophical learning testifies to a kind of scopic cogito produced through the exercise of spatial practices recorded in the survey and other forms of travel writing popular in the early modern period. As Howell describes it,

> to run over and traverse the world by *Hearesay,* and traditionall relation, with other mens eyes, and so take all things upon courtesie, is but a confused and imperfect kind of speculation, which leaveth but weake

and distrustfull notions behind it; in regard the *Eare* is not so authentique a witnesse as the *Eye*, because the *Eye*, by which as through a cleare christall Casement, wee discerne the various works of *Art* and *Nature*, and in one instant comprehend halfe the whole Universe. (12)

For Howell, seeing is transparent, a window on the world through which the viewer in an instant "comprehends," that is, grasps in the double sense of understanding and taking in or encompassing.[72] Howell's praise of the eye and the eyewitness dramatizes the importance of a scopic drive in producing the effects of a hegemonic, often colonizing, subjectivity that depends on being there, on presence. As Howell memorably puts it, speaking of Alexander the Great, "he had surveyed more Land with his Eye, than other Kings could comprehend with their thoughts" (13). Yet Howell's own project is contradictory; it disrupts the very hegemony of presence he praises, since his book forms part of what he terms "auricular" (13) knowledge, a locution that reminds us that early modern "readers" were sometimes listeners to whom books were read aloud. Subjectivity is produced not by moving literally through space—through the city, through Europe, through the so-called new world—but by the observing I/eye that recounts that peripatetic journey. Space is negated in the very act of inscribing it, in writing that offers mastery not in presence but in absentia.

How did early modern writing circulate in London and Paris?[73] Writing in the abstract, theoretical sense in which I use it here found its way to readers and audiences in material forms both new and traditional in early modern Europe. Print culture and the book trade were organized differently in the two cities with important and differing effects. Stow, for example, received three pounds for his *Survay of London* and forty copies of his book, which he likely offered as gifts to potential patrons. Later, as I have noted, his book would be expanded, in 1618 by Anthony Munday and in subsequent editions into the eighteenth century. Once they had sold a manuscript, authors no longer had control over its printing and distribution; even English printers themselves sometimes found that works they had purchased might be appropriated, printed, and sold by others. Though England had a system of short-term "privileges" whereby the Crown gave monopolistic rights to certain books to certain printers, as did France, most books were not covered by any privilege or system of copyright. In 1557, Queen Mary and King Philip granted a charter to what came to be known as the Stationers' Company, the group of printers, publishers, booksellers, and binders that regulated the book trade and granted its members control over the printing and selling of books in England. Before any book could be printed, it had to be approved by some governmental or ecclesiastical authority, and registration served to record licensing and was evidence of the publisher's copyright.[74] Books required sanction of the authorities and often of titled patrons and dedicatees whose names appeared in their opening pages and represented protection, gratitude, hope of reward or advancement, or assurance of merit, to their readers or purchasers.[75]

England's book trade expanded prodigiously in the course of the sixteenth century and was situated almost entirely in London.[76] Guidebooks and surveys such as Stow's saw print as did Bibles and sermons, conduct books, pamphlets, and ballads, but shorter forms and writing directed at specialized or aristocratic audiences, such as Donne's poems to which I will turn in chapter 3, circulated in manuscript.[77] Not only Donne but other writers from the gentry and aristocracy, including Sidney and Ralegh, shunned the so-called stigma of print and circulated their poetry in handwritten copies among friends, acquaintances, and potential patrons.[78] Though professional scribes plied their trade in the city and produced copies of all sorts, most copies were made by readers or their amanuenses. Personal miscellanies encouraged the participation of readers as writers and editors, as the manuscript histories of some poems demonstrate.[79] The manuscript medium enabled poetic competitions in various milieus including universities, aristocratic households, the Inns of Court, and the court itself. Nevertheless verse became, in John Harrington's words, "merchantable ware" and appeared as well in printed anthologies such as *Tottel's Miscellany* and other collections as printers and publishers began to see a market in poetry.

As is well known, initially plays were more likely to be performed than printed in early modern England. Shakespeare famously never saw any of his plays into print, but publishers saw a market for drama and began publishing them, including those by Shakespeare.[80] Shakespeare's plays appeared in so-called pirated quartos from a variety of putative sources, in early editions often without attribution.[81] Ultimately, as drama gained in cultural prestige, important editions appeared such as Ben Jonson's *Workes* (1616), which he notoriously saw into print himself and which contemporaries mocked: "What others call a play you call a work."[82] What is now known as Shakespeare's First Folio (1623), the result of a joint venture between two of Shakespeare's fellow actors and two London publishers, brought together for the first time both plays already in print and most of the unprinted plays as well.[83]

Across the channel, writing found its way into print in ways both similar to and different from the English case. Paris printers and booksellers, like their English counterparts, formed a corporation with restricted membership and elaborate regulations initially dependent on the University of Paris. In 1521, Francis I required all books to be licensed and authorized by the university before printing, with severe penalties prescribed for the printing and distribution of unlicensed books. The *privilège* or license to print was used by the authorities to regulate and repress texts that were deemed dangerous, particularly during the religious wars of the late sixteenth century. During the Fronde, this function was transferred to salaried royal censors, and the practice of granting general licenses to particular authors was abolished (1659). The extraordinary proliferation of unlicensed and incendiary political pamphlets and broadsides available in the streets of Paris and on the Pont Neuf during the Fronde demonstrates the difficulty the authorities had in regulating print.[84] Though in England size was a standardized feature of the penny chapbooks, in France the *bibliothèque bleue*, which evolved during the same period, shared neither length nor subject matter, but low price, typographic devices friendly to basic readers, and the ubiquitous blue paper covers.[85] Though Paris was the center of the printing and book trades, in France books were also printed outside the capital in Lyon, Troyes, Toulouse, and elsewhere.[86]

Texts also circulated in manuscript and were read aloud in the burgeoning culture of salon and academy in Paris.[87] Though Richelieu's establishment of the Académie française (1635) represented an attempt to regulate the circulation of letters and culture, a rich array of rival salons and academies assured the circulation of other forms of literary production not sanctioned by the Academy. In short, many of the texts examined in the chapters to follow illustrate the multiple forms in which cultural capital in the form of literary and cultural production circulated in early modern London and Paris: in printed books sanctioned by the authorities, in scandalous, unlicensed pamphlets and broadsides sold in the streets, on alehouse walls, in manuscripts circulated in special milieus of various kinds, in commonplace books in households, performed or read in salons and academies, and on the public and coterie stages.

Travel writing circulated both in manuscript and in print and was one of the most popular genres of the early modern period, both in the form of the survey or guidebook discussed earlier, and in travelers' accounts of their sojourns in foreign cities and climes. It depended on a metropolitan readership or audience and an urban, mercantile economy for its success. Even critics of travel recognized its popular and lucrative appeal, as in this remarkable address to the reader in Samuel Purchas's celebrated *Hakluytus Posthumus, or Purchas his pilgrimes* (1625):

> As for Gentlemen, Travell is accounted an excellent Ornament to them; and therefore many of them comming to their Lands sooner than to their Wits, adventure themselves to see the Fashions of other Countries, where their soules and bodies find temptations to a twofold Whoredom, whence they see the World as *Adam* had *knowledge of good and evill*, with the losse or lessening of their estate in this *English* (and perhaps also in the heavenly) Paradise, and bring home a few smattering termes, flattering garbes, Apish crings, foppish fancies, foolish guises and disguises, the vanities of Neighbour Nations . . . without furthering of their knowledge of God, the World, or themselves. I speake not against Travell, so usefull to usefull men, I honour the industrious of the liberall and ingenuous in arts, bloud, education: and to prevent exorbitancies of the other,

which cannot travell farre, or are in danger to travell from God and themselves, at no great charge I offer a World of Travellers to their domesticke entertainment.

Travelers' accounts and journals of the sort Purchas gathered together and modeled on Hakluyt as well as the guidebooks written by Corrozet, Du Breul, and others were produced for a literate metropolitan audience and its armchair recreation.[88] Purchas's address to his reader looks backward in its fear of foreign travel and at the same time forward to the grand tour when travel was not only the prerogative, but also the prerequisite, of a gentleman's education. And though the gentleman's circuit encompassed all of Europe, his destination par excellence was Paris.[89]

A young man came to Paris to become, as a contemporary put it, an "honnête homme and worthy of the name he bears."[90] In the seventeenth century, Germain Brice's *Description nouvelle de ce qu'il y a de plus remarquable dans la ville de Paris*, first published in 1684, was the most popular guidebook of the period. Already by 1687 it had been translated and published in England. In the notice "To the Reader," the translator claims the guide is the first of its kind in English, useful to those who have already visited Paris by reminding them of its beauties, useful to those interested in painting, sculpture, and architecture, and finally necessary to "such young gentlemen who go over; (as some do almost daily) in regard [that] this Book in their Pocket with them, will be, as their Informer, so their Guide, and lead them directly to such sights as they most fansie." Brice's indispensable guide presents the capital's principal monuments and collections, its private houses (who built them, how much they cost, what is collected and displayed within) in extraordinary detail, including the king's "Garde Meuble" and library with descriptions of its books and prints, medals and stones, mummy and magnifying glass. He even includes in its account of places worth visiting the earliest so-called salon, the "Hotel de Montausier, formerly called the Hotel de Rambouillet, heretofore the most delightsome seat of the muses, and which still serves at this day as the Retreat and Sanctuary to all ingenious persons" (Bxii'). The sixteenth and seventeenth centuries saw a sharp increase, prompted by religious persecution, in the number of French and European immigrants and visitors to London; the Stuart court's exile to France and the Royalist exodus brought members of the English elite to Paris, as did the promise of its increasingly prestigious cultural capital.[91]

Bernini's Bridge

At the end of July, midway through Bernini's stay in Paris, Chantelou collects his charge one evening for their daily outing:

Le soir, la promenade fut assez courte; il a voulu aller sur le pont Rouge, et y a fait arrêter la carrosse un bon quart d'heure, regardant d'un côté et d'autre du pont, puis m'a dit:"C'est là un bel aspect, je suis fort ami des eaux; elles font [du bien] à mon temperament." Après nous nous en sommes revenus.

Our evening drive was rather short; he wanted to go on the pont Rouge and stopped the coach on it for a good quarter of an hour looking first from one side of the bridge and then the other. After a while he turned to me and said,"It is a beautiful view; I am a great lover of water, it calms my spirits." Then we returned home.[92]

Chantelou's account of this moment is richly evocative of what I will call the *topographic imaginary.* Bernini—sculptor, architect, painter, dramatist—takes his evening promenade in the city. Comfortably ensconced in a coach with his cicerone, he admires the Seine from the pont Rouge, the little bridge that joined the Île de la Cité with the Île St. Louis. He lingers before the arresting sight of the river's waters with their affective power, waters crucial to Paris's expansion, development, and position as a capital city. As far as we know, Bernini never alights from the safety and comfort of the coach and thus misses the street life recorded in ballads, pamphlets, and plays and hawked on streets and bridges. Furthermore, our access to his privileged artist's sight is available only through the mediating voice of the narrator, Chantelou, who recounts their pause on the bridge and Bernini's judgment of the view framed by the coach window. Bernini returns from his promenade to the Hôtel Frontenac, seemingly refreshed and renewed by his moment on the bridge overlooking the city prospect and its river. Paris's less privileged inhabitants striving to survive and to succeed, who make up the teeming life of the city, he sees only from a distance.

CHAPTER TWO

Toward a Topographic Imaginary

Magna civitas, magna solitudo
—ERASMUS

Paris had been for many years the goal of my longings, and
the bliss with which I first set foot on its pavements I took
as a guarantee that I should attain the fulfillment of other
wishes also.
—SIGMUND FREUD, *The Interpretation of Dreams*

To contemplate the urban prospect of early modern Paris, Bernini chooses a
bridge, the pont Rouge, built between 1627 and 1634 to join the Île de la
Cité and the Île St. Louis. A bridge is first and foremost a connector. Two
bridges, one each from the Right and the Left Bank to the Cité, served Paris
until circa 900; two more were built across each arm of the Seine by 1420 to
make four bridges in all (see fig. 2). By the end of the seventeenth century,
urban growth had prompted bridge building such that ten bridges reached
across the Seine, but up until the late sixteenth century, the Right Bank was
in part dangerous territory consisting mainly of fields and woods. The Pont
Neuf, now the oldest bridge in Paris, helped to transform the Right Bank into
urban space by connecting the Louvre and Tuileries with the Left Bank and
the Cité, or Paris proper (fig. 6). Begun by Henry III in 1578, work on the
bridge was interrupted by the religious wars and money problems, and then
taken up again by Henry IV as part of his vast reconfiguration of public space
in Paris that included extending the Louvre, beginning the Collège de France,
building the Hôpital Saint Louis and the Place Royale, now the Place des
Vosges, and completing the Pont Neuf in 1604 when people began to use the
bridge.[1] In 1608, the poet Malherbe writes to a friend of these changes:"si
vous revenez à Paris d'ici à deux ans, vous ne le connoistrez plus" (if you come
back to Paris two years from now, you won't know it anymore).[2]

Situated in the center of the city, just outside the Palais (de Justice), between
the Louvre and Palais-Royal on the Right Bank, and the Hôtel de Luxembourg
and its gardens on the left, the Pont Neuf was the most frequented place in
seventeenth-century Paris and the city's most frequently represented urban
landmark by far.[3] Represented in guidebooks, visual topographies, and books
of all sorts, in engravings and advertising, on fans and ceramics, the Pont Neuf
was the privileged sign of seventeenth-century Parisian modernity. Scholars of

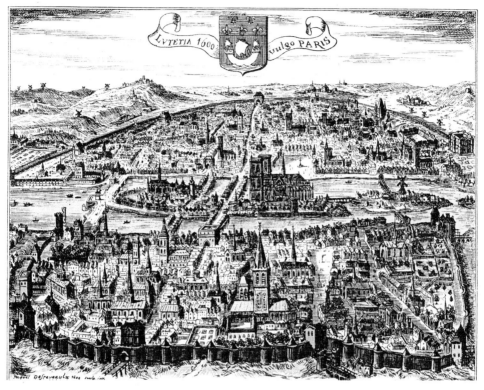

Figure 6. Lutetia 1600, Jacques Defrevaulx. Musée Carnavalet

early modern Europe have made much of the early modern fascination with the so-called New World, its wonders and spectacles of strangeness, but travelers to early modern Paris were often amazed at marvels closer to home. Opposite the title page of the English version of Germain Brice's popular guidebook, *A New Description of Paris,* the Pont Neuf appears in an engraved view (fig. 7) looking toward the Île de la Cité. Brice highlights the bridge in a long and emphatically positioned verbal description:

> We are now arrived at the last article of this description, which cannot be better concluded than with the Pont Neuf. . . . this bridge is one of the most beautiful that can be seen for its length which extends over the two arms of the Seine . . . for its breadth, which is divided into three ways, one in the midst for Coaches and great carriages, and two on each side raised higher for those who go on foot, and lastly for its structure, which is of such solidity and of such ordinance, that has but few equals. . . . Among [its] advantages one must also add the delicate Prospect which the Passenger has from it: a view which passes for one of the most pleasing and finest in the world.[4]

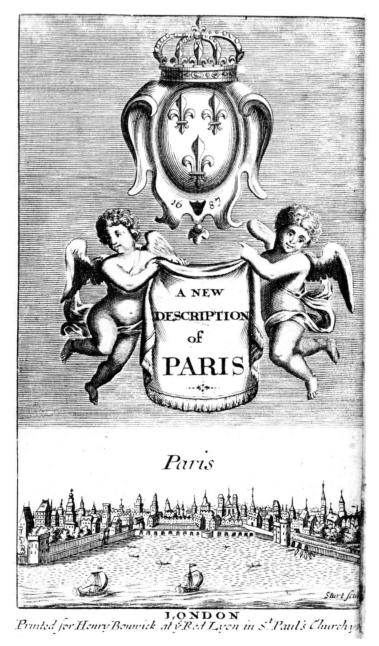

Figure 7. Frontispiece, Germain Brice,
A New Description of Paris (London, 1687) Folger Library

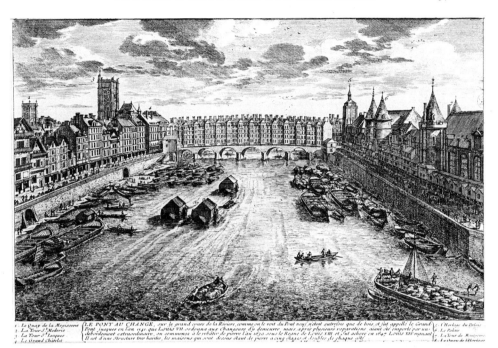

Figure 8. Le Pont au Change, from the Pont Neuf, anonymous engraving,
early seventeenth century. Musée Carnavalet

Brice goes on to compare the Pont Neuf with two wonders of the early modern
world, the port of Constantinople and Goa in India. The Pont Neuf helped
to organize and rationalize space on both sides of the Seine by reducing the
river's role as barrier and enhancing its utility for trade, sociability, and communication. Like Brice, his predecessor Jacques Du Breul also gives pride of
place to the Pont Neuf by making its description the climax of his section on
the Cité. Both Brice and Du Breul recognize the social, aesthetic, and economic consequences of the reconfiguration of urban space effected by the
building of the Pont Neuf. Du Breul, for example, observes that the tip of the
Île de la Cité had been *inutile* (useless) before the building of the bridge, but
since its completion it had become "la plus belle et la plus utile place de Paris."[5]
Both Parisians and foreign visitors alike marveled at the bridge: its length
across the Seine, its breadth, its structure, and its water pump, La Samaritaine.

What immediately distinguishes the Pont Neuf from previous bridges is its
open plan, part of the reconfiguration of the street as public space for the flow
of traffic that began to characterize urban development in the early modern
city. Unlike its predecessors, the Pont Neuf was not lined by several stories of
shops and houses like the Pont au Change (fig. 8) or London Bridge. Whereas
such bridges with their rows of houses and shops rising several stories initially

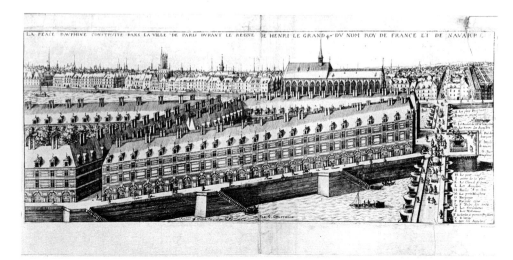

Figure 9. Pont Neuf and Place Dauphine, 1607–15, engraving
after Claude Chastillon. Musée Carnavalet

promoted trade and communication and represented a vast investment in physical infrastructure, they were less well suited to the city's burgeoning population, traffic, and commerce that promoted the accumulation of capital.[6] Though the Pont Neuf was initially designed for such buildings, Henry IV is said to have insisted on an open plan so as not to obscure the view of the Louvre from the bridge (Du Breul, Hhiiii'). Thus the Pont Neuf provided the nonelite with an urban prospect, a space from which to gaze out and encompass the metropolis often reserved for the privileged. Contemporaries describe the bridge's division into three parts with what we would term sidewalks on each side of a central wider path for "carosses & cheveaux" (coaches and horses, Du Breul, Hhiii'). The bridge thus accommodated the new vehicular traffic that both plagued the early modern city and also fostered its development (fig. 9).[7] The king himself is said to have first crossed the bridge in June 1603 to demonstrate its safety to his subjects, but Pierre de l'Estoile notes in his *Journal* that initially few would hazard crossing the bridge, apparently suspicious of the new technology.[8]

On the bridge itself Henry commissioned another technological marvel, the Samaritan water pump (fig. 10), designed and installed by engineers imported from the Low Countries.[9] Contemporaries recognized the importance of water to urban life and remarked upon the moment the pump began to deliver water to the Louvre: the poet Malherbe wrote portentously to a friend that "l'eau de la pompe du Pont Neuf est aux Tuileries."[10] Water from the Samaritan pump was designated only for the palace and a select few privileged by the king, a state of affairs that provoked bitter disputes with city officials who demanded water from the pump for the city's inhabitants.[11] The Samari-

Figure 10. La pompe de la Samaritaine (Samaritan Pump), ca. 1635,
nineteenth-century rendering. Musée Carnavalet

tan pump was embellished with yet another wonder of early modern technology, an elaborate clock that marked the hours and days that increasingly regulated work and everyday life in the early modern city.[12] Still another sign of
the bridge's state-of-the-art technology was the equestrian statue of Henry IV
commissioned by Marie de Medici following the assassination of the king, the
first such monumental, freestanding bronze in France (fig. 11). Both connector and destination, the bridge fostered commerce by facilitating traffic and
supporting lively market stalls, criers, hawkers, and colporteurs who sold political pamphlets, the new *gazettes* or news-sheets, and street poetry on its pavements; it connected the court with the city, the royal palace with the Palais
de Justice; and it was, notoriously, the site of burgeoning urban crime.

Demographic growth and the reconfiguration of urban space effected by
the Pont Neuf had aesthetic, cognitive, psychic, and social effects traced in
visual and verbal representations that make legible the actions, practices, and
experience of urban life in early modern Paris. Guidebooks, pamphlets and
ballads, poetry and engraving all represent the "continual press of people passing over this Bridge, by which," as Brice puts it, "one may guess at the infinite

Figure 11. Equestrian statue of Henry IV, ca. 1614, Pietro Francavilla
and Pietro Tacca, anonymous engraving. Musée Carnavalet

number of inhabitants in Paris."[13] Both high-cultural artifacts and popular materials including a whole subgenre known as "les ponts neufs" represent life in early modern Paris.[14] Accounts of comets, prodigies, miracles, crimes and their punishment, of fires, earthquakes, monsters, and monstrous births were all sold on the bridge. Broadsides record the bridge itself as a site of class warfare between pages and apprentices, bourgeois and gentlemen. In a popular poem entitled "Les aubades aux petits maîtres," for example, middling sort husbands of "filles et femmes d'honneur" who have been molested by loitering gallants defend the honor of their citizen wives and their right to use the bridge without being manhandled. They form a battalion "hermaphroditte" of husbands and wives who march across the bridge arm in arm and rout the offenders. The bridge was also known for performances of charlatans, the most famous and popular of which were Tabarin and his partner/master Mondor, purveyor of pomades and unguents, who made jokes, often scatological, about gender, sex, religion, work, politics, health, and more.[15] Countless poems and pamphlets represent thieves prowling the crowded bridge as in this example in which the speaker is a "crocheteur" (literally picklock carrier, but by extension, thief) who finds himself transported to the top of the Samaritan whence he views the teeming bridge below:

> C'est pourquoy vous voyez tous les jours telle afluence de personnes de toutes sortes, de tous sexes, de toutes nations, de tous aages, & de toutes lunes, qui me viennent visiter, afin d'apprendre quelque chose de nouveau.[16]

> That's why you see daily such a crowd of people of all kinds, sexes, nations, ages and humors who come to see me to find out what's new.

Written in the vernacular, these poems and pamphlets are filled with Latin tags and mythological allusions, topical and topographic references that place their authors at least on the fringes of the legal milieu nearby at the Palais (de Justice). They often use as a pretext a speaker giving a foreigner—from the provinces, proverbially Gascony, but sometimes from abroad including exotic locales such as Turkey—a tour of Paris. In the "Dialogue d'un Turc et d'un François sur la Statue Royale de Henry le Grand mise sur le Pont Neuf" (1614), which is set on the bridge, as its title indicates, and apparently written soon after the statue of the king was installed, a Turk visiting Paris asks the native "Quelle statue est celle-là?" (What is that statue there?), to which the Frenchman responds, are you blind, deaf, have you lived long at sea, not to recognize this prince "si rare / que toute la terre a cognu" (so renowned that the whole world knew him). Later during the uprising known as the Fronde, the statue of Henry IV becomes the speaker lamenting the state of France in a long diatribe directed at his son Louis XIII's equestrian statue in the Place Royale, now the Place des Vosges.[17]

During the seventeenth century, the Pont Neuf became known as "la bibliothéque de Paris" (the library of Paris), the place where inhabitants and visitors to the city could always buy the latest scandal sheet or political pamphlet, particularly, as this contemporary notes, during the Fronde:

> Oüy certes, depuis cette mal-heureuse guerre la Samaritaine est devenuë la Bibliotheque commune de tout Paris; c'est l'Academie où l'on dispute de toutes les affaires du temps; la licée [*sic*] où toutes les difficultez du monde se resoudent; l'Escolle où l'on traite de toutes sortes de matieres; la Sorbonne vniverselle. . . . C'est là où se trouvent & se vendent tous les liures de l'Université, plus les meschans que les bons, plus ceux qui calomnient, qui noircissent, qui rauissent, qui dechirent la reputation que les autres qui la deffendent ou qui la protegent.

> Yes, really, the Samaritan has become the public library of Paris since this unhappy war began; it is the academy where all that is happening is debated; the college where all the difficulties of the world are resolved; the school where all sorts of matters are taken up; the universal Sorbonne. . . .There all the university books can be found and are sold, more the wicked than the good ones, more those that slander, blacken and libel, that ruin a reputation, than those that defend or protect it.[18]

As Christian Jouhaud observes in his study of the *mazarinades*, pamphlets written against Cardinal Mazarin and his party during the Fronde years, "La polyphonie littéraire est l'instrument privilégié d'une politique qui n'a pas d'autre expression publique" (Literary polyphony is the privileged instrument of a politics that has no other means of public expression) (fig. 12).[19] Even the most inconsequential events seem to have inspired writing.[20] In his massive study of printing and the book trade in early modern Paris, Henri Martin has demonstrated that the mid–seventeenth century—the period of the Fronde— was a time of crisis resulting from the cost of paper, fewer opportunities for apprenticeship, power struggles among printers, and conflict with the authorities over "privilège" or licensing.[21] Authorities struggled in vain to prohibit the sale of pamphlets and libels on the bridge by regulating or banning colporteurs or itinerant booksellers.[22] Nevertheless, the trade flourished; the bridge's parapets were lined by open-air stalls, the precursors of today's *bouquinistes*; it was also the place most frequently used to affix ballads and broadsides, signs, edicts, ordinances, convocations, and recruitments. News of all sorts was not only sold on the bridge; the bridge itself was the stage on which news became spectacle.

Not only verbal forms but also visual culture grapples with representing and ordering metropolitan social variety. To represent this newly constituted metropolitan space with its mix of persons and activities, seventeenth-century artists distorted the space of the bridge by inflating it, by making the Pont Neuf larger than life, larger than it actually was. Though a general inflation of perspective is characteristic of the visual conventions of some seventeenth-

AVIS QUE DONNE UN FRONDEUR AUX PARISIENS QU'IL EXORTE DE SE RÉVOLTER CONTRE LA TYRANNIE DU CARDINAL MAZARIN .

Figure 12. Frondeur advising Parisians to revolt against Mazarin, mid–seventeenth century. Bibliothèque nationale

century art, particularly engraving, distortion of this overdetermined space of the early modern Parisian metropolis testifies to the cognitive and visual impact of urbanization.[23] Figure 13, an engraving by Adam Pérelle entitled *La place du Pont Neuf,* represents only the area immediately before the equestrian statue of Henry IV and not the entire bridge; his inflation of space can be gauged by comparing it to a recent photograph of the same area taken from the Place Dauphine (fig. 14). Pérelle's engraving shows some six coaches, each drawn by numerous horses (a mark of status in the early modern period), two sedan chairs, ten individual horsemen, nine booths for selling goods, three additional tables for street sellers, two open-air theatrical entertainments taking place on platforms with substantial audiences, five criers and hawkers, three dogs, one duel—well over three hundred persons in all with ample space to spare. Figure 15 shows a reverse shot of the same space looking toward the Place Dauphine. Single-point perspective and symmetry manage the hurly-burly of urban life, at once stimulating and threatening—the tradesmen, entertainers, transients, criers, vagabonds, and the poor that made up the lion's share of the Parisian population and that frequented the Pont Neuf alongside the elite and middling sort.

Not only Pérelle but many other artists and engravers of the period, including Israel Sylvestre, Stefano della Bella, and Aveline, to name a few, represent

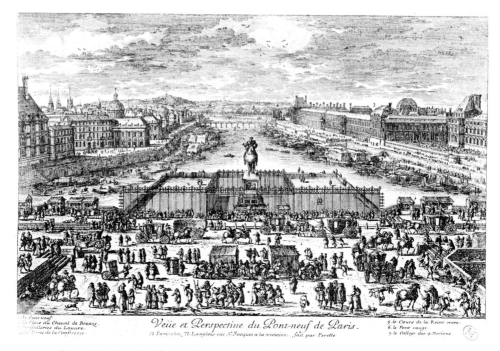

Figure 13. Pont Neuf, ca. 1650, engraving by Adam Pérelle. Musée Carnavalet

this Parisian landmark and the crowds that frequented it (figs. 16 and 17). Such images aestheticize the mix of persons that characterizes urban life; they not only were produced in response to urbanization but also produced an ideology of the urban—traffic, the crowd, the mix of classes, the mingling of work and leisure, economic exchange, and conspicuous consumption. For the inhabitants of early modern Paris, wealthy and impoverished alike, the Pont Neuf was the privileged sign of the city; its image was reproduced in various media and contexts, from Abraham Bosse's engraving of Paris's *petits métiers* (fig. 18) to the illustration of mathematical textbooks and fashionable fans. By the early eighteenth century, when the bridge was no longer the novelty it once had been and the representation of urban experience was no longer visually new, such distortion of perspective diminishes (fig. 19).

In these engravings, the Pont Neuf, a bridge some twenty-eight meters wide, expands to represent the entire hierarchical spectrum, from street singer to carriage-borne aristocrat, by connecting city to palace, estate to estate, in heretofore unimagined proximity—a democratizing feature of urban life Georg Simmel and others ascribe to the nineteenth-century city.[24] These various representations helped to produce a distinctive urban discursive space in which persons of different status and degree mixed, in which the "rights of man" could be imagined, a public space Jürgen Habermas, in theorizing the

Figure 14. Present view from the Place Dauphine toward the statue
of Henry IV. Photograph, Thomas R. Brooks

Figure 15. Pont Neuf, ca. 1650, engraving by Adam Pérelle. Musée Carnavalet

Enlightenment, has termed the *public sphere.*[25] Put another way, I am tracing an emerging psychic, cultural, and material logic that leads to the Enlightenment, with its notions of individualism, liberalism, and democracy.

In a chapter of his powerful reading of contemporary culture, *Postmodernism, or the Cultural Logic of Late Capitalism,* Fredric Jameson reads new historicism not by way of its Renaissance performers, usually said to have instituted its practice, but by reading Walter Benn Michaels's book *The Gold Standard.*[26] Jameson claims that new historicism does not constitute a methodology but is merely engaged in the production of homologies. According to Jameson, then, this chapter would merely show how the Pont Neuf is linked homologically to absolutism, urbanization, and the Enlightenment discourse of rights, and would then, in the classic new historicist move, turn briefly, as in fact it does, to a canonical author. Though Jameson is certainly justified in making this charge in the case of many examples of what passes for new historicist practice, he is wrong theoretically. New historicism is not merely the production of homologies between the social and the literary; it works, on one hand, to delegitimate older, purely formalist, literary hermeneutics and, on the other, to legitimate a different hermeneutic practice fully engaged with both formal and historical problems.

Consider, for example, the seventeenth-century French polemicist and poet Nicolas Boileau, perhaps best known as the exemplar of French neoclassi-

Figure 16. Pont Neuf, 1646, engraving by Stefano della Bella. Musée Carnavalet

La statue de Henry IV. et de l'Isle du Palais.
A Paris Chez I. Vander Bruggen rüe S. Iacques au grand Magazin. Auec priuilege du Roy.

Figure 17. Pont Neuf and statue of Henry IV, ca. 1660. Musée Carnavalet

cism.[27] Boileau took the side of the ancients in the late seventeenth-century culture wars by attacking women writers of romance novels and the salon culture in which they flourished. His poetry has been considered mainly in terms of neoclassical canons, imitation of the ancients, and, despite his own bourgeois origins, as staunchly exemplifying "high culture." His well-known Satire VI, for example, modeled on Juvenal's Satire III, is invariably discussed in terms of imitation.[28] But Boileau's Satire VI is about a Parisian traffic jam and warrants comparison not only with Juvenal and high-cultural artifacts but also with the guidebooks of Corrozet, du Breul, and Brice, with urban topographies such as Stow's *Survay* and Howell's *Londinopolis*, and with popular street poetry of the period such as *La ville de Paris en vers burlesques* (ca. 1652) attributed to François Bertaut or "Sieur Berthaud," onetime reader to the child Louis XIV, brother of the memoirist Madame de Motteville, and longtime Parisian.[29]

Despite his privileged status, Bertaut's popular poem was cheaply printed in numerous editions and may have been hawked on the bridge itself. It begins with a preface, "A mes amis de la campagne," in which the author claims that so many people write to friends in the country about the beauties of Paris that they no longer entertain or stand out. Instead the speaker recounts what he reveals to a recent new arrival: not only the Palais Royal, the Cours de la Reine, and the Comédie, the Paris of the elite, but the Pont Neuf and the Galerie du Palais (the Palais de Justice) with its merchant stands and boutiques, lawyers and cases, the traffic jam in front of the Palais, criers and

Il n'est point d'instrument qui vaille   Iamais soubs le faix ie ne tremble,
    Les crochets que j'ay sur mon dos;   Ma force est esgalle à ma voix;
Cest auec eux que je trauaille,   Ie crie, et scay porter ensemble
    Et sur qui ie prends mon repos.   Et des fagots, et du gros bois.

Figure 18. Parisian *cri* with Pont Neuf in background, engraving
by Abraham Bosse. Bibliothèque nationale

Figure 19. Pont Neuf, ca. 1700. Bibliothèque nationale

hawkers of all sorts, in short, the lively mix of places and persons that was early modern Paris. The French guide who is the poem's main speaker uses a middle style, but his Gascon visitor, the perennial provincial gawker/bumpkin, speaks in virtually incomprehensible dialect. Each person they meet speaks as fits his or her place, status, and work or profession. This poem of some eighteen hundred lines is a walking tour of the city, its places and monuments, but more important its working populace, that ends:

> He, bien, adieu, car je te quitte:
> Dans un autre jour je t'invite
> A voir le reste de Paris.
> Cependant chante, dance, et ris.

> And so adieu, for I leave you,
> Another day I will invite you
> To see the rest of Paris, but
> In the meantime, sing, dance, and laugh.

Sieur Berthaud's poem is populated by a host of urban types plying their trades, from thieves and prostitutes to shopkeepers and lawyers, from lackeys and gallants to secretaries and churchmen. Movement through space is its organizing principle of textual development. In both *La ville de Paris* and Boileau's

Satire VI, the speakers move peripatetically through the streets of early modern Paris, but whereas Bertaut's speaker and his visitor enjoy the city spectacle with its lively variety and multiple encounters, Boileau's persona is buffeted by noise, crowds, and urban crime. Whereas Bertaut's burlesque retails the *copia* of city life, in the case of Boileau, the satire form, like single-point perspective in the images of Paris's Pont Neuf, manages the threatening hurly-burly of urban life. Formal satire is usually said to present an encounter between an "I" and its adversary who drives the satirist to speech; in Boileau's sixth satire, that encounter is with the city itself. The poem opens with a question:

> Qui frappe l'air, bon Dieu! de ces lugubres cris?
>
> Who beats the air, dear God, with these mournful cries?[30]

"Ces lugubres cris" assault even the air; they point to their perpetrators—stray cats—but they also indicate those who apparently hear these cries, speaker and addressee. The next line offers another question, but one that furnishes the poem's first personal pronoun:

> Est-ce donc pour veiller qu'on couche à Paris?
>
> So is it to stay up that one goes to bed in Paris?

Here the oxymoronic juxtaposition of *veiller* and *coucher* surrounds the pronoun, *on,* which would seem to refer to the urban populace. Boileau's speaker is awakened by an unknown, unavailable other and leaves his sleepless bed for the streets of Paris; there he finds no one in particular, no differentiated addressee, but pressing, teeming crowds: gutter cats and thieves, coaches and carts, lackeys and blacksmiths, groans and gunshots, hue and cry. Bombarded by sense impressions in his itinerary through urban space, the speaker is continually assailed by the populace into whose space he unwittingly stumbles:

> En quelque endroit que j'aille, il faut fendre la presse
> D'un people d'importuns qui fourmillent sans cesse;
>
> Wherever I go, I have to fend off the crowd
> Of an importuning populace that swarms nonstop;

Not even bodily contact admits of differentiation among faces in the crowd; no relation between the "I" and the swarming, antlike mass can be established. Boileau's poem ends with an acerbic recognition of the power of money in metropolitan life: sleep, he opines, can only be bought for a price:

> Ce n'est qu'à prix d'argent qu'on dort en cette ville.
>
> Only money buys sleep in this city.

The rich, the speaker tells us, can turn the world upside down; they can change the noisy urban Paris of crowds and traffic into the quiet of the countryside; their gardens are "peuplé d'arbres verts" rather than by the undifferentiated mass, the *peuple* the speaker encounters in his nightmarish, toponarcotic plunge through urban space. Satire, with its opposition of an "I" and an adversary, is the formal means here of differentiating between persons of different social statuses and degrees, a differentiation that metropolitan space erodes, yet the "I" is produced paradoxically through the very anonymity of the urban crowd: Paris is at once the object of satire and of anxious desire. The technology that allowed the building of the Pont Neuf reorganized the subject in urban space, provided new arenas for the distribution and dissemination of cultural capital, and fostered its accumulation, both cultural and material.

Boileau, of bourgeois origins, produced himself as a defender and producer of high-cultural forms, and he has been read since the seventeenth century in precisely those terms, as exemplifying neoclassical canons. Commentators invariably point out his classicism and his debt to Juvenal in the satires, but as I have demonstrated, this poem plays its part in the reconfigured cultural logic I am analyzing: to situate Satire VI in relation to the urbanization of early modern Paris is to challenge readings of Boileau as simply a high-cultural, elite author harkening back to the classical past; it is to read him instead as part of that configuration we call modernity—the "je" of the sixth satire is never a unified subject but is bumped and buffeted, jostled and shoved, knocked down and run over, divided and individual, with all the complexities of meaning that word accretes in the course of the seventeenth century.[31] The implications of my claims here are important not so much for reading a particular author—Boileau—but for refuting, on one hand, Jameson's criticism of the new historicism and, on the other, the constitution of cultural studies in today's academy. Cultural studies continues to operate as if "politics" inheres in the object of study, and it has been therefore focused almost exclusively on late nineteenth-century and twentieth-century mass culture and, less frequently, on popular culture of the past. Renaissance studies, for example, has been preoccupied with popular cultural forms, most notably, of course, Shakespeare. Hence my own perverse choice of Boileau to make my argument. The fundamental arena in which political struggle is waged is the legitimacy of concepts, of ideologies.[32] Politics inheres not in the object of study but in the way we *read*. Pace Jameson, new historicism does not merely produce homologies but legitimates ways of reading that are neither narrowly literary nor historical and that depend not on the content or provenance of a text for their political valence but on reading both high- and low-cultural forms.

The second epigraph to this chapter records Freud's memorial account of his early sojourn in Paris in 1885–86 and returns us to the cognitive and psychic consequences of urbanization. There he first met Charcot, an encounter that Ernest Jones claims in his biography turned Freud from neurologist to psychopathologist and which thus is represented as a founding moment of psychoanalysis.[33] In Freud's letters of this period, Charcot is oddly figured in terms of Parisian monuments and pastimes: after his lectures, Freud goes out "as from Notre Dame, with new impressions to work over," and his brain, he relates, "is sated as after an evening at the theatre."[34] He refers frequently to Notre Dame as emblem of the city and twice recounts climbing its towers. He even came to admire Hugo's *Notre Dame de Paris* more, Jones recounts, than neuropathology, though Freud claims not to have appreciated the novel before his sojourn in Paris. On departing, he carried back to Vienna as a souvenir a photograph of the Parisian cathedral. Not only Notre Dame but other city landmarks figure prominently in Freud's letters from Paris, from the Louvre to Père Lachaise. Jones also reports that Freud wrote a long, illustrated account of Paris's topography and sights to his betrothed, Martha Bernays, that included a sketch of the city.[35]

But Freud's letters from this period are far from presenting Paris in the nostalgic, even ecstatic terms of my epigraph's retrospective depiction. In the letters to Bernays during his first months in Paris, he recounts being bewildered by its crowds, paranoid of his surroundings (he apparently tested the green curtains around his hotel bed, fearing they contained arsenic); he records meticulously the cost of lodging, food, and books; he disparages the city's inhabitants whom he dubs arrogant, inaccessible, shameless cheats. They are hostile, subject to psychical epidemics and mass convulsions, allusions to the continuing, anxious preoccupation with the French Revolution displayed by European visitors observing the French scene. In a telling anecdote from his first day in Paris he recounts feeling so isolated and lonely that had he not, as Jones reports, had "a silk hat and gloves he could have broken down and cried in the streets."[36] Only his sense of his separation from the crowd, marked by class—silk hat, gloves—prevents psychic breakdown. In other words, Freud's later topolatry, that is, reverence or excessive adoration for a particular space or place—Paris—is retrospectively produced in the register of the imaginary, a topographic imaginary in which he also locates the fulfillment of his ambitious wishes. He writes at this time to Bernays from densely populated Paris: "I feel it in my bones that I have the talent to bring me into the 'upper ten thousand.'" Freud's retrospective bliss at traversing the streets of Paris begins as topophobia, a topophobia produced by a xenophobic intensification of the peripatetic experience of city noise, demographic menace, metropolitan space, and urban anonymity.[37]

Topophobic Coda: Cade's Rebellion and London Bridge

Silk as a status or class distinction, fear of mass convulsion, disorder and the urban street, xenophobia, the world turned upside down—thus Boileau, Freud, and Shakespeare's Jack Cade come together. The Jack Cade rebellion in *2 Henry VI* rehearses early modern anxieties about urbanization: the mix of persons, disorder, threat, the crowd. My interest here is the representation of London in the play, the role of London Bridge in the action, and the temporal disjunction between the play's account of events that took place in the mid–fifteenth century and the many anachronistic London place-names Cade and his followers invoke. Though Cade's rebellion makes up less than one act in Shakespeare's *Henry VI* plays that chronicle the so-called Wars of the Roses, the protracted struggle of the houses of York and Lancaster for the English throne following the death of Henry V, Cade and his revolt have garnered voluminous commentary among Shakespeareans. Critics have used the play to speculate about Shakespeare's attitude toward popular rebellion and have argued on both sides of the question: on one hand, Shakespeare, it is claimed, registered "the sneering impatience with the language of peasants and artisans of the literate bourgeois" and represented Cade's rebellion "as a grotesque and sinister farce, the archetypal lower class revolt both in its motives and ludicrousness"; or, on the other, that Shakespeare was acquainted with and deployed the language of the egalitarian tradition to express social inequity and reveal certain social distinctions as "corrupt social practice."[38] William Carroll offers a middle ground: "In these plays, disorder from below is invariably condemned, though its causes are admitted."[39]

The action of *1–3 Henry VI* chronicles events that took place over the course of Henry's reign during the middle of the fifteenth century. *2 Henry VI* is generally thought to have been written in the early 1590s, before parts 1 and 3. Episodic in structure, it recounts the fall of Duke Humphrey of Gloucester, Lord Protector and uncle to the king, and a series of treasonous incidents that beset Henry's reign, including the Cade Rebellion that attempted to topple the monarchy by capturing London. Though act 4 of Shakespeare's play purports to represent the events surrounding the Kentish rebellion of June 1450, commentators have long recognized the playwright's conflation of a series of peasant revolts and, more important for our purposes, urban protests in the 1590s, in his presentation of Cade's rebellion.[40] Jack Cade's rebellion is presented anachronistically, situated not in the mid-fifteenth-century London of Henry VI but in Shakespeare's London, a city, as Roger Manning insists, "troubled by popular protest. . . . Between 1581 and 1602, the city was disturbed by no fewer than 35 outbreaks of disorder. Since there were at least 96 insurrections, riots and unlawful assemblies in London between 1517 and 1640, this means that more than one-third of the instances of popular disorder during that century-and-a-quarter were concentrated within a 20-year period."[41] Manning attributes this rash of outbreaks of disorder and riot not, as has often been claimed, to hunger and famine following the harvest failures of the 1590s but to "extraordinarily rapid population growth" and the host of problems it precipitated in the city.[42]

For the rebel Cade and his "ragged multitude" from Kent to succeed, they must capture London, and from Cade's first appearance on the scene, he is determined not merely to take London but to arrest the changes brought about by urbanization and mercantile expansion that have led to the desperate poverty recorded in Simpcox's wife's line "Alas! sir, we did it for pure need" (2.1.150). Instead, he seeks to establish a utopic state in which all "shall be in common." Famously, Cade vows to reverse inflation, to criminalize the watering down of beer he associates with town trade, to stop enclosure, and to pull down London's chief commercial district, Cheapside, where he intends instead to graze his horse: "There shall be in England seven halfpenny loaves sold for a penny; the three-hoop'd pot shall have ten hoops; and I will make it felony to drink small beer. All the realm shall be in common, and in Cheapside shall my palfrey go to grass."[43] "Come; let's march towards London" (4.3.16–17), he cries. Only when it is reported that "Jack Cade hath almost gotten London Bridge" (4.4.48) does the king finally agree to flee the city. The taking of the bridge provokes the citizens to "fly and forsake their houses; / The rascal people" to "Join with the traitor; and they jointly swear / To spoil the city and your royal court" (4.4.49–52). Cade's brief victory and rampage are chronicled by London place-names: Cheapside and London Bridge, Southwark, the Tower, London Stone, Cannon Street, the Little Conduit, Pissing Conduit, Smithfield, the Savoy, the Inns of Court, the Standard, Billingsgate, Fish Street, Mile End Green, Saint Magnus' Corner, Saint George's Fields, the White Hart in Southwark, Bedlam, the Thames. Some date from the fifteenth century, but others anachronistically from Shakespeare's London: Bedlam, Billingsgate, Southwark, the Standard, and London Stone were already place-names in the reign of Henry VI, as was Smithfield, the Savoy palace, that dated from the thirteenth century, and the White Hart, for which there is a reference as early as 1498. But Cannon Street, Cheapside (earlier Chepe, Cheap, or West Chepe/Cheap), possibly Fish Street, and the Pissing Conduit are sixteenth-century usage.[44] No play of Shakespeare's recalls so many London place-names, and no place is mentioned more frequently than London Bridge, the point of entry to the city from the south that Cade "has almost gotten," then wins, orders burned, contradictorily orders saved, and across which he parades the heads of the executed Lord Saye and his son-in-law, kissing, and whom Cade has ordered executed on the anachronistic grounds that Sayre had "caused printing to be used" and "built a paper mill" (4.7.30–33).[45] Though some critics have seen Cade's attack on printing and literacy as entirely negative, one more episode of grotesque low comedy that works to deflate social critique and undermine the legitimacy of complaints by the poor, others have recognized in its attack on lawyers, records, and literacy not "a farcical assault on literacy designed to discredit Cade, . . . [but] an attack on the records and recorders whose presence permitted and promoted the oppressive collection of revenues."[46]

London Bridge, like most medieval bridges, was dark and narrow, built up several stories on both sides with houses and shops, and it remained so well into the seventeenth century. Thus it was closer in use and appearance, though

not in size or material construction, to the Parisian bridges that preceded the
Pont Neuf. Whereas Parisians crossing the Pont Neuf enjoyed a broad, open
bridge with sidewalks built for traffic from which they could survey the burgeoning city on both banks of the Seine, early modern inhabitants of London
were met with a startlingly different sight. Instead of a clock mounted on a
modern waterworks reminding them of urban time—not the time of the seasons, or night and day, but time divided and quantifiable, the time of workdays
and appointments—in Shakespeare's day Londoners traversed a narrow passage and were confronted with the remains of executed traitors and criminals
whose heads were commonly mounted on the bridge and are clearly visible in
Visscher's famous view of the city (fig. 20, detail). Whereas the French king
Henry IV was among the first to cross the newly opened Pont Neuf to demonstrate to his subjects its safety and utility, English monarchs often went to
extraordinary lengths to avoid London Bridge. Though Henry V famously
entered the city by crossing London Bridge after his victory at Agincourt in
1415, again in 1421 following his marriage to Katherine, and a final time
when his funeral bier crossed the bridge on its way to London from France in
1422, Queen Elizabeth showed a topophobic aversion to the bridge. Though
the bridge was a place of ritual celebration and pageantry for Londoners themselves which John Norden described as "comparable in itselfe to a little Citie"
and "one of the wonders of the world," Elizabeth, who famously enjoyed
mingling with her people, apparently found its narrow passageway, overhanging shops and houses, and snarl of traffic menacing. Following her accession
in 1558 until 1579, Elizabeth seems to have entered the city over London
Bridge only once.[47] In that year, she planned an elaborate entry into the city
across the bridge but seems to have canceled at the last moment, thus proving,
according to the Spanish ambassador, "how little confidence these rulers have,
even in their own people, and that many are watching for an opportunity of
shaking off the yoke."[48] The queen seems to have preferred arriving by water
even though "shooting the bridge," or passing beneath it through one of its
narrow arches, often led to overturned barges and drowning—Wolsey notoriously disembarked, climbed onto a mule and rode through Thames Street
before dismounting and renewing his journey by water.

Far from the spacious sign of urban modernity that was the Pont Neuf,
London Bridge in the sixteenth and seventeenth centuries remained the medieval bridge it was in Cade's day, a narrow, crowded, almost tunnel-like passage
from Southwark to the city of London. Whereas "medieval London's population, commercial activity, and significance was concentrated in the city north
of the river, and Southwark, on the south bank, was only a minor and satellite
settlement," as Vanessa Harding has observed,[49] by 1630 urban historians
believe inhabitants of Southwark may have numbered 20,000, while the population of the city north of the river had reached at least 120,000. The eastern

Figure 20. London Bridge, detail from Visscher's long view of London, ca. 1600.
Bibliothèque nationale

and western suburbs probably doubled that figure. Unlike Paris, where the court and fashionable quarters developed on the Right Bank across from the long-established governmental, judicial, religious, and university institutions on the Left Bank and the islands of the Seine, which made the Pont Neuf an arterial link between two major and increasingly equal parts of one urban entity, London and its population developed unevenly until well into the eighteenth century. The court and fashionable Westminster and the Inns of

Court expanded to the west of the City; both were north of the Thames, while Southwark grew more slowly.[50]

Southwark was separated from the City in other ways as well: notoriously, to cross the bridge meant leaving the City's jurisdiction and entering the suburbs and liberties, a different county and diocese that housed the brothels and theaters to which London's city fathers so frequently objected.[51] Though Southwark became a ward of the City in 1550, it was not fully integrated until much later. It offered space for institutions such as hospitals and prisons, as well as for the city estates of nobles. The bridge provided residents on both sides access, but its narrow passage could accommodate neither the city's burgeoning pedestrian nor its increasing vehicular traffic. To an even greater extent than in Paris, London's watermen who plied the river offered the principal means of crossing from the city to Southwark.

There is no consensus concerning the origins and mode of construction of London Bridge, but by the fourteenth century it was an established feature of life in London.[52] A medieval bridge built up some five stories high with each story stepped out over the one below, thus creating a virtual tunnel, it was dark, dangerous, and conducive to ambush from both filth and crime. In one way it was like its French counterpart: Nonsuch House, said to have been erected during Elizabeth's reign, like the Pont Neuf's Samaritan, was built by the Dutch; in 1582 a Dutch engineer constructed four water wheels at the bridge that conveyed water to Thames Street, Leadenhall Street, and the neighborhoods of Aldsgate.[53] No more than twenty feet wide at its broadest and in some places as narrow as twelve feet, it offered no quarter for pedestrians. Home to merchants and enterprises of various sorts, including at one time or another both the book and cloth trades, and to one John Allan at the "Lock of Hair" who sold hair, "curled and uncurled, bags, roses, cauls, ribbons, weaving, sewing, silks, cards, blocks with all goods made use of by peruke makers at the lowest prices," London Bridge was a busy commercial street.[54] It burned in 1632 and was not rebuilt for almost a decade, but when Charles II returned from exile to England, he entered his capital city across London Bridge; in fact, London Bridge remained the only bridge across the Thames until the eighteenth century.

Long associated with rebellion, London Bridge was, as chroniclers recount, often graced with reminders of treason—the heads of traitors displayed on pikes at what was originally Traitor's Gate: Wat Tyler, Jack Cade himself, Sir Thomas More, Guy Fawkes, and many more. Jean Froissart relates how, after Henry IV, then Duke of Lancaster had imprisoned Richard II, the Lord Mayor caused to be beheaded knights of the king's household, and "their heads affixed to spikes on London-bridge";[55] in 1554 when Sir Thomas Wyatt led an uprising against Mary I and threatened to lead his troops across the bridge into London, the queen appealed to the City for her defense. Members of the livery companies held London Bridge against the rebels, and Wyatt was forced to enter the city the long way round via Kingston some fifteen miles upstream. A visitor to London in 1602 described "the heads of 30 gentlemen of high standing who had been beheaded on account of treason and secret practices against the Queen" exhibited on the bridge.[56] No wonder, then, that London Bridge was associated not with urban development, vehicular traffic, and the burgeoning English nation-state but with fear, mutiny, and rebellion.

Traversing urban space, as I have argued, was the chief pastime of the early modern city dweller regardless of social rank, but urban space was also the site of contest, riot, and conflagration long before 1848 or the Paris Commune. Shakespeare registers the significance of urban space to rebellion in his transference of the riot and disorder of late sixteenth-century London to Cade's charge through what was then a medieval city. In his work on everyday life, Michel de Certeau compares traversing the city to speech acts and describes its "triple 'enunciative' function: it is a process of *appropriation* of the topographic system on the part of the pedestrian . . . ; it is a spatial acting-out of the place . . . ; and it implies *relations* among differentiated positions" (97–98).[57] Boileau in his Satire VI, Sieur Bertaut in *La ville de Paris en vers burlesques*, Freud in his letters to his wife, and Shakespeare in *2 Henry VI,* all witness this enunciative function of moving through the city. Though psychoanalysis is sometimes imagined as privileging time over space in its concern with theories of the subject as constituted in and through the past, psychoanalytic processes have, of course, a resolutely spatial dimension. That spatial dimension is not merely etymological, as in *displacement* or *transference*, but gestured at in Virginia Woolf's famous phrase describing psychoanalysis and the unconscious: "The moment of importance came not here but there." Past trauma is presented spatially—"there, not here," rather than "then, not now," by what linguists term *spatial deictics*, expressions that specify spatial location "relative to the location of the speaker or the addressee."[58] Though the space of psychoanalysis is, of course, profoundly a mental and, for Freud, a neurological, space, we need also to consider that space prosaically, to refuse its figurality and to look at the urban spaces in which the human sciences, including history, psychology, and psychoanalysis, came to be produced.

CHAPTER THREE

Walking Capitals

Traversing urban space—the streets and bridges, squares and fairs, markets and exchanges of the city—was, as I have argued, perhaps the chief pastime of the early modern city dweller regardless of social rank. The inhabitants of and visitors to seventeenth-century London and Paris frequented in particular certain sites that become the subject of literary and visual representation as well as of historical record. The bridges of Paris, its fairs, the Palais (de Justice) with its more than two hundred boutiques, the Luxembourg Gardens, the Cours la Reine, and the Tuileries were among the most frequented places of seventeenth-century Paris. Though some catered to or were reserved for the elite, others such as the newly built Pont Neuf or the popular foire Saint-Germain, which, with its named streets and places of resort, modeled the city itself and inspired an entire literature (fig. 21),[1] served inhabitants and visitors from across the social and economic spectrum who mixed there in unprecedented proximity. Londoners frequented Saint Paul's, the Exchange (fig. 22), the Strand, Moorfields, and somewhat later Covent Garden, as well as Smithfield at fair time, of which John Taylor, the Water Poet, wrote: "Hither resort people of all sorts, High and Low, Rich and Poor, from cities, town and countries; of all sorts . . . [and] all conditions."[2] With regard to green space, both cities shifted from peripheral fields, meadow and pasture for walking to gardens and more ordered, formal sites.[3] Walking the city was undertaken for myriad purposes—to carry on business, to shop and consume, to encounter those whom one cannot hope or expect to encounter elsewhere in more exclusive interior spaces, to see and to be seen, in short, to absorb the social knowledge offered in streets, shops, by criers and street sellers, in outdoor theaters, by passersby.[4]

As we saw in chapters 1 and 2, many different kinds of texts directed to very different audiences depict moving through the city space of early modern London and Paris, texts we ordinarily separate generically: not only the survey and guidebook, the verse satire of Boileau, the masque and other forms of elite entertainment, but also street poetry and pamphlets, the diary or journal, city comedy and the comic novel. However important generic differentiation for formalist analysis, such segregation and the distinction popular/elite it entails preclude questions of the sort I wish to raise here. The characteristic strategy of these texts on Paris and London is, as I have shown, to present a pedestrian/speaker/narrator who moves through urban space undergoing a

Figure 21. Plan of the foire Saint-Germain, engraving by Iollain,
late seventeenth century. Bibliothèque nationale

series of encounters characteristic of metropolitan life. Often he is accompanied by someone else, frequently a visitor to the city—provincial or foreign—whom he introduces to urban sights and pleasures and warns of urban ills and dangers. Donne's Satyre I, Boileau's Satire VI, Charles Sorel's *Polyandre* and the collaborative *Le parasite mormom*, Robert Greene's cony-catching pamphlets, Everard Guilpin's "Of Caius," Paul Scarron's short poem on the foire Saint-Germain and John Taylor's poem "Bartholomew Faire," Ben Jonson's "On the Famous Voyage," D'Avenant's "The Long Vacation," and popular poetry such as the "Ville de Paris en vers burlesque" all variously present a speaker / narrator who moves on foot through city space encountering its sites and inhabitants, frequently describing particular places of resort and detailing the dangers and pleasures on offer in both capitals.

What is the relation of this poetic strategy to the notion of the *flâneur* said to be inspired by the nineteenth-century city? Though the first uses of the word *flâneur* do in fact date from the early part of the nineteenth century, *flânerie* and the verb *flâner*, meaning "se promener sans hâte, au hasard, en

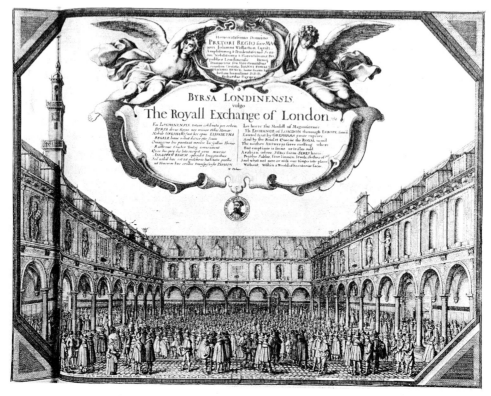

Figure 22. The Royal Exchange, London. Bibliothèque nationale

s'abandonnant à l'impression et au spectacle du moment" (to walk in a lei-
surely fashion, wherever, giving oneself up to the impressions and sights of
the moment) date from the early seventeenth century and are linked to the
Scandinavian *flana*, meaning to run here and there. The word *flâneur* itself
seems initially to have been a synonym for the older term *badaud*, which meant
someone who stops to look or gape at the spectacle of the street. The word was
proverbially linked to the inhabitants of Paris: Rabelais uses it with reference to
Parisians, whom he accuses of being so "badaud" that common city sites—a
waterman, a mule with its bells—make them stop, stare, and form a crowd
more readily than a preacher. *Robert* even gives as an example of the adjectival
form "Le Parisien est badaud." The word has a certain pejorative cast in the
sense of connoting a dumbstruck gawker. Walter Benjamin's inflection of
Baudelaire's *flâneur* is a flattering reading of the older word *badaud* in which
the gaze of the subject is no longer dumb wonder but seeks to fix the spectacle
of the urban environment in a safe relation to the subject's desires, to confer
meaning and "depth" on the appropriated sight.[5] The notion of a certain sort
of pedestrian movement through city space in which the subject's attention is

arrested by the spectacle of the street—the idea of *flânerie*—thus dates from the early seventeenth century when Paris and London become major metropolitan centers whose streets are filled with sights that capture the attention of passersby. In Satire VI, which we have already considered in some detail in the preceding chapter, Boileau emphasizes the speaker's haphazard movement through the city: "je me mets au hazard," "sans songer où je vais," he stumbles through the streets, caught up in the crowds, traffic, and noise, accosted by thieves that roam the city after dark. His walk through the streets of Paris, however directionless, is far from the strolling *flâneur* whose gaze is caught by urban spectacle and chance encounters; there is little to suggest the attractions of urban life. In contrast, Bertaut's speaker and his visitor enjoy the spectacle of urban life, their various encounters, and the *copia* of Parisian life.

Donne's first satire provides a compelling demonstration of the temptations and attractions of the London streets and *flânerie*. Donne's satires are generally attributed to the period he spent living at the Inns of Court in the early 1590s. His biographer Bald dates his entry into Lincoln's Inn May 1592 when, he opines, "all the life of the metropolis beckoned to him."[6] The city's expansion from east to west produced new social topographies, and the inns, located between the City and Westminster, became centers of intellectual and, especially, literary activity, where young men congregated to pursue distinction, pleasure, and advancement.[7] A contemporary described the inns as "a kind of academy of all the manners nobles learn," and Francis Lenton in his *Characterisimi* (1631) avers that young men of the inns showed a marked preference for "Shakespeare's plaies instead of my Lord Coke" (sig. F4).[8] Membership in the inns expanded in the 1590s and became increasingly divided between those students in pursuit of "civility" who privileged amateurism and leisure over professionalism, and the more serious students of law. Commentators have consistently allied Donne with the former, with the circle of young men at the inns seeking preferment at court and in letters through mastery of gentlemanly codes of wit and manners.[9]

Satyre I opens in medias res with the speaker banishing his interlocutor, dubbed a "fondling motley humorist," who is apparently importuning him to leave his study and take to the streets.[10] The opening lines oppose two kinds of "consort," the speaker's with his books, the humanist's cultural capital made up of works of divinity, Aristotle, history, and poetry and which he calls "constant company," versus an outing accompanied by his importunate, changeable companion. This opposition is also worked out spatially through the juxtaposition of the speaker's study, which is likened to both a prison and a coffin, and the city's peopled streets.[11] Commentators usually divide the poem into two sections, the first fifty-two lines before the speaker acquiesces to his companion's desire that he go out, and the next sixty lines in which the two men move through the streets of London. But already while still in his study, before he takes to the streets with his companion, Donne's speaker

retails a few of the temptations and encounters the London streets afford: the
wealthy and fashionably dressed (a gilt-clad captain, a perfum'd courtier, and
a "velvet justice" with liveried entourage), plump muddy whores, prostitute
boys, London heirs and heiresses, even meteorological prognosticators. The
poem's opening sixty lines present a cross section of the city's inhabitants and
their ranks: the court, the military, the judiciary, apprentices, schoolboys, and
people living off the streets.

   Once in the street, they meet a "well favour'd youth" (84) famed in the
capital for dancing divinely, and another who excels "Th'Indians, in drinking
his Tobacco well" (88). Tobacco, so ambivalently popular in the 1590s, was
one of many foreign luxury imports newly available in the capital.[17] The
speaker and his companion next encounter a decked-out fashion maven, then
an urbane traveler who "seeme[s] to be / Perfect French, and Italian." Consumer goods and services are retailed on persons and in the grammatical series,
as at line 97 ("To judge of lace, pinke, panes, print, cut, and plight") and the
poem makes allusion to popular London sights of the 1590s, including an
elephant being exhibited in 1593–94 and "Morocco," a numerate bay gelding
said to be able to add, to tell the number of coins in a purse, to dance, and
to bite and strike if you mentioned the despised king of Spain. Despite the
variety of persons encountered, the London population of Donne's satire,
unlike many urban poems of the period, is peculiarly homogeneous: it is "men
of sort, of parts, and qualities" (105); in moving through the London streets,
they encounter few of the shopkeepers and small craftsmen, the criers and
watermen, the beggars and urban poor that made up the largest proportion
of the city's population; in Donne's poem such people are distinguished rhetorically; they are represented by analogy in simile: "like a needy broker" (30),
"As prentises, or schoole-boyes" (75), or by the city's sexual underworld represented synecdochically by muddy whore and prostitute boy (40). Merchants,
shopkeepers, and artisans appear metonymically through the goods they trade,
sell, or produce. For the speaker's companion, however, the homogeneous
"men of sort, of parts, and qualities" (105) they meet as they walk out perhaps
from the Inns and toward the Strand are by no means alike; much of the
poem's action turns on the humorist's valuation of the various persons they
meet whom he judges particularly by their apparel. The satire's first simile
compares him to a pawnbroker shrewdly appraising goods:

> When thou meet'st one, with enquiring eyes
> Dost search, and like a needy broker prize
> The silke, and gold he weares, and to that rate
> So high or low, dost raise thy formall hat. (29–32)

The humorist hails each according to his conspicuous consumption, but he
will consort with none "untill thou have knowne / What lands hee hath in
hope, or of his owne" (33–34). Even walking in the street itself has its own

status protocols. The humorist claims the privileged place: he walks inside, "to the wall," presumably protected by overhanging eaves from the ever-present danger of mud and filth jettisoned from windows or clogging conduits and city streets. So confined and thus unable to address "every fine silken painted foole we meet," instead he solicits them with "amorous smiles," "grins," "smacks," and "shrugs," stooping low "to the most brave" (78).

C. S. Lewis, in his commentary on Donne's satires in the *Oxford History of English Literature*, complained that "everything that might make his lines come smoothly off the tongue is deliberately avoided. Accents are violently misplaced and some lines defy scansion altogether. The thought develops in unexpected and even tormented fashion." Lewis attributed this metrical irregularity to what he terms the "old blunder which connected *satira* with *satyros*"—in short, to classical influence. But Donne's metrical audacities in Satyre I evoke "headlong, wild uncertaine" (12) movement through the urban cityscape, jostling, unexpected encounters, peripatetic confrontations, and propulsive hustle, in short not so much blundering etymology as rhythm and meter before urban planning.

Movement through urban space ceases abruptly in the satire at line 106 when the "motley humorist" "his Love he in a windowe spies." This urban window frames not the beloved of courtly poetry glimpsed on a balcony or in a casement, but spied out, its commercial character displayed to passersby, a part of that "Shew" of consumer goods that according to the antiquarian John Stow characterized London and prompted pedestrians both to gaze and to buy. The line alludes both to the practice of prostitutes advertising their wares in urban windows and to tradesmen's wives pranked up and sitting at the door or in the window of their shops to entice customers, a practice frequently remarked in city comedy.[13] Having abandoned the speaker for his "Love," another example of sexual capital purveyed in London's streets, the roving companion finds himself apparently in a crowd of customers quarreling and fighting until, wounded and turned out again into the streets, he comes in the poem's final couplet directly "to mee hanging [his] head, / And constantly a while must keepe his bed."

Traditional commentary on Donne's first satire denies any specificity to the urban space through which the two men move. Instead, critics point to Horace's Satire I, 9 and, in the words of Donne's editor Milgate, the "idea of a walk in the street with a wearisome companion." Critics claim that Donne reworks the Horatian pretext to present an allegorical debate between "soul and body, spiritual endeavor and physical appetite."[14] Or in a similarly binary interpretation, the satire is said to dramatize the dilemma of a character faced with a choice between "the moral and philosophical values of a scholar and the self-indulgent morality of the society."[15] Typically in such readings, the specificity of the capital city and its seductive forms of cultural capital are ignored or relegated to the editorial apparatus, barely accorded the dignity of

literary history. Despite his own careful glosses of the varied topical allusions
to London in the 1590s in his edition of the satires, Milgate claims Donne's
satires are "in the worst sense, imitative," his subjects "the stock-in-trade of
Roman satire, and indeed of sermons, homilies, and moral writings throughout the ages."[16] The streets through which the speaker moves with his companion are consigned to the putatively generic street of classical satire. But Horace's Satire I, 9 differs from Donne's from its opening line. Whereas Horace
evokes Rome by punctuating his poem with place-names—"ibam forte via
Sacra," the Tiber, Caesar's gardens, the temple of Vesta—place is conspicuously absent from Donne's satire. Instead, Donne's London is evoked through
a series of peripatetic encounters that register demographic anxiety and what
Simmel in his consideration of the metropolitan type termed "the intensification of nervous stimulation" characteristic of the metropolis. In fact, Donne's
poem illustrates the impact of an emergent metropolitan market society on
both the authorizing tropes of classical satire and the received terms of humanist discourse. The poem contrasts different kinds of cultural capital—books
and reading, religious, philosophical, historical, and poetic, that is, the conso-
lations of the study—with the luxuries of the capital and a developing world
market: fashion and sartorial variety, perfume, tobacco, exotic animals, French
and Italian manners, the theater, and sex.[17] Here urbane London is a space of
sexual encounter where one meets, apparently indiscriminately, whores and
prostitute boys, where one seeks to seduce the rich or useful with "amorous
smiles" (73). Even the humanist learning the speaker leaves behind in his
study, which is presented as opposed to the urban world outside, subtly foreshadows his walk through the city streets: his books are "Gods conduits,"
urban water pipes as well as figuratively the channels through which knowledge flows, and the Aristotle to which he refers would seem to be the *Politics*,
since it teaches "of a cities mistique bodie" (8) or the body politic. Not even
the speaker's study is a safe space of contemplative retreat cut off from the
city beyond.

Whereas Horace's speaker seeks to ditch the bore at every turn, Donne's
relation to his companion is quite different. Though the speaker chastises his
companion for his toadying, fickle, headlong movement through the London
crowd, an attitude initiated in the opening plosive imperatives ("Away" and
"Leave mee") and marked by the shift from "thou" to "he" (67), a strategy of
satire Lawrence Manley characterizes as "the degeneration of second-person
confreres into third-person targets,"[18] the speaker finds the humorist tempt-
ing. That temptation is marked by the pun on "fall" in his question, "Shall I
leave all this constant company, / And follow headlong, wild uncertaine thee?"
Seduced by his attraction to his companion of whom he is jealous and whose
desertion, termed adultery, he fears, lured by the crowded streets, he leaves
his study and the inherited terms of humanist discourse to walk the streets.
Critics influenced perhaps by Walton's Dr. Donne claim that Christian duty

drives Donne's persona to satire. The speaker/scholar decides to accompany the humorist as he walks the London streets because, we are told, the humorist is "a man worthy of and in need of counsel." The speaker is said to be insistent "on showing the fop the spiritual significance of his actions" and to "reclaim the soul of his worldly friend."[19] Readings less determined to interpret the satires through Walton and Donne's later career in the church, but nevertheless focused on the corrective impulse of satire, point to the speaker's attempts to reform his companion and to censure his behavior. Certainly the poem provides ample evidence of his exasperated, critical judgments and rebukes, a pattern Manley claims characterizes Elizabethan satire and distinguishes it from its classical counterpart. The speaker is engaged, he claims, in an "urgent but futile attempt to win over a young companion . . . at the very moment he is being lost to the world's folly."[20]

In *The Cankered Muse*, Alvin Kernan analyzes the ambivalence characteristic of the satirist who, though a "foe of vice," also envies "the fools he despises and castigates" (116). Kernan points out the satirist's taste for the sensational, his exposure of sins of which he too is guilty, and his melancholy at that recognition, but oddly Kernan claims Donne an exception to this tradition. Donne's satirist/speaker is, according to Kernan, free of such taint.[21] But in Satyre I, Donne seems at pains to reveal if not the speaker's complicity in the humorist's vices, then his desire for his foppish, flirtatious, socially aspirant companion, his "fondling," which means both fool and one who is fondled and loved.[22] Even as the speaker dissociates himself from his *adversarius*'s fawning obsequiousness and social climbing, he is his accomplice and more. His imperatives and contemptuous judgments belie an ambivalence that mixes revulsion and attraction toward his companion and the urban crowd. He demands that the humorist "sweare by thy best love in earnest. . . .Thou wilt not leave mee in the middle street" and alludes to their relation in terms of marriage ("For better or worse take mee, or leave mee: / To take, and leave mee is adultery" [25–26]); he obsesses over his companion's "ranke itchie lust, desire and love" (38) for naked whore and prostitute boy, and in the final lines of the poem he can only imagine his companion's desertion jealously as a kind of rape: "He flings from mee / Violently ravish'd to his lechery" (107–8). Even the poem's arguably most conventionally Christian moment, lines 42 through 52, in which the speaker muses on "Mans first blest state" and his subsequent fall, he is preparing to sally forth into the city streets, playing Adam in his "course attire" to the humorist's better-dressed Eve.

Though commentators usually take the "Love" of the final lines to be a woman, there is nothing to indicate the sex of the beloved, and certainly the satire makes casual allusion to both same-sex and cross-sex relations. At line 24, for example, in characterizing the humorist's putative obsequiousness in encountering the velvet-clad justice, he asks, "Wilt thou grin or fawne on him, or prepare / A speech to court his beautious sonne and heir." Uncomfort-

able with the characterization of the heir as beauteous and the humorist's
actions as courtship, Milgate glosses this line as follows: "The 'humorist,'
impressed by the judge's splendour, will think of cultivating his son and heir
as a way into high society, or as a source of wealth . . . or as a potential ward:
for any of these reasons, the heir would seem beauteous" (120). In general,
critics eschew mention of the "prostitute boy" and the speaker's apparent
desire for his companion. This instability of sexual allusion makes the final
lines particularly interesting: the action moves from study to street to an oddly
unlocated bed, a spatial trajectory also marked by abrupt temporal shifts.
When the humorist returns hanging his head, injured, from his encounter
with the suitors, he "directly came to mee," the speaker. Where is the speaker
when his companion regains his company? is he still in the street? has he
walked back to his study? to his companion's own quarters? In his first undevi-
ating act in a poem of movement and encounter, the "fondling motley humorist" "constantly a while must keepe his bed" (112). How do we move from
street to bed? Past, present, and future are compressed in the verb forms of
the poem's last several lines. And though the pronoun *his* gives possession of
the bed to the companion, the previous line of this rhymed couplet with its
emphatic first-person pronoun "mee" ties the bed to the speaker:

> Directly came to mee hanging the head,
> And constantly awhile must keepe his bed (111–12).

Here the humorist's hanging head, on the one hand, offers bawdy sexual
innuendo, but on the other betrays shame, an affect unlike any registered
earlier in the poem, an affect perhaps unexpected in satire. Both sexual joke
and affective gesture register the speaker's vexed relation to his companion
and the seductive urban life he represents. Walton's account of Donne's life
of study while at the Inns of Court outlines succinctly the entire action of
Satyre I: "In the most unsettled days of his youth, his bed was not able to
detain him beyond the hour of four in the morning; and it was no common
business that drew him out of his chamber till past ten; all which time was
employed in study; though he took great liberty after it."[23] Here Donne's bed
is unable to detain him from his studies, whereas in Satyre I the humorist's
bed at last detains him from London's urban attractions. But even here the
constancy of his keeping his bed is undermined by the adverbial—"constantly."
    The streets of late sixteenth-century London proffer cultural, social, and
sexual capital. They are filled with, in Bourdieu's phrase, systems of "mutually
reinforcing and infinitely redundant signs of which each body is the bearer—
clothing, pronunciation, bearing, posture, manners . . . the basis of 'antipa-
thies' or 'sympathies' " (241). On the one hand, the speaker's denigration of
his companion's obeisance to social and cultural capital would seem to distinguish him from that companion, but that distinction is betrayed by the speaker's own desire. At once fascinated and repulsed by the urban world of luxury

goods and the sophisticated jet set—or rather coach set—that consume them, the speaker's "I" is produced through a series of mediated encounters with the well-heeled, the well-traveled, and the well-connected in which the humorist is positioned as a buffer. The London streets are purged all but rhetorically of the city's sexual low life, its teeming commerce, and its motley crowd, which are not directly encountered but appear only putatively in simile or comparison. From those maligned but enticing encounters he wrests words. Christian humanist diction ("God," "Divines," "contrite penitent," "sinnes," "repent," "vanities") is opposed to the language of urban commerce and cultural capital; that world is displayed through the peripatetic urban encounter.

In the conclusion to *Postmodernism, or, the Cultural Logic of Late Capitalism*, Fredric Jameson reflects on the materialist dimension of demography and the "radical cultural effects" of "this enlargement of the peopled universe" associated with urbanization, globalization, and globalization's apparent celebration of difference.[24] Jameson produces the postmodern challenge to Enlightenment individualism as a demographic problem: "The more other people we recognize, even within the mind, the more peculiarly precarious becomes the status of our own hitherto unique and 'incomparable' consciousness of 'self' " (358). "Too many people begin to cancel my own existence with their ontological weight" (363), he writes. Others, notably Frances Ferguson, consider this question in relation to Malthus, the population debate, and the Romantic consciousness that "emerges in reaction to the proliferation of other consciousnesses" in the late eighteenth and early nineteenth centuries.[25] In seventeenth-century London and Paris, inhabitants confronted a similar "horror of multiplicity" located not in global difference, in "natives," people of color, religious "minorities" turned majorities, Bushmen and Hottentots, Kurds and Serbs, nor in the "claims of other consciousnesses" that provoked Wordsworth's cultivation of solitude, nor in some existential fear of number, but a horror of the motley crowd. Scholars of early modern England and France have often detailed the fearful responses of monarchy and municipal governments to the demographic explosion that swept London and Paris in this period, the futile attempts to prevent migration to both capitals and the legislation concerning housing, traffic, filth, and crime.

In the early modern capital, demographic number endangered not what would be in early modern London an anachronistic enlightenment "self" but what we would now term a classed subject, the "I" produced by order and degree. In the newly burgeoning capitals of seventeenth-century Europe, with their ever-expanding range of social and cultural capital from fashion to tobacco and their new forms of *civilité*, distinction became available to greater and greater numbers, but those very numbers affronted in the metropolis jeopardized elite identity.[26] The new space of the metropolis, the relentless saturation of what had been only recently empty and open spaces, the promiscuous encounters of the urban pedestrian, and the need to reduce spatial barriers and provide access to newly developing market spaces breached status boundaries and not only generated profound anxiety about order and place but also fueled the production of "the *subject* as an *individual*" that will eventually become Jameson's enlightenment subject and Ferguson's romantic consciousness.[27] In early modern London, Donne, Marston, Guilpin, and the other verse satirists used satire, with its structures of encounter and address, to manage the burgeoning multitude of persons and behaviors that characterized early modern London and troubled its inhabitants and city government. So in Donne's Satyre I, though the speaker walks on the outside in closer proximity to the social world of the London streets through which he and his companion move, the satire protects the speaker rhetorically from peripatetic encounters and insists on his disconnection from the persons, sights, and things that people the city. The initial enumeration of "Captaine," "Courtier," "Justice," and his "sonne and heire" is presented in an anaphoric series of putative contacts the speaker fears may lure his companion away; the "needy broker," "cheape whore," "prentices," and "schoole-boyes," as I have already pointed out, appear only through simile. "Plumpe muddy whore" and "prostitute boy" enter the poem interrogatively as an ethical opposition to virtue posed by the speaker to the humorist. The urban sights—Morocco and the elephant—are not seen and encountered but compared to the humorist. Though they do see the "well favour'd youth," they see him only from afar; only in the last twenty-five lines do they meet anyone at all. The speaker's street encounters are negotiated and mediated by the humorist and by means of trope and poetic figure.

Donne's satire offers a compelling view of the temptations and attractions of the London street for young men of the Inns of Court in the 1590s, but sartorial splendor, tobacco, and urbane travel were inaccessible to most of the city's inhabitants. For its apprentices and servants, schoolboys and muddy whores, such luxuries were out of reach, and even necessities were sometimes difficult to come by. Isabella Whitney's "Wyll and Testament" to London, published in 1573 as part of her *A Sweet Nosgay, or Pleasant Posye*, provides a pointed contrast to Donne's satire. Whitney is believed to have come to London from the country to work as a servant; from one of her "familiar Epistles" included in *A Sweet Nosgay* we learn that she lost her place working in service for "a virtuous Ladye."[28] Unable to find another, Whitney's speaker presents herself as driven from London reluctantly by poverty. Before her departure,

> I whole in body, and in minde,
> But very weake in Purse:
> Doo make, and write my Testament
> For feare it wyll be wurse.
> And first I wholly doo commend,
> My Soule and Body eke:
> To God the Father and the Son.

Though Whitney begins and ends her poem conventionally, with the legal and religious language of wills, the greater part is made up of her walk through the streets and lanes of London, apparently through her neighborhood in the southwest of the city. She describes its markets and shops, the Fleet, Bridewell, Bedlam, the Thames, Cheape, and the Mint. The speaker makes her way through the city on foot, past the buildings, landmarks and places, streets and shops that a woman in service would have known or frequented.[29] Whitney's poem dramatizes the "particular kind of urban femininity" Laura Gowing has described in early modern London "constructed around the social and cultural shifts of high migration, economic pressures, changing civic cultures, an expanding domestic service sector, and changing patterns of consumption."[30] Her movement is far removed from that of the leisured *flâneur*; she is excluded economically, socially, and by her sex from the kind of walk Donne's speaker undertakes with his friend.

By presenting her walk through London as her last will and testament, Whitney dramatizes her plight as an impoverished woman who has lost her place in the multiple senses of that word.[31] As she moves from place to place in the city, she bequeaths goods and services, activities, professions, even crimes, to their appropriate location in London: wool to "Watlyng Streete, and Canwyck streete," linen to Friday Street, jewels and plate to Cheape, hose she leaves in Birchin Lane, tailors to Bow Street, and artillery at Temple Bar. She lovingly describes the fashionable luxury goods for sale at the Royal Exchange: "French Ruffes, high Purles, Gorgets and Sleeves," and, as Ann Rosalind Jones observes, she is "wishfully participatory rather than critical."[32] To the booksellers "because I lyke their Arte" she leaves money, to wealthy widows, she leaves young gentlemen, and so forth through the city streets. At the Inns of Court she leaves young gentlemen

> For whom I store of Bookes haue left,
> at each Bookebinders stall:
> And parte of all that London hath
> to furnish them withall.
> And when they are with study cloyd:
> to recreate theyr minde:
> Of Tennis Courts, of dauncing Scooles,
> and fence they store shall finde.
> And every Sonday at the least,
> I leave to make them sport.
> In divers places Players, that
> of wonders shall reporte.

Whitney's bequest to the gentlemen of the Inns testifies to its reputation as a gathering place for young men pursuing civility, letters, and preferment like Donne. In these lines she envisions the speaker of Donne's poem, "with study cloyd," but her young gentlemen take pleasure in the city's recreations rather than seeking to evade them. Her bequest at the Inns is Whitney's final legacy and one that offers a perspective on the poem's rhetorical stance in which London is represented as a rejecting lover. Whereas Donne's speaker walks at will through the streets judging what he sees, and it is the aspiring humorist who abandons him, not the city itself, Whitney's walk through London communicates her loss at being forced out of the city by want.

Whitney's speaker conveys a powerful sense of the city's consumer pleasures and the variety of goods for sale in its shops and streets. Her enumeration of those goods has prompted one critic to label her poem "a crowded shopping list,"[33] a view that discounts the poem's sense of the speaker's exclusion and loss. Though inaccessible to her in life, in death she can bequeath those very goods she could never possess while also sharing her pleasure in the city's urban landmarks and its well-known streets and shops. Her role as guide and "promoter of its wares allies her imaginatively with its prosperous buyers and sellers," but she also acknowledges urban crime, violence, and exploitation.[34] Having read Whitney's poem, the reader acquires an insider's knowledge of commercial London, a sense of all the speaker has and will miss, but also of urban poverty and the suffering it causes. Though Dick Whittington, like Whitney's speaker, is briefly driven from the city by mistreatment while in service, Whittington's is ultimately an urban success story of upward mobility. It is also a story of wish fulfillment, since the features leading to his success would seem to be contradicted by much of what we know about gaining the freedom of the city and the route to success of its governing merchant elite.[35] In contrast, the contours of the history recounted in Whitney's poem seem, from the historical record, to have been all too common.[36] Whittington's, then, is a gendered success seemingly unavailable to a young woman in service.[37] No wonder Whitney's speaker leaves to poor maidens rich widowers "to set the Girles aflote." The poem negotiates a gendered subjectivity in its movement between symbolic and concrete spaces: Whittington's career takes him through the broadest London streets, the streets of civic celebration, whereas Whitney traces a different route that includes not only the everyday commercial city but also Bridewell, Bedlam, and the Fleet.[38] Whitney's spatial story is quite different from that traced by Dick Whittington or by Donne's speaker and his friend. Though, like John Stow, she is nostalgic for the London she knows, she can neither succeed like Whittington nor find solace in her study or with a friend.

In the decades following Whitney's stay in London and Donne's at the Inns in the 1590s, when both wrote of walking the city's streets, changes brought about by early modern urbanization produced new technologies of movement in cities across Europe that had psychic, social, and literary effects. The increasing importance of law and finance, the development of centralized shopping spaces such as the Royal and New Exchanges in London and the

Galerie du Palais and the installation of the foire Saint-Germain in covered, permanent halls with named "streets" in Paris, the rapid expansion of both London and Paris to the west, all required new forms of transport, first elite coaches and carriages but rapidly hackneys, *diligences*, and omnibuses.[39] The medieval streets, sometimes no more than a mere two meters wide, could ill handle the growing number of vehicles that began to crowd both cities: famously in Boileau's Satire VI, a coach making a turn catches its wheel and rolls over into the notorious Parisian mud; another, trying to pass the first, finds itself in the same spot. Soon twenty more are backed up with more than a thousand, according to the speaker's hyperbole, lined up behind; this traffic snarl is compounded by the arrival of a large herd of cows:

> Chacun pretend passer: l'un mugit, l'autre jure.

> Each one tries to pass: one moos, the other swears.

Here the parallelism turns men into lowing cattle, and both men and cattle alike into vehicles vying for passage in the crowded city street. Boileau's traffic jam with its putative thousand-plus coaches witnesses the enormous increase in vehicular traffic that plagued early modern Paris.

The coach was a new form of mobility in the late sixteenth and early seventeenth centuries, a novel spatial practice that helped to produce newly configured urban environments—broader streets, sidewalks, and bridges designed for vehicular traffic rather than pedestrian commerce. According to Stow, the first coach was brought to England for the queen in 1564, but coaches quickly spread through the aristocracy and gentry. By 1636, there were said to be some six thousand coaches in London.[40] In sixteenth-century Paris, coaches were also initially confined to the royal family; the eighteenth-century French memoirist Henri Sauval reports that Marie de Medici extended the privilege to a few others, but Paris, like London, was soon overrun by coaches and carriages of all sorts. In the anonymous pamphlet *Advis aux bourgeois de Paris, sur la réformation des carrosses*, the speaker claims to have gone one evening to the Cours la Reine after dinner to find it overrun with coaches—some 1,868, he claims. He goes on to decry the fact that coaches have made leather expensive: in 1611, he claims, shoes cost twenty-eight to thirty sols; now they cost fifty-five, or even an écu, all because of "ces maudits carrosses" (these wicked coaches).[41] By 1701, the anonymous author of *A View of Paris, and Places adjoining with an Account of the Court of France* reports that not only noblemen and men of great estate keep coaches but gentlemen of indifferent fortunes, such as lawyers, players and others, "starve their families at home to make a great figure abroad."[42]

The coach's popularity needs to be understood in part as a means of reestablishing the social distinctions put in jeopardy by the "promiscuous sociability" of the newly congested, burgeoning urban environment of the street so powerfully evoked in Donne's satire and in more popular writing by Dekker, Lupton, Middleton, and others. Coaches, according to Henry Peacham in his *Coach and Sedan, Pleasantly Disputing for Place and Precedence* (1636), make "a publique difference between *Nobilitie,* and the *Multitude.*"[43] The newly fashionable sedan claims it allowed its occupant to exit his dwelling and move through the city streets to enter directly "a Ladies chamber [and to be] had to the fire," without ever being obliged to set foot in the city streets (B3ʳ). In the words of Sir William Cavendish, the fashionable could visit "the most publique, and most received places of entertainment" and then "retire to their coach, and so prepare for another company."[44] The privacy coaches afforded quickly came to be used for other purposes as Laxton and the coachman make clear when the aptly named gallant meets Moll at their assignation in Gray's Inn Fields in *The Roaring Girl* (1611). In the satiric *Le parasite mormom,* a careful distinction is drawn between the beau monde that frequents the gardens of Paris in coaches, and also thereby avoids the filth of the city streets, and the people of the street who pass to and fro on the Pont Neuf, drawn by the charlatans and lively street life. Coaches, carriages, and sedan chairs led to congested city streets and prompted regulation, but the new technology also reorganized the subject in space by separating their elite passengers from unwanted encounters with the heterogeneous urban walking crowd and the urban filth that filled the city streets of both capitals. As the gallants' guidebook, *Les lois de la galanterie* (1644, 1658), insists, filth in the streets and traffic have made it impossible to go about in Paris except in a coach.[45] One speaker in Peacham's allegorical pamphlet mentioned earlier would seem to remember Donne's London of the 1590s when he asks, "Why our Nobilitie and Gentry cannot in faire weather, walke the streetes as they were wont . . . when a coach was as rare almost to be seene as an Elephant" (C4ʳ).

Coaches inevitably changed the perception of urban space, at least until one encountered an overturned cart or some other obstacle that produced a traffic jam—so fabled in early modern Paris as already to have merited a name, "l'embarras de Paris," also the popular title given to Boileau's Satire VI. By 1619, the traffic in London had inspired petitions complaining of the "multitudes of Coaches . . . [such that] inhabitantes there cannott come to their howses, nor bringe in their necessary provisions of beere, wood, coale or haye, nor the Tradesmen or shopkeepers utter their wares, nor the passenger goe to the common water staires without danger of their lives and lymmes."[46] Enclosed in a coach or carriage, the privileged occupant was safely segregated from the hurly-burly of the street. John Taylor writes of being overcome with "a Timpany of pride" while riding in a coach looking down on the hoi polloi: "In what state I would leane over the boote and looke and pry if I saw any of my acquaintance."[47] From a coach window, riders saw a moving picture, a framed series of images, a refigured perception of the urban cityscape quite different from that of the pedestrian. In the texts that present movement through city space in a coach, that movement is rendered not through description or the list, not through peripatetic encounters on bridges, in shopping areas, or in streets, but as in Chantelou's account of Bernini's visit to Paris, by myriad verbs of motion that record the comings and goings of an elite. Riders pass to and fro, seeing and being seen, from palace to cathedral to garden, skipping places and dangers outside the aristocratic loop, enacting a kind of class-determined peripatetic asyndeton. Journals, diaries, and other texts represent the interpersonal relations of power and the movement to and from those confrontations through verbs of coming and going. The substantive *coach*, which abruptly appears in nearly every European language in the sixteenth century, itself becomes a predicate in English: Londoners coach the streets, they "coach to the Exchange" in Richard Brathwait's words in *The English Gentleman* (1630); "All the Gentry coacht it up to the City," says Thomas Fuller (1632).[48] What I call pedestrian poems, whether from the perspective of high or low, and including Boileau's Satire VI, Bertaut's *La ville de Paris en vers burlesque*, Whitney's "Wyll and Testament," and Donne's Satyre I, by contrast, represent city space through the encounter, through description, substantives, lists of consumer goods, street life with its enumerated pleasures and dangers. Both sorts of texts retail a newly metropolitanized subject negotiating financial and cultural capital in France's and Britain's burgeoning capitals. Donne's speaker's encounters with tobacco, perfume, the numerate horse Morocco, an elephant, all drawn from dispersed, sometimes exotic, locations, demonstrate how persons and objects are increasingly estranged from their immediate and distinctive spatiality and organized and disposed of in new ways within urban space.[49] When in 1657 in the title to his *Londinopolis*, the seventeenth-century traveler James Howell dubs London that "Imperial Chamber, and chief Emporium of Great Britain,"[50] he witnesses this changed mode of encountering objects and commodities in the newly centralized shopping spaces of early modern London and Paris that will be the subject of chapter 5. Howell also describes in sensual detail the hazards and dangers that the elite sought to avoid and the plebeian populations suffered: filth, stench, and noise.

CHAPTER FOUR

"Filth, Stench, Noise"

Jonson's seldom-read poem "On the Famous Voyage," from which I take this chapter's title, traces a mock epic journey up Fleet Ditch from Bridewell to Holborn through the London sewers represented as a grotesque, polluted, and gendered urban body. Of Jonson's poem, Swinburne famously opined, "Coprology should be left to the Frenchmen. . . . It is nothing less than lamentable that so great an English writer as Ben Jonson should ever have taken the plunge of a Parisian diver into the cesspool."[1] Swinburne's opinion, for all its national prejudices, nevertheless initiates the work of comparison I develop here. Rapid urban growth, population concentration, and the development of large scale, coordinated activities such as centralized markets and state bureaucracies in seventeenth-century London and Paris fostered an unprecedented accumulation of both financial and cultural capital and promoted, as we have seen, distinctive urban behaviors, social geographies, and new forms of sociability in both cities. This demographic explosion also produced a host of urban ills usually associated with the modern, industrial city—filth, stench, noise, disease, starvation, immigration and crowding, traffic, violence, and crime.

Urban historians have studied much of this litany—immigration and crowds, disease and famine, violence and crime, but filth, stench, and noise have been largely ignored.[2] Simmel explains this omission, and its political effects, as a function of the senses. Solidarity with the proletariat as an ethical ideal, he claimed, was impossible "simply because of the insuperability of impressions of smell."[3] He makes his own sensitivities a measure of the modern: "The modern person is shocked by innumerable things, and innumerable things appear intolerable to their [*sic*] senses." For Simmel, "Life in stench, noise, and filth appeared as something pre-modern."[4] The late British urban historian H. J. Dyos makes an important material and theoretical claim about this omission: "The most direct aesthetic effects of concentrated numbers, noise and smell," he writes, "have no historical dimension whatever."[5] In the years since Dyos made that claim, a new generation of historians has begun to study stench and noise, but I want to pause carefully over Dyos's statement itself. First, what is meant by "direct aesthetic effects"? We usually associate the "aesthetic" with the perception of the beautiful—its primary lexical meaning—but *aesthetic* comes from the Greek *aisthánesthai,* which means "to perceive." A secondary meaning of *aesthetic,* then, is "concerned with or pertaining to sensation," and it is that meaning associated with Kant's *First*

Critique that Dyos seems to have in mind: the sensation and perception of noise and smell, he claims, have "no historical dimension whatever." Certainly there is no disputing that the filth, stench, and clamor produced by the "concentrated numbers" that characterized urban life in the past have left few if any physical remains.[6] But Dyos's claim inevitably raises questions—what forms of evidence are deemed to have, as he puts it, a "historical dimension"? What is allowed to count as "historical"?

The pioneering work of the French historian Alain Corbin inspired the study of archival materials, including journals, diaries, treatises, and the like by doctors, scientists, and others concerned with the stench and filth of Paris, histories of polluted waterways, of refuse dumps and sewers, and the theories their odors generated.[7] But English historians, as Mark S. J. Jenner observes, have been squeamish about such topics. He quotes Frank Kermode's review of Corbin's work, which created a stir partly "because no respected historian had ever before written . . . so explicitly about shit."[8] Such reluctance suggests cultural difference articulated as nationalist prejudice, which we find registered in the observation of a Briton traveling in France in the late eighteenth century, amazed at the olfactory tolerance shown by Europeans: "In England," he claims pompously, "your senses may not be gratified, but they will not be offended."[9] Jenner resists the tendency to generalize about the sensory regimes of particular periods or entire nations. Instead, he seeks to trace a history of smells through "multiple ethnographies" that demonstrate how filth and stench, and I would add noise, are culturally relative concepts. In what follows I argue for the historicity of the senses by considering how aesthetic effects are registered in writing and by asking what the relation of cultural production, particularly what we call literature, is to sense experience. How do texts register sensation, sensory phenomena, and affect?

La boue de Paris

Perhaps no detail of urban Paris has inspired more commentary than Paris's fabled mud, *la boue de Paris*, which had become proverbial long before the advent of what we term *modernity*. Translated as "mud," *la boue de Paris*, from the early modern period until at least the end of the nineteenth century, meant not simply mud, but sewage, the sludgy, smelly, staining shit that filled the streets and open conduits of both London and Paris and provoked satire, farce, lament, calls and plans for public works, and all manner of commentary. *Boue*, or *crotte*, as it was often called, was an obstacle to the newly developing forms of sociability and social mobility that characterized early modern Paris—impoverished gallants and bourgeois hoping to pass as gallants, but without the means to hire a coach, were exposed by the telltale signs left on their clothes by their pedestrian travels through the Parisian streets. The litera-

ture of the period abounds with allusions to the Parisian mud and the dangers
it posed to sartorial display and aristocratic identity: in his sixth satire (see
chapter 2) Boileau's speaker describes a coach overturned in "un grand tas de
boue." Claude Le Petit, Colletet, La Bruyère, Scarron, Sauval, Sorel, Madame
de Sevigné, and Furetière, to name only a few writers from widely differing
social strata, describe the perils it posed.

Reference to the telling detail that was *la boue de Paris* was a regular feature
of satiric, anti-idealist writing in the early modern period. Such satire set
itself aggressively against the *roman gallant* associated with Mademoiselle de
Scudéry, La Calprenède, and the *précieuses*. In seventeenth-century Paris, for
example, the allegorically named *Polyandre* or Everyman of Charles Sorel's
comic novel of that name heads to the Luxembourg Gardens upon his arrival
in Paris after time in the provinces to get all the news. The fenced and gated
gardens were famous as a place to see and be seen, the shadows of its allées
notorious as a scene of assignation (fig. 23).[10] Only the well-heeled were allowed to enter and promenade its walks.[11] Polyandre makes his way to the
gardens, carefully avoiding *la boue de Paris*. Clothes marred by the Parisian
mud reveal their wearer as a social climber, since, as we have seen, the privileged could afford a coach, a new sign of status and social differentiation in
this period. Coaches delivered their passengers unscathed to the gardens, their
silks and laces unmarred by *la boue de Paris*. The coach, as we saw in chapter
3, protected the elite not only from filth but also from the promiscuous encounters suffered by urban pedestrians. In conduct books and treatises such
as *Les lois de la galanterie*, young gallants of both sexes are exhorted to avoid
the Parisian mud that would stigmatize them by sensorily revealing their lack
of material means. Where once a gallant could ride abroad on horseback in
silk stockings and caparisoned in velvet, now "les crottes s'augmentent tous
les jours dans ce grand ville avec un embarras épouvantable" (the dung piles
increase daily in this great city producing an unbelievable impasse) such that
gallants can no longer go about except by coach "où ils seront plus en repos,
et moins en péril de se blesser, ou de se gâter" (where they can rest easy and
will be in less danger of wounding or spoiling [their attire]).[12] Such fear of
urban sensory experience writes the ideological history of status and desire in
early modern Paris.

Antoine Furetière's *Le roman bourgeois*, as its then oxymoronic title adver-
tises, depicts the impact of salon society and its codes of gallantry and *civilité*
on the bourgeois world of urban Paris. "Je chante les amours et les aventures
de plusieurs bourgeois de Paris" (I sing the loves and adventures of several
bourgeois of Paris), Furetière announces, parodying Virgil and Ariosto in his
first line.[13] In book 1, Furetière recounts two *historiettes*, as he calls them, the
diminutive another way of marking his generic distance from epic and romance. Both tales satirize the conventions of romance and love poetry. Situating the action in the place Maubert, "le plus bourgeois" quarter of Paris,

Figure 23. Le jardin de la noblesse françoise, 1629, engraving
by Abraham Bosse. Bibliothèque nationale

Furietière launches a *recusatio* in which he regales us, using many of the conventions of urban description, with all he claims he will not tell us about the square. Dispensing with describing the square, its architecture, or its church, while all the while displaying his knowledge of more fashionable city landmarks, haunts, and classical architecture, Furetière introduces a young man whom he dubs *amphibe*, lawyer by day, aspiring courtier by night and on weekends, a reader of *Cyrus* and *Clélie*, the best-selling romances of gallantry by Scudéry that Molière famously satirizes in *Les précieuses ridicules*, and wearer of judicial robes by day and laces and ribbons by night. Nicodemus sees his beloved in a church, but rather than admire her from afar and then celebrate her in verse, he woos her by putting gold in her collection purse, which a spurned suitor has filled with small change. Here the conventional Dantesque and Petrarchan love at first sight in church is transformed into a commercial transaction–cum–beauty contest, since whichever *quêteuse* collects the largest sum is recognized as the most beautiful.

In the second story, a young marquis, having glimpsed the beautiful bourgeoise Lucrèce in church, determines to find someone to introduce him into her household when an accident saves him the trouble. Driving down her street, he spies her standing in her door. Leaning out his window to salute her, at the same moment a horse trader passes, goading his horse along the narrow street with a rusty spur, and "il couvrit de boue le carrosse, le marquis et la demoiselle."[14] Blaming this calamity on his desire to see her up close, the marquis turns mishap into compliment, and Lucrèce invites him in, where she quickly changes to demonstrate her possession of the real property clothes represented in the early modern period; the marquis, unable to change his soiled clothing (we learn he has been lax with his valet and left him to his own devices while out, which means he is unavailable to be commanded to bring a clean change of clothes), is so shamed that he seeks out an obscure corner in order to hide what are termed his wounds (*ses plaies*). Never, we are told, in all his amorous adventures, had he suffered so painful an accident as to appear in such a state at a first encounter with his beloved. Though passionately smitten, he is unable to declare his love out of shame: he imagines his honor to be as stained as his suit. At that moment, some neighboring girls arrive and, seeing him covered with shit, take him for some poor provincial and begin to mock him: "Vraiment, Monsieur est bien galant aujourd'hui; il ne manque pas de mouches" (Really, Monsieur is debonair today; he doesn't lack beauty marks), one teases, calling the stains on his clothes the "beauty marks" then in fashion, to which another responds, "But is it fashionable to wear them on one's linen?" Still another jokes that he has been sprinkled with holy water.

Both love stories parody the literary conventions of romance, which in turn depend on the Petrarchan tradition, but I want to analyze the second encounter in greater detail. There, social success and success in love depend on staying clean; the exaggerated responses of the company to the filth of urban Paris expose the codes of *civilité* that governed not only aristocratic but increasingly, as Furietière's stories show, also bourgeois life, codes in which contingency is invested with significance.[15] Furetière moralizes mud and at the same time sharpens the reader's sense of the micro-present in the place Maubert. The comedy of the scene and the ensuing conversation on how to judge persons— by what they wear and how they wear it—depend on the distance between the exaggerated language Furetière uses to describe the affect provoked by this mishap and the event itself. In language that exaggerates the admonitions of *Les lois de la galanterie* quoted earlier ("en péril de se blesser"), the marquis is *wounded*; in response to the jibes of Lucrèce's visitors, he *suffers*, he cannot *defend* himself because he feels *remorse* knowing he is *guilty* (104ff.). He tells the company about a friend who suffered a similar fate despite all his efforts to cross town by taking refuge in shops and alleyways and avoid *la boue de Paris*, but who, for all his care, is soiled nevertheless and, once soiled, hurries home ashamed, hiding his face in his cloak and henceforth narrows his acquaintance to the immediate neighborhood, determined to avoid risking the city's filthy streets. Gallant conversation in all the senses of the word—not only talk but also amorous relations—is prevented by the filth encountered in the streets. The company trade reflections on the gallant and his predicament and on how merit is to be judged. Furetière parodies the idealist novels of Scudéry, which I will consider in chapter 6, in which her characters converse at length defining gallantry, merit, and love. In the bourgeois world Furetière depicts and in the courtly world he mocks, cleanliness is equivalent to wit, urbanity, success, the good, in short, to all things. Dress makes the man and a soiled suit provokes insult, shame, and defeat. What made the Parisian mud so horrific?

Already in 1596, an Italian visitor remarked on the filth that ran through the Parisian streets: "Il circule dans toutes les rues de la ville un ruisseau d'eau fetide, où se déversent les eaux sales de chaque maison et qui empeste l'air" (Filth runs through the streets where each household throws out its filthy waters that poison the air).[16] In this historical account, the stink of the city streets is registered not only by description but by the measures it forces on passersby who are obliged to carry flowers or some perfume "pour chasser cette odeur" (to banish the smell).[17] An English visitor to Paris in 1620 describes *la boue de Paris* at greater length. James Howell, the renowned seventeenth-century traveler whom we encountered in chapter 1, helped produce the English vogue for travel to the Continent that issued in the grand tour.[18] Author of a number of texts, including *Londinopolis*, a praise of London modeled on his predecessors that ends with a comparison between that city and Paris, and of *Instructions for forreine travell* (1642), a defense of travel as philosophical learning in which, you will remember, he argues that "*Peregrination* . . . may be not improperly called a *moving Academy*, or the true *Peripatetique Schoole*,"[19] Howell traveled through Europe during the 1620s and subsequently published a series of familiar letters to friends and family describing the sights and cities he visited.[20] The sixteenth letter of book 1, written upon his arrival in Paris, describes the city but lingers at some length on the filth that filled its crowded streets, threatening the silks and laces of its elite and the sober attire of its middling sort, and soiling the simple garments of the lowest estate. Paris, Howell writes, is the "Epitome" of France, the "Rendezvous of all Foreigners," but its streets are "foul all the four Seasons of the year."[21] Because Paris is situated with its suburbs high above the city, he claims,

> the Filth runs down the channel, and settles in many places within the body of the City, which lies upon a flat; as also for a world of Coaches, Carts, and Horses of all sorts that go to and fro perpetually, so that sometimes one shall meet with a stop half a mile long of those Coaches, Carts, and Horses, that can move neither forward nor backward, by reason of some sudden Encounter of others coming a cross-way; so that often-times it will be an hour or two before they can disintangle. In such a stop the Great *Henry* was so fatally slain by *Ravillac*. Hence comes it to pass, that this Town . . . is always dirty, and 'tis such a Dirt, that by perpetual Motion is beaten into such black unctuous Oil, that where it sticks no Art can wash it off of some Colours; insomuch, that it may be no improper Comparison to say, That an ill Name is like the *Crot* (the *Dirt*) of *Paris*, which is indelible; besides the Stain this Dirt leaves, it gives also a strong scent, that it may be smelt many miles off . . . this may be one cause why the Plague is always in some corner or other of this vast City, which may be call'd, as once Scythia was, *Vagina populorum.* (43)

In this account, filth is exacerbated by traffic jams; a traffic jam leads to royal assassination and the roiling up of *la boue de Paris* into "such black unctuous Oil" that "no Art can wash [it] off." An ill name is like the "Crot" or *boue de Paris*, indelible—it mars reputation. The mud's odor is so strong it may be smelled many miles off, which is why Paris is constantly visited by the plague. Here Howell expresses the early modern belief that disease was carried by air, fear of bioterrorism *avant la lettre*. In Howell's final comparison, he dubs Paris—the crowded city with its black, oily, stinking filth—"Vagina populorum." In Howell's account of his travels to Paris, the filthy, stinking, crowded city becomes a seething sheath, a vagina. The feminine becomes the overdetermined site of urban filth. Howell remarks upon the stinking filth of the Parisian street but conveniently ignores the mud of his own capital, which an Italian visitor described in 1617 as foully smearing clothing "with a sort of soft and very stinking mud, which abounds here at all seasons, so that the place deserves to be called Lorda (filth) rather than Londra (London)."[22] Not only well-off foreign visitors but popular native jests record the foul-smelling streets of London in which the city's sewage collectors, euphemistically dubbed "goldfinders," offer a satiric riposte to gentlemen offended by the stench of their carts: "Some gentlemen, not able to endure the smell and were to pass that way, flung their cloaks over their faces; which one of them observing, said, 'If you would always keep your tails shut, you should not now have occasion to stop your noses.' "[23]

The unctuous, smelly, black mud of Paris, the soft, stinking mud of London. Both descriptions insist on sensory perception—tactile, olfactory, visual—to epitomize the city and its snarl of coaches, horses, and carts. In his *Economic and Philosophic Manuscripts of 1844*, Marx reflects on the senses: "The forming of the five senses," he writes, "is a labour of the entire history of the world down to the present."[24] Sensory perception, Marx insists, is not natural or simply "experienced," but is formed and has a history. How sense experience is organized and the medium through which it is communicated are determined not by nature alone but by historical circumstances. Marx goes on in this passage to condemn sense experience in pursuit of individual consumption and resorts, as he does elsewhere, to the feminine to illustrate his argument: he inveighs against false forms of communism that call for the communal, hedonist exchange of women, that would make woman, as he puts it, the "spoil and handmaid of communal lust." Instead, only the articulation of "human needs," he claims, not individual sense experience "in which man exists for himself," enables the transcendence of private property. His is a constructivist account that argues that the senses have a history only knowable in their articulation as need, desire, pleasure, pain, or suffering (I repeat): "The forming of the five senses is a labour of the entire history of the world down to the present." Susan Stewart has recently used this aphorism from Marx to argue for the necessity and power of what she terms "aesthetic activity," and specifically lyric: "intelligible meaning is made from sense experiences and generates sense experiences" she writes, "freed from the goals of use and appetite alone."[25] In representation, sense experience becomes knowable and eschews mere use value; through literary representation, sense experience becomes at once knowable and historical.

Adorno develops Marx's point in relation to the literary when he insists that "a poem [by which he means *poesy* in the early modern sense of literary forms, not only poetry or lyric] is not merely an expression of individual impulses and experiences. Those become a matter of art only when they come to participate in something universal by virtue," paradoxically, "of the specificity they acquire in being given aesthetic form."[26] The specificity of aesthetic form preserves sense experience in the past, gives sensory phenomena and their perception a history; the attempt to articulate sense experience and give it the specificity of artistic form participates in the universal. To return to *Le roman bourgeois*, Furetière represents the sensual onslaught of the city synecdochically—the Parisian mud assaults its inhabitants and allows no distinctions, between subject and object, between aristocrat and bourgeois, as Furetière's serial triplet insists: "il couvrit de boue le carrosse, le marquis et la demoiselle." *La boue* defines their social place, determines their actions and relations to others, and produces emotion. We understand the power of certain aristocratic norms by the feelings of suffering, remorse, and guilt such offenses inspire. Through the comic distance produced by the disjunction between the language of affect he employs and the events themselves, Furetière registers his critique of such aristocratic norms and *civilité* in early modern Paris. In the excess of affect he assigns to *la boue de Paris*, sense experience exceeds itself and becomes available for understanding. In representing sense experience not as natural, solipsistic, mere individual experience but as constructed, readable, Furetière's mud-stained silks and lace make a universal claim for the performance of desire and its articulation for another as a feature of the senses.

Morose's Room

Long before Proust famously took to his cork-lined room to insulate himself from domestic, environmental, and metropolitan distraction, Ben Jonson's Morose devised "a room with double walls and treble ceilings, the windows close shut and caulked" (1, 1, 178–79) where he lives shut off from the invasive, fearsome noise of the city.[27] Act 1, scene 1 of *Epicoene or the Silent Woman* regales its audience with the sounds early modern Londoners encountered as they made their way through city streets or endured indoors as part of daily life in the city. Morose, as we learn in the play's opening scene, "can endure no noise" as below (1.1.141–42). To protect himself from acoustic attack, he wears nightcaps buckled over his ears, which Jonson exoticizes by dubbing them a "turbant." Among the noises Morose seeks to shut out are the cries of street vendors memorialized visually in woodcuts and engravings (fig. 24) and verbally in lively ballads and songs. One such ballad, "Turner's Dish of Lenten Stuff," records the myriad criers that enlivened the London streets and which Morose seeks so doggedly to avoid:

> My Maisters all attend you,
>   if mirth you loue to heare:
> And I will tell you what they cry,
>   in London all the yeare.
>   . . . .
> The fish-wife first begins,
>   nye Musckles lylly white:
> Hearings, Sprats, or Pleace,
>   or Cockles for delight.
> Nye welflet Oysters:
>   . . . .

Figure 24. London criers, early seventeenth century. Magdalene College, Cambridge

Ould shoes for new Broomes,
 the broome man he doth sing:
For hats or caps or buskins,
 or any ould Pooch rings.
[Buy] a Mat, a bed Mat,
 [a pad]lock or a Pas,
A couer for a close stoole,
 a bigger or a lesse.

Ripe Chery ripe,
 the Coster-monger cries,
Pipins fine, or Peares,
 another after hies,
With basket on his head,
 his living to aduance,
And in his purse a paire of Dice,
 for to play at Mumchance.

Hot Pippin pies,
 to sell unto my friends:
Or puding pies in pans,
 Well stuft with Candles ends,
Will you buy any Milke,
 I heare a wench to cry,
With a paile of fresh Cheese and creame,
 another after hies. [28]

The ballad gives a lively sense of London's animated streets filled with people hawking and bartering their wares, with foodstuffs of all sorts for sale, with games (mumchance was a game like hazard) and everyday life, in short, with the physical, commercial, and ludic world Morose's hatred of noise represents. Morose, we learn, has signed "treaties" with these London's criers, its fishwives (figs. 25 and 26) and orange-women, but the city's chimney sweeps and broom men have refused to sign. [29] Costardmongers make him swoon. Morose is at war with the London noise, a war he attempts to win not only through traditional military means ("divers treaties," "long sword," "rust without action") but through urban zoning. Neither brazier nor armorer is permitted to live in his parish, and the "waits" or street musicians maintained at the city's charge Morose pays not to come near his ward. He deliberately avoids the newly broad streets like the Strand built to accommodate vehicular traffic and instead has chosen "a street to lie in so narrow at both ends that it will receive no coaches nor carts nor any of these common noises" (161–63). By 1609, when the play was first performed, coaches are apparently widespread enough

Figure 25. London fishwife, seventeenth century. Huntington Library.

to make up the "common noises" of the city that Morose would avoid. In *The seuen deadly sinnes of London*, Dekker writes that "carts and / Coaches make such a thundring as if the world ranne vpon wheeles."[30]

Morose's obsession with noise provokes mockery, insult, and trickery, particularly on the part of his nephew, Dauphine, whom he is threatening to disinherit by marrying, and of Clerimont. Both Dauphine and Clerimont have apparently arranged a series of assaults on Morose's quiet: Clerimont's

Buy my dish of great Smelts,

Figure 26. London fishwife, seventeenth century. Huntington Library

boy plays bellman and sounds the hours at his uncle's door, a bear baiter with dogs from four parishes cries his game beneath Morose's window, a fencer is directed down his street with his drummer, and more. The bells that pealed the hours, plague, feast days, and celebrations, and that young people apparently rang at length in competitions, contribute to the noise pollution that Morose abhors.[31] Jonson portrays Morose as absurd, the classical *senex* opposed to change and the sounds of modern London. Dogs, drums, even a squeaking new pair of shoes drive him mad. To disinherit his newly knighted kinsman Dauphine, Morose has determined to marry, and the play's plot, as its subtitle, *The Silent Woman*, suggests, turns on the conventional assumption of women's talkativeness and the difficulty of finding a silent wife.

Traditional commentary locates the sources for Jonson's plot in Aretino's *Il Marescalco* (1533), which provides the device of the wife who turns out to be a boy in disguise, and in two declamations by the Greek sophist Libanius that Jonson may have known through an edition published in Paris from the 1590s that includes both the original Greek and a Latin translation. In Libanius XXVI, the speaker, a hater of noise named in the Latin text Morosus and who, at the behest of a meddling friend, has married a supposedly quiet wife, declaims to an assembly of senators his anguish at discovering at his wedding that she is raucous and talkative. The apparent purpose of the declamation is to request permission to commit suicide by drinking hemlock. As modern commentators have pointed out, the declamation provided much material for the play: its central occasion, the wedding feast filled with noisy guests, the prompt for the comic bits with Morose's servants whom he has enjoined to silence, the irritations of snoring and coughing, and a pattern of imagery Jonson uses repeatedly to represent noise: rushing waters and flood. Conspicuously missing from the declamation and from the playwright's borrowings is the very urban noise that so exercises Morose in Jonson's play: the "common noises" detailed in the play's opening scene by Clerimont. In Herford and Simpson's commentary and Holdsworth's section on sources in his introduction to the New Mermaids edition, no mention is made of the changes Jonson makes in his source material that insist on metropolitan sound and the changing acoustic urban scene in late sixteenth-century and early seventeenth-century London. From Jonson's comic rendering of all the sounds Morose suffers and fears we learn a great deal about urban noise pollution. Jonson's play provides a brief, aural register of the sounds that assaulted the senses of inhabitants of the early modern city regardless of their socioeconomic status and which, as both Boileau and Jonson remind us, the rich sought to control and avoid.

At one moment in their dialogue about Morose's phonophobia, Truewit asks about the effect on Morose of trumpeters or "the hau'boys" (oboes); Clerimont answers, "Out of his senses." The onslaught to his senses Morose encounters in London drives him out of his senses, makes him mad—he swoons, duels with the air, sends the bear baiter advertising his trade away from his window nursing head wounds Morose has inflicted. Though we laugh at Morose's opposition to games, festivity, and urban hurly-burly, we also register his resistance to the street sounds produced by urbanization. At act 4, scene 4, after his marriage and the discovery his wife's loquaciousness, which is marked in the play by her immediate plans to sally forth with the Collegiates to the Exchange and shop, Morose proclaims his willingness to do what he terms "penance" by submitting his offended senses to London's

streets and landmarks. When Dauphine exclaims against his uncle's sugges-
tion that he might geld himself to anger his new wife, Morose answers: "So
it would rid me of her! And that I did supererogatory penance, in a belfry, at
Westminster Hall, i' the cockpit, at the fall of a stag, the Tower Wharf—what
place is there else?—London Bridge, Paris Garden, Belinsgate, when the noises
are at their height and loudest. Nay, I would sit out a play that were nothing
but fights at sea, drum, trumpet, and target!" (12–18). Here each city landmark and pastime figures city noise: the innumerable church bells, the noisy
crowds in shops, law courts, at the docks, on London Bridge, the thundering
ordnance at Tower Wharf, the cockfights and bearbaitings, bawling fishwives,
and, last and worst, the sound effects of battles enacted at the theater. When
Morose goes to the law courts to seek redress for his calamitous marriage, he
hurries home, driven by noise that makes his wedding feast seem a "calm
midnight" (4.7.18). Jonson represents this judicial jangling that makes "noise
here" into silence by a string of Latinate legal maneuvers and instruments
strung together pell-mell: "citations, appellations, allegations, certificates, at-
tachments, intergatories [sic], references, convictions, afflictions" (4.7.15–16).
The play ends only when Morose signs an agreement to provide for Dauphine
during his lifetime and assure him of his inheritance at his uncle's death. His
signature enables the discovery that his wife Epicoene is in fact a boy. In the
play's final lines, Truewit comes forward, asks the audience for the traditional
applause that ends classical and so much Renaissance comedy, and assures us
Morose having gone in, "It may be that noise will cure him."

But Morose is not the only urban victim in *Epicoene*, nor noise the city's
only danger. In a strange passage at act 3, scene 2, the social-climbing Mistress
Otter, the remarried widow whose fortune was made in the china trade, recounts her "dream o' the city." Her oneiric reveries apparently chronicle her
nightmarish fears of the accidents that may befall her efforts at social success
in the city: a stained damask tablecloth, a singed satin gown, a wilted ruff
heavy with candle wax, a crimson satin doublet and black velvet skirt splashed
with mud. Her quest for cultural capital in the city and at court leads her to
gallivant through London attending dinners, meetings of the collegiates, and
a masque. She even sets up an assignation in Ware, apparently a favorite spot
for trysts. Before she can make her way there by coach ("I was taking coach
to go to Ware"; 66–67), like Furetière's marquis, she is dashed with mud by
a brewer's horse. Like Lucrèce, she is driven inside to change, and the results
of this encounter with city filth produces shame, an excess of emotion: she
"kept her chamber a leash of days for the anguish of it" (70). It is difficult to
determine if these events have actually befallen Mistress Otter or if she has
only dreamt them, thus registering her fear of social rejection, but the scene's
comedy is produced by the exaggeration of the distance between what Mistress
Otter actually suffers and the language of affect used to describe and respond
to it. Dauphine sympathizes satirically, "These were dire mischances, lady,"

and Clerimont declares, "I would not dwell in the city, and 'twere so fatal to me." Urban life can be lethal—though she must continue to dwell in the city where she hopes to make her way, she avows that she takes her doctor's advice to "dream of it as little as I can" (73–74).

In *The Civilizing Process*, Norbert Elias outlines a theory of modernity in which shame plays a central role.[32] In the course of the early modern period, he claims, attitudes toward the body and its functions, including sex, cleanliness, appearance, table manners, and all sorts of behaviors, changed and began to produce shame. Codes of sociability and *civilité* are culture specific; they change over time and vary according to class, gender, age, and social aims.[33] As Elias argues, changing shame thresholds enabled social groups to distinguish themselves from others and helped to refine and enforce status distinction. Mrs. Otter's shameful nightmares reveal such culture-specific codes of correct behavior and appearance in early modern London, but the mocking responses of Dauphine and Clerimont expose her exaggerated fears of urban contamination as absurd. The city is *scene* and its inhabitants the audience before which both the socially aspirant and the comfortably urbane perform; but at the same time, the urban environment jeopardizes those performances with its filth, stench, and noise. In his massive section on shame in *Affect Imagery Consciousness*, Sylvan Tomkins argues that shame depends not simply on contempt and judgment from or by the other but on "the expected good feelings," the "excitement" or "enjoyment" one had expected, but that turns to shame. "Shame-humiliation is the negative affect linked with love and identification," he writes.[34] Eve Kosofsky Sedgwick, reading Tomkins, insists on the performativity of shame: "Shame and pride, shame and dignity, shame and self-display, shame and exhibitionism are different interlinings of the same glove: shame, it might finally be said, transformational shame, *is performance*."[35] Mrs. Otter's humiliation, like that of Lucrèce's suitor, depends on the desire for approval, recognition, admiration, and love. Both perform their shame, a shame inspired by their very desires, provoked by urban life, and acted out in the scene that was early modern London and Paris.

CHAPTER FIVE

Courtship and Consumption
in Early Modern Paris

English city comedy, as we have seen in Jonson's *Epicoene*, represents vividly changes brought about by urbanization: the filth, stench, and noise of the city streets, the rivalry among city gallants, and the increased availability of consumer goods in shops and the Royal and New Exchanges (see fig. 22). The renewed interest in historical scholarship within English studies long since dubbed the new historicism has prompted work not only on the city comedies of Jonson but on those of Heywood, Middleton, and others.[1] Commentators have addressed the impact of urbanization, consumerism and new markets, information and communications, credit, capital accumulation, and political economy in a number of plays set in early modern London. Though lip service is occasionally given to the European context of these historical formations, with few exceptions they have been considered primarily in the context of early modern England and English drama.[2] In previous chapters, I have considered the impact on cultural production of demographic growth, structural urbanization, related urban cultural practices including social mobility, the demand for luxury goods, the preoccupation with fashion and display, and urban leisure pastimes such as theater, collecting, walking, and the promenade. I have analyzed representations of mercantile aspiration and of the urban poor in various forms of cheap print. In the previous chapter, I considered the urban ills and dangers that beset inhabitants of early modern Paris and London, rich and poor alike. Here I will explore how the development of a consumer society and its attendant cultural practices were manifested across the Channel, not in early modern London but in early modern Paris.

The dominance of classical tragedy in French seventeenth-century literary history and of Moliere's comedy, influenced by the commedia dell'arte tradition, has eclipsed plays appropriately called French city comedies that were written, performed, and printed in Paris in the 1630s and 1640s, most notably by Pierre Corneille. Corneille's comedies have received considerably less attention from critics, readers, and the theater than his tragedies; an occasional article, a survey in an early chapter of a book devoted to his tragedy, and recent interest in and revival of the convoluted, baroque *Illusion comique* constitute the extent of critical and theatrical attention accorded Corneille's earliest dramatic successes.[3] Critics overwhelmingly study the tragedies, meditate on "héroisme cornélien," and, given the preoccupation with history and ideology in recent critical practice, produce Corneille as a political thinker concerned with power and the state, legitimacy, ambition, rivalry, and the family in its relations to the state. Books by André Stegmann, Georges Couton, Jean-Marie Apostolidès, and, in English, by David Clarke, all consider Corneille's theater in such terms, ones that suggest political and diplomatic history continues to reign untroubled by the many histories that have so changed not only the discipline of history itself but of literary and cultural studies: social, economic, urban, women's history, and the history of sexuality, histories that offer strikingly different narratives through which to understand Corneille and "politics."[4] In my analysis of Corneille's city comedy, I draw on those various histories not to dispute the claim for Corneille as politically engaged but to extend the range of what is termed politics in the commentary on Corneille's theater. By doing so, I hope as well to trouble conventional assumptions about French neoclassical tragedy and the codes of *bienséance* (decorum) and *vraisemblance* (verisimilitude) that came to dominate seventeenth-century theatrical aesthetics and practice. But my primary aim is to provoke interest in Corneille's early city comedy, which deserves critical attention in its own right.

English city comedy is famously concerned with urban subcultures, with con artists and grifters, tradesmen, artisans and apprentices, pickpockets, prostitutes and petty criminals, country bumpkins and young heirs, dupes agog at the city with its street life, exchanges and fairs, its lively commerce. Elaborate plots involve what a commentator of an earlier age dubbed "the old English love of felonious ingenuity and humorous knavery" undertaken by "the versatile London thief, a modern type whose existence was bound up with the development of the capital."[5] Its characters flock to London in search of fortune, preferment, and cash, and its characteristic mode is satire. French city comedy is quite different from its English counterpart. Instead of tricksters, thieves, and young gallants on the make more often for money than for love, its characters are members of a young urban elite in search of romance, intent on urban pleasures, on fashion, entertainment, and amatory adventure. Its plots depend on confusion, intrigue, and mistaken identity, features of English comedy as well, but rarely on gulling, theft, and roguery. Nevertheless, both English and French city comedy employ a language of exchange and value in the realm of human relations that suggests the impact of what has been termed the "consumer revolution" taking place in Europe over the course of the seventeenth century.

Historians have begun to study not only the accelerating pace at which goods were produced and acquired in early modern Europe but also "consumerism as a *mentalité*, informing attitudes not only towards goods and belongings, but also personal relations and political philosophies."[6] This chapter traces the impact of new developments in commerce and consumption in early seventeenth-century Europe on Corneille's city comedy and on the language of courtship he employs. That impact is registered in a number of ways, in where plays are set, on character, but particularly, I argue, in changing uses of the word *objet* (Eng. *object*) in the language of love and courtship. *Objet* has a long and complex semantic history in the French Renaissance and appears in a variety of both discrete and overlapping discursive contexts. *L'objet* in Petrarchism and in its seventeenth-century appropriations in the pastoral romance is the beloved, frequently though not always a woman; she is the object of a lover's passion, its aim and goal, that which is thrown before his eyes (Lat. *obiectus*). Within the syncretic discourse of Neoplatonism and Petrarchism, the love of earthly beauty epitomized in the beloved mistress was, of course, one stage in the journey toward the divine, a trajectory traced in countless sonnet cycles and other texts, perhaps most famously in book 4 of Castiglione's *Il Cortegiano*. In the English lexicographer Randle Cotgrave's important *Dictionarie of the French and English Tongues* (1611), *objet* is spelled *object* as in English, thus highlighting its etymological link to the Latin *obiectus*, "putting against, opposing," the plural of which means "things objected, charges, accusations."[7] Cotgrave defines *object* as "the subiect of the sight, anything one lookes on directly; anything that is before the eyes." That definition is linked in turn to the Latin *objectum*, in scholastic usage "something thrown before the mind or thought." An object is that toward which action, thought, or feeling is directed: an objective in the sense of an ambition or goal. This complex of meanings is admirably illustrated in the title of Maurice Scève's poetic sequence of decasyllabic ten-line stanzas or *dizains: Délie, objet de plus haute vertu* (1544), with its anagram of the beloved's name: *Délie = l'idée*. Scève's poems trace the richly ambivalent literary and philosophical meanings of the word *objet*: the beloved toward which the lover aspires, but also the Neoplatonic *idea*, which in Scève is imbued as well with syncretic Christian meanings.

But by the late seventeenth century, *objet* is used increasingly, as in modern usage, in relation to things and that revolution in the world of goods that social and economic historians have traced in early modern Europe.[8] In what follows, I sketch the outlines of this shift in meaning and usage in relation to questions of urbanization, commerce, and gender by looking at two exemplary, untranslated comedies of Corneille, *La galerie du palais* (1632) and *Le menteur* (1643). In *La galerie du palais* he foregrounds the question of what constitutes a beloved object by situating his comedy in the newly urbanized, bourgeois commercial spaces of early modern Paris. Similarly, *Le menteur* is set in the city, but not in a bourgeois Paris of shopping and commerce but in a demanding capital of fashion and gallantry in which the question of the object figures a changed social cityscape.

Classical tragedy, with its strict codes of decorum in relation to persons and place—Corneille's undifferentiated theatrical space dubbed by critics his *lieu théatrale*—disables consideration of this shift in setting and linguistic usage. *La galerie du palais* depends on and uses the old meanings of *objet* in the idiolect of Neoplatonic love, of sonnets, love poetry, and pastoral romance, but as its title, which names what might be termed an early modern Parisian shopping mall, already hints, the play is symptomatic as well of that new world of objects Arjun Appadurai, Mary Douglas, Chandra Mukerji, and others have recently analyzed.[9] Since the play is not widely read and is unavailable in English, a brief plot summary is in order: Lisandre loves Célidée, Célidée loves Lisandre, and already in the second scene of the first act, we learn that Célidée's father supports their marriage. The action of the play involves elite games of gallantry or *civilité*, in which the young lovers pass their time shopping, attending the theater, dining, teasing and feigning with one another, dueling, and conversing about books, fashions, goods, and feelings. The conflict comes about because Célidée's friend Hippolite, the rival of the play's subtitle, *L'amie rivale/The Rival Friend*, also loves Lisandre and has enlisted the aid of Lisandre's squire (Fr. *écuyer*), Aronte, in winning Lisandre's love away from her friend. In an attempt to wrest Lisandre away from Célidée, Hippolite convinces Célidée to test her lover by pretending not to care for him. Meanwhile, Lisandre's friend Dorimant falls in love with Hippolite. After a series of confusions and misunderstandings, even a duel, and a great deal of flirtatious *badinage*, the lovers are at last sorted out, and the play ends with the promise of a double, perhaps even a triple, marriage, since in the final lines it is suggested that Hippolite's mother and Célidée's father may join their progeny in tying the marital knot.

As even this short account of the plot and its characters suggests, the play recalls countless Renaissance comedies of mismatched lovers, but in this urban *Midsummer Night's Dream*, the lovers are sorted out not by a magic potion and sojourn in a fairy-populated Athenian forest but in the urban shopping spaces of early modern Paris while handling and buying merchandise from various tradespeople—a draper, a bookseller, and a haberdasher—characters who appear onstage in their boutiques discussing their goods and mercantile schemes.[10] The most frequent observation made by modern commentators about Corneille's comedy is to note this so-called *pittoresque parisien*. Though Corneille did not introduce mercantile scenes and characters to the seventeenth-century French stage, that his setting of the play in the Galerie du Palais was remarkable is witnessed by a contemporary mocking allusion in a pamphlet from the controversy surrounding *Le Cid*. There Corneille's theater is censured with the charge:

> Il a fait voir une *Mélite, la Galerie du Palais* et *la Place royale*, ce qui nous faisoit espèrer que Montdory annonceroit bientôt le *Cimetière Saint-Jean*, la *Samaritaine* et la *Place aux Veaux*.

He has presented us with a *Mélite*, *The Court Exchange*, and *The Place Royale*, which makes us expect Montdory will soon present *The Cemetery of St. John*, the *Samaritan Waterpump*, and *Cattle Square*.[11]

As this derisive enumeration of the public spaces of early modern Paris suggests, with its pun on *veau*, which also meant "ninny" or "dodo," contemporaries reproached Corneille for his Parisian settings. The playwright evidently smarted from such attacks, for in his *Examen* to *La galerie du palais* added in 1660 for the publication of his collected works, Corneille appeals to the ancients, both Greek and Roman, on two different counts to justify his urban setting: he claims setting and title have no more to do with the action than the ancients' habit of naming plays for the chorus, and he points out that their plays are typically set in public places—on the street or in a doorway, even though the action might more appropriately transpire indoors. But his principal reason for the scenes in the Galerie du Palais, he claims, is

> parce que la promesse de ce spectacle extraordinaire, et agréable pour sa naïveté, devait exciter vraisemblablement la curiositè des auditeurs; et ça été pour leur plaire plus d'une fois, que j'ai fait paraître ce même Spectacle à la fin du quatrième Acte, où il est entièrement inutile, et n'est renoué avec celui du premier que par des valets qui viennent prendre dans les boutiques ce que leurs Maîtres y avaient acheté, ou voir si les Marchands ont reçu les nippes qu'ils attendaient.

> because the potential of this extraordinary spectacle, so pleasing in its liveliness, would likely excite the audience's curiosity, it was to please them more than once that I had this same Spectacle appear again at the end of the fourth act, where it was entirely unnecessary and is only linked to the first by the valets who come to pick up in the boutiques what their masters had bought there, or to see if the tradesmen had received the haberdashery they were expecting.[12]

Title and setting, Corneille claims, are mere advertising, pandering to the excitations of an audience imagined as hungry for the quotidian spectacle of commercial Paris. But the setting of Corneille's comedy in the Galerie du Palais is far from gratuitous; it is crucial to the play's conflation of different categories of objects, mercantile, cultural, amatory, and linguistic. Before looking more closely at that conflation of objects, however, we need to consider in some detail what is known about the Galerie du Palais itself in order to understand why that setting matters to the play's social and sexual politics.

Within the space bounded on the east by the rue de la Barillerie and on the west by the rue de Harlay was the little world of the Palais de la Cité, subsequently the Palais de Justice.[13] Virtually all the major judicial offices and the administrative offices of the state and the Parlement of Paris were located in its precincts; it was frequented by an array of members of parliament, magistrates, officers, lawyers, clerks, process servers, and the like. Tradesmen were quick to take advantage of this concentration of *noblesse de robe, bons bourgeois,* and their dependents, all with money to spend. In the *grande salle* and the *cour du palais* were located some 225 boutiques built in wooden galleries strung from pillars, squeezed between the buttresses of the Sainte Chapelle, and leaning against the walls of the *palais,* some less than two meters across: haberdashers, drapers and lace merchants, glovers, cobblers, ironmongers, booksellers, and other assorted *métiers.* Along the quay and in the court were goldsmiths, watchmakers, and engravers. The Galerie du Palais was the most important commercial shopping space in seventeenth-century Paris, not unlike London's Exchanges, a place where the well-heeled and powerful of the city went to do business, to see and be seen, and to buy the latest in luxury goods. Known as the center of fashion, the Galerie du Palais offered gloves, ribbons, lace, linen, silk, belts, fans, masks, handkerchiefs, the latest novels, plays, poetry, maps, engravings, and pamphlets. Not only French goods but objects from the world over were available for sale in the Galerie du Palais, as a merchant details in the nearly contemporary popular poem *La ville de Paris en vers burlesques* (Sieur Berthaud, ca. 1652) discussed in chapter 2:

> Des couteaux à la Polonoise;
> Des colets de buffle à l'Angloise;
> Un castor qui vient du Japon;
> Venez voir un futre fort bon:
> Il est excellent pour la pluye,
> C'est de ceux qu'on porte en Turquie.

> Knives à la Polonaise;
> Leather collars à l'Anglaise;
> A beaver from remote Japan
> Come see a felt hat oh so grand
> That it repels the rain with ease
> Just like those they wear in Turkey.[14]

Another shopkeeper goes on to offer "de belle Holande, / Des manchettes, de beaux rabats, / De beaux colets, de fort beaux bas, / Achetez-vous quelque chemise, / Voicy de belle marchandise" (Beautiful linen, cuffs, fine bands, handsome ruffs, lovely hose / Buy yourself some shirt or blouse / Here is my choice merchandise). The *galerie* was memorialized (fig. 27) by Abraham Bosse in his well-known series of Parisian scenes. There we can see the variety of goods available for sale and observe a young urban elite, strolling through the palais, shopping. Beneath Bosse's image are verses that describe the scene he portrays:

> Tout ce que l'art humain a jamais inventé
> Pour mieux charmer les sens par la galanterie,

Figure 27. La Galerie du Palais, engraving by Abraham Bosse. Bibliothèque nationale

Et tout ce qu'on d'appas la grace et la beauté
Se découvre à nos yeux dans cette galerie.

Ici les cavaliers les plus aventureux
En lisant les romans s'animent à combattre
Et de leur passion les amants langoureux
Flattent les monuments par des vers de théâtre.

Ici faisant semblant d'acheter devant tous
Des gants, des éventails, du ruban, des dentelles,
Les adroits courtisans se donnent rendez-vous,
Et pour se faire aimer galantisent les belles.

All that human art has ever invented
Better to charm the senses [with pun on *sens*] through gallantry
And all there is of grace and beauty
Are discovered to our eyes in this arcade.

Here the most adventurous cavaliers
In reading novels are provoked to fight

And languorous lovers flatter
Those deaf to their passion [statues] by reciting dramatic verse.

Here seeming to buy in front of everyone
Gloves, fans, ribbons, laces
Clever courtiers keep rendezvous
And to make themselves loved, gallantize the belles. (trans. mine)[15]

The palais is a place where one goes to shop for *tous*, and that *all* clearly includes "les belles," or "tout ce qu'on d'appas la grace et la beauté" (all there is of charm and beauty). Figure 28, another contemporary engraving of the Galerie du Palais, appears as the frontispiece of Corneille's play in the collected edition of his theater (1660). Two young women shop for collars and lace while across the way two young men shop for books; more important than any shopping they are doing at the stalls themselves is the series of looks passing between one of the women and one of the men emphatically preoccupied with one another rather than with the objects on offer.

In act 1, scene 4 of Corneille's play, which takes place in the g*alerie*, Dorimant sees Hippolite shopping and is smitten; as the scene opens, Aronte pledges that his master, Lisandre, "changera d'objet" (will change objects). The word *objet* has, as I have already noted, a long and complex discursive history in the French literary Renaissance. Aronte's pledge that his master will "changera d'objet" puts in play the question this play raises repeatedly: what is an *objet* in the theatrical and commercial space of early modern Paris? Whereas in the traditional narrative of courtly and Petrarchan love, the lover first encounters his Laura or Beatrice in a church or garden, at court or, perhaps, at a window, here Dorimant sees Hippolite and is wounded by her beauty while she shops for linen and Dorimant himself browses for books. The mercantile and the idealizing amatory collide in this scene in which Hippolite herself becomes an object in both senses of the word. In an amusing stichomythic interchange, Hippolite asks the lace merchant, "Madame, montrez-nous quelques collets d'ouvrage" (Madam, show me some worked collars). As she promises to do so, Dorimant comments to the bookseller, "Ceci vaut mieux le voir que toutes vos chansons" [107] (Seeing this is worth more than all your poems).[16]

Corneille sets up direct equivalences between women as objects of erotic desire and not lace or ribbons, but cultural *objets*, poems and plays, for *La galerie du palais* is also an allegory of the commodification of literature itself, in which consumerism is gender specific: women shop for fashionable ribbons, lace, and collars while men seek out the books that display their taste and distinguish them from common readers. Corneille establishes Dorimant's *honnêteté*, his gentlemanly distinction, by having him prefer poetry to the *romans* "que notre peuple en était idolâtre" [137] (that the people are mad for).[17] Hippolite is equated with generically defined cultural capital (*vos chansons*) in an ironic equation, since women were associated with novels both as writers

Figure 28. La Galerie du Palais, anonymous frontispiece, vol. 1, Pierre Corneille,
Le théâtre (1660) Bibliothèque nationale

and as imputed readers. The equivalence between persons and cultural capital is witnessed in the line and the pronoun *ceci*. In the earliest edition of the play, the pronoun substituted for Hippolite is that used for things, not persons; in 1660, Corneille changes the line to read "Ce visage vaut mieux que toutes vos chansons"; the synecdoche values Hippolite in relation to the bookseller's poems and ballads. The lace merchant reiterates that equivalence later in the scene when she comments to the bookseller, "Ce cavalier sans doute y trouve plus d'appas / Que dans tous vos Auteurs" [131–32] (This cavalier doubtless finds more charms here [in my stall] than in all your authors), thereby commodifying cultural production (*vos Auteurs*) and producing a slippage between literature as goods and the newly beloved Hippolite. Following this interchange, Lisandre arrives on the scene to find his friend reading as he awaits the return of his *écuyer* sent to discover the identity of his newly beloved. Before Dorimant confesses his love for Hippolite to Lisandre, the two gallants expend some fifty lines in literary critique. They ridicule the conventions of love poetry ("l'amour à la façon des poètes") and lament the negative effect on comedy produced by its clichés: love as madness (*fureur*); its "langueurs," "ravissements," and "tendresses"; its metaphors, "Venus," "Flore," "lis," "roses"; and the reputed imperial power exercised by the beloved's regard ("un bel oeil peut s'étendre l'empire"). Lisandre criticizes those writers who "veulent parler d'amour sans aucune pratique" [149] (speak of love without having experienced it). But ironically both he and Dorimant censure precisely the Petrarchan conventions that, in the very next scene, they use to describe the debuts of their respective loves and their subsequent feelings. *La galerie du palais* represents not only the seriality of objects in its enumeration of ribbons, lace, the collars and books displayed in its boutiques, but of language itself, here the paraphernalia of Petrarchism that is also commodified. Its provenance and workmanship, value and usefulness, are weighed and found wanting but ultimately recirculated in the immediately following scene.

Comparison with shop scenes in English city comedy highlights the differences between the French and English genres. In Middleton and Dekker's play *The Roaring Girl* (1611), for example, at act 2, scene 1 the audience is presented with a similar scene in which city gallants, Laxton, Greenwit, and Goshawk, shop for upscale goods, including tobacco, feathers, holland, and lace. The scene is set in three shops, an apothecary, a feather shop, and a sempster's (seamstress's) shop, which are inhabited, as in Corneille's play, by their proprietors. Whereas Corneille uses the interactions between his pastorally named gallants and the unnamed shopkeepers as backdrop to the young lovers' plot, and to reveal their possession of cultural capital in the form of literary and sartorial taste and connoisseurship, in *The Roaring Girl*, the aptly named Gallipots, Tiltyards, and Openworks take part in plots of attempted seduction but ultimately triumph, for the citizen couples, like the roaring girl Moll herself, finally get the better of the city gallants. Instead of picturesque backdrop, Middleton and Dekker's shopkeepers have their own subplot of adultery, uxoriousness, and mercantile exploits. Whereas in Corneille's comedy the proprietors argue over custom and commercial space and deal mainly with the young lovers' servants, the English citizens are substantial businessmen who own "barns and houses" (3.2.91), are literate, and emulate behaviors of those higher up the social hierarchy as when the citizen wives venture out on the town masked.[18] Though these differences may be explained in part by differing dramatic conventions, in what can be dramatized on the English stage—multiple plots, a mix of persons—versus the French neoclassical tradition that demanded a unified action, the separation of high and low, and so forth, they need also to be understood in the context of different urban contexts. In London in 1611, neighborhood remains powerful, and the comings and goings of the roaring girl Moll, the gallants, and the citizens are intertwined and scrutinized by all, whereas Corneille's Paris of the 1630s would seem to be a larger, more anonymous urban environment of rigid hierarchies.

In Corneille's comedy following the two scenes in the *galerie*, his *jeune premier* Dorimant recounts his first view of Hippolite and his determination to discover her identity. Lisandre warns him that curiosity will soon give way to desire, and his speech is filled with the conventional diction of Petrarchan love: "flamme," "Notre ame blessée," "trouble," "un sommeil inquiet," "souhaits," "coeur," "voeux." Seeing her has doctrinaire effects: "Voyant je ne sais quoi de rare en sa beauté" [207] (Seeing something exceptional—it's unexplainable—in her beauty) excites in him a determination to know "quelle est sa qualité, son nom, et sa demeure" [205] (what is her condition, her name and her address). In other words, just as in the previous scenes in the *galerie* where the young privileged Parisians have asked of tradesmen and shopkeepers the provenance of goods, considered their workmanship and price, not only material objects like collars and ribbons, but also cultural goods and the relative merits of genres and styles, so Dorimant wishes to appraise the object of his affections. The word *objet* is repeated in this brief comedy of some eighteen hundred lines sixteen times in the 1637 edition and nineteen times in the 1660 revision. In the three additional incidences in the 1660 edition, in each case *objet* has been substituted for *sujet* used in reference to the woman/beloved. Lisandre perhaps best exemplifies the slippage between *objets* as goods and the beloved as *objet* in a desperate soliloquy at act 2, scene 9 in response to Célidée's feigned indifference: "Et tout ce que Paris a d'objets ravissants/ N'a jamais ébranlé le moindre de mes sens" [671–72] (All Paris possesses of ravishing objects/Never excited my senses in the least). Paris is filled with "objets ravissants," both women and goods. This scene and the earlier encounter of Dorimant and Hippolite also demonstrate the importance of the visual both to courtship and to commerce. Though Cotgrave's definition of *obiect* quoted earlier ("the subject of the sight, anything one lookes on directly; anything that is before the eyes") stresses its philosophical meaning and only secondarily hints at its usage in love poetry, here the insistence on seeing and love, on seeing goods, the visual display of goods/*objets* in the boutiques of the *galerie*, and the equivalence set up between women and goods demonstrates the shift in the meaning of the word that takes place in the course of the seventeenth century. These scenes also gesture toward the power of the visual in consumer culture that cultural commentators have analyzed in studying the development of the arcades and department stores of nineteenth-century Paris and London.

Critics have, of course, often observed the conflation of a language of value with the idealizing language of love poetry, a conflation already clichéd in Corneille's day.[19] But words like *posséder, trésor, gagner, valoir*, though they witness a coded language of value, of possession and ownership, of the dear and the precious used to represent desire and emotion, are not precisely mercantile; they register no market exchange or monetary transaction and entail no merchant or tradesman. Furthermore, Corneille's city comedy, unlike his tragedy, enables us to see this conflation of the rhetoric of love and value, the impact of which is considerably diminished when used outside a bourgeois, commercial setting such as the Galerie du Palais or the Royal or New Exchanges in London. If we consider *Le Cid*, for example, we find that at the outset of the play's action Chimène faces, as many commentators have noted, the same dilemma as does Rodrigue; like Rodrigue, she struggles with conflicting loyalties, on the one hand, to her family's honor, on the other, to her love for Rodrigue; like him, she is a subject who must choose.[20] But in the course of the play she becomes, notoriously, an object, until in the final judicial determination, she is given to Don Rodrigue: "Rodrigue t'a gaignée, et tu dois être à lui" [1841] (Rodrigue has won you, you must be his); she is "le prix de sa victoire" [1841] (the prize/price of his victory).

Critical protocols that demand that we distinguish between tragedy and comedy generically, that observe that *Le Cid* takes place in medieval Spain dominated by an aristocratic code of honor, that situate the play in relation to debates about dueling and aristocratic bloodlines in seventeenth-century France, or that claim that "le tragique amoureux cornélien n'est pas le tragique social mais celui de l'esprit" (Corneille's tragedy of love is not social, but a tragedy of the spirit)[21] hold to and perpetuate critical postures that prevent our observing certain relations of power and the gendering of both subject and object. Outside the commercial setting of seventeenth-century urban Paris's Galerie du Palais, such tropes signify *Poésie*; they have no power to evoke concrete situations of exchange such as are enacted in *La galerie du palais*.[22] In other words, in a historical epoch of urbanization in which relations to goods and to space are changing profoundly, the critical codes of *bienséance, vraisemblance*, and the like are gatekeeping concepts that uphold certain interpretations while obscuring other different readings of gender, class, and the newly commodified status of literature itself. Our critical view is turned away from persons and books as objects exchanged like the other luxury goods sold in the Galerie du Palais, away from a new specificity of space—urban and

public, *intime* and private—and away from the seventeenth-century revolution in the world of goods that so changed not only aristocratic and privileged
milieux but also a broader urban populace.[23] In *Le Cid*, Chimène is the price
of victory; women are possessed, given, won within a tightly circumscribed
aristocratic world of rank, blood, race, and power set in the historical past,
not in the marketplaces of early modern urban Paris. The *bienséance* of place
shrouds the expanding commercial world of mercantile and erotic exchange
familiar to Corneille's audience, that "extraordinary spectacle" that was the
Galerie du Palais.

In Corneille's comedy, what troubles his critics is precisely the effects of
place, the way in which the idealizing language of love, desire, the soul, and
so forth is undercut by the commercial language of goods, workmanship,
provenance, price. Timothy Reiss, for example, complains that the mise-en-
scène of *La galerie du palais* "is designed with no attempt at *vraisemblance*"
and results in a "conflict between the action and the set." The thick forests of
pastoral better support such action, since they "seem to echo the complicated
tangles found in the speeches and plots of the lovers."[24] I argue that this
juxtaposition, epitomized by the shift that I have traced in the meaning of the
word *objet*, enables interested rather than purely formal reading practices in
which questions of gender, status, and exchange are foregrounded.

But in this comedy, men are also beloved objects, and Hippolite bargains
and negotiates on behalf of her love of Lisandre as forcefully as Dorimant
solicits her. She rejects his attempted courtship as adamantly as earlier he and
Lisandre had ridiculed the conventions of love poetry with a brusque critique
of his gallantry:

> Ne me conte point tant que mon visage est beau,
> Ces discours n'ont pour moi rien du tout de nouveau,
> Je le sais bien sans vous, et j'ai cet avantage,
> Quelques perfections qui soient sur mon visage,
> Que je suis la première à mon apercevoir:
> Pour me galantiser il ne faut qu'un miroir
> J'y vois en un moment tout ce que vous me dites. (331–37)

> Stop going on and on about the beauty of my face,
> That line does nothing for me, it's completely debased,
> I know well enough without you, and anyway, for me
> Whatever perfections in my face there might be
> I'm the first to perceive them, for court to be paid
> All I need is a mirror, there I see all you've said. (translation mine)

Hippolite's forceful action on behalf of her love, like Chimène's handling of
her dilemma early in *Le Cid*, would seem to call into question the gendered
status of the beloved *objet*. Yet the play ends with the promised marriage of

Hippolite and her wooer Dorimant, a marriage to which Hippolite accedes by disavowing her own choice, a disavowal marked by Hippolite's speaking of herself in the third person and agreeing to marry him: "Si ma mère y consent," she tells him, "Hippolite est à vous" [1720] (If my mother agrees, Hippolite is yours). In early seventeenth-century Paris, young lovers promenade, taking in the mercantile sights of the city, choosing books and lace, professing love to whomever they choose, but daughters are finally disposed of to suitors at their parents'—mother's or father's—discretion. Both men and women are objects of desire, and yet the gendering of objects in the play is significant: Hippolite shops for collars and lace, for the latest in sartorial workmanship and fashion, while Dorimant and Lisandre shop for books, for the cultural capital that ensures them a place in the expanding public space of early modern Paris.

The male protagonist of Corneille's later comedy, *Le menteur*, arrives in Paris intent on acquiring the cultural capital he needs to cut a figure in the capital. Banished ("banni"; 1.1.18) from his native city to Poitiers to study the law, on his return Dorante is determined to shed any vestige of the provinces. Instead of the Galerie du Palais, much of the action takes place in the Tuileries, "le pays du beau monde, et des galanteries" (the land of the fashionable and of amorous adventures) as he characterizes the gardens in his and the play's opening lines. Dorante is the liar of the title, a new urban variant of the braggart soldier who boasts not only of martial exploits or of the women who adore him, but of extravagant fantasy entertainments, the ten languages he can speak, and the stories (*nouvelles*) he can tell that compete with those of writers. The play's action depends on Dorante's series of lies and on mistaken identities in which the object of his errant desire changes from one moment to the next. It ends with paired lovers soon to be married but swerves away from that convention in a final, enigmatic exchange between Dorante, who, at the very moment he is united with the object of his love, Lucrèce, seems to turn in yet another direction, toward Lucrèce's *suivante*, Sabine. The ending foreshadows Corneille's *La suite du menteur*, which opens with putatively the same Dorante having fled Paris on the eve of his marriage to Lucrèce. He absconds with the money from her dowry and recounts to his valet Cliton his second thoughts about marriage:

Que j'eus considéré ses chaines de plus près,
Son visage à ce prix n'eut plus pour moi d'attraits.
L'horreur d'un tel lien m'en fit de la Maîtresse,
Je crus qu'il fallait mieux employer ma jeunesse.

When I had considered those marital chains more nearly
At that price her face no longer seemed to me charming,
The fear of such a bond made my mistress horrible in truth
And I believed I could much better employ my youth.[25]

In both *Le menteur* and *La suite du menteur*, Corneille uses the same language of commerce and exchange found in *La galerie du palais*, and, as in the earlier play, the word *objet* appears numerous times and in similar contexts. Women are charming objects, love is worth the price. At the end of act 4, Clarice and Lucrèce discuss Dorante, who has wooed Clarice believing her to be Lucrèce and thus unknowingly woos Lucrèce by letter and at her window. Lucrèce admits she has begun to believe Dorante, and Clarice responds: "Qui se croit aimée aime bientôt après" [1408] (Whoever believes herself loved will love soon after). The two women initially use the Petrarchan language of fire and flames, but Lucrèce makes an interesting shift: "La curiosité souvent dans quelques âmes / Produit le même effet que produiraient des flammes" [1409–10] (Often in some souls curiosity / produces the same effect as do the flames of desire). The two young women bicker about whether they are in love or whether simple curiosity has prompted their willingness to listen to Dorante's compliments. *Curiosité* in early modern Paris is linked to the collecting of sought-after, unusual objects and here extends the language of exchange for courtship so typical of Corneille's comedies.

The preoccupation of the play's antihero, the liar Dorante, is to accumulate and display the social knowledge and cultural capital that will enable him to succeed with Paris's fashionable set.[26] Worried he will seem a bore in the capital, he solicits advice from his valet, Cliton, who tries to reassure him:

Vos lois ne réglaient pas si bien tous vos desseins
Que vous eussiez toujours un portefeuille aux mains. (55–56)

Your principles have not paid for / regulated so well all your plans
That you don't still have a portfolio available in your hands.

However much he has "paid out" during his apprenticeship in Poitiers, Cliton assures him he still has plenty in his "portefeuille." In the seventeenth century, *portefeuille* referred to one's negotiable physical and moral assets and is linked to commerce and technical financial instruments, *les effets de commerce*. Though Dorante admits he has been successful in Poitiers, he fears that success will not travel: "Ce qu'on admire ailleurs est ici hors de mode, / La diverse façon de parler et d'agir / Donne aux nouveaux venus souvent de quoi rougir" [62–64] (What is admired elsewhere is out of fashion here / The different way of speaking and acting / Often gives newcomers reason to blush). Every gesture and word requires knowledge of urban style and forms of sociability and is negotiable on a market. As the conduct book *Les lois de la galanterie* (1644, 1658) puts it, "Ce ne sera que dans Paris, ville capitale en toutes façons, qu'il faudra chercher la source et l'origine de la vraie galanterie et où l'on croira que sont les vrais galants, que les provinciaux ne pourront jamais avoir l'air du grand monde s'ils n'ont demeuré quelque temps dans ce superbe lieu, qui est un abrégé du monde universel" (It will only be in Paris, capital city in every sense, where one will find the source and origin of true gallantry, where the true gallants are to be found, and provincials will never have the manner of the fashionable world if they haven't spent some time in this superb place which is an epitome of all the world).[27] The play offers a glimpse of the pastimes, places, and objects fashionable in the capital: not only the Tuileries and the Place Royale but "du Temple," where the Théâtre du Marais in which Corneille's plays were performed was situated, and the newly built Palais Royal and Saint-Germain des Près mentioned earlier. The characters read the newly popular newspaper, the *Gazette*, and Dorante fantasizes throwing a party aboard five hired boats with music and dancing, a twelve-course banquet, and fireworks that emulate the extravagant aristocratic entertainments of the period. Embedded in Dorante's lies are references to chic consumer goods, medical discoveries, and new technologies. He claims he is discovered in the bedroom of his beloved when his watch sounds. Personal watches begin to be available in France in the second half of the sixteenth century and were among the fashionable luxury goods increasingly available to the well-off. Dorante's watch, then, indicates his status and consumption of luxury goods. In another lie, having made up a duel in which he pretends he has left his onetime friend Alcippe for dead, he claims Alcippe is miraculously healed by means of "poudre de Sympathie" or "weapon-salve," a remedy in vogue to cure wounds by applying vitriol to the weapon that had caused the injury. It is said to have first been used in France in 1642, less than two years before the publication of Corneille's play. In short, *Le menteur* retails new forms of cultural capital in early modern Paris.

The action unrolls not in the commercial shopping spaces of early modern Paris, as in *La galerie du palais*, but in the favored places of resort of a young urban elite: the Tuileries and the Place Royal (now the Place des Vosges). Dorante and his father make their first appearance together onstage in the Tuileries after a "promenade." Their heart-to-heart in which Géronte tells his son he has chosen him a wife takes place in outdoor Paris after an initial exchange about recent alterations in the urban landscape. Géronte marvels at the symmetry and beauty of the buildings to which Dorante replies

> Paris semble à mes yeux un pays de romans
> J'y croyais ce matin voir une île enchantée;
> Je la laissai déserte, et la trouve habitée.
> Quelque Amphion nouveau, sans l'aide de maçons,
> En superbes Palais a changé ses buissons. (552–56)

> Paris seems to my eyes a land of romances
> This morning I imagined seeing an enchanted island
> When I left it was deserted, at my return, I found it inhabited
> Without the help of masons another Amphion
> Has transformed bushes into superb palaces.

Géronte responds by saying that one sees such transformations (*métamorpho-ses*) throughout the city and proceeds to detail them: Saint-Germain des Près, le Palais Royal. According to Géronte, the universe has seen nothing to equal the changes afoot in Paris; it seems a miracle arisen from an old ditch. Looking at the "superbes toits" (superb roofs), one would assume its inhabitants were all gods or kings. Here urban development is represented first by Dorante as the work of another Amphion, the poet and musician whose playing was said to have raised the walls of Thebes, and then by Géronte as so astonishing as to seem unreal, a fiction, a miracle, and the beauty and splendor of its build-ings offer sights fit for a king. The conventional comic formula of arranged marriage is subordinated to the marvelous description of the newly configured space of the capital, a capital produced by the magic of poetic fiction.

If we return to Corneille's introduction to his 1660 collected works, we can trace a changing attitude toward space, a developing sense of differentiated spaces, a perceived relation between certain kinds of talk, certain genres, and certain spaces. Corneille admits that some of what his characters say to one another, particularly the young lovers, might better be said not in the public space of the street, shopping mall, or garden but in a *chambre* or a *salle* (302). Literary *bienséance* or decorum, then, can be seen as part of a move not only to differentiate literary genres, comedy from tragedy, but toward a new differ-entiation of space. Jürgen Habermas analyzes this differentiation of space as the demarcation in the late seventeenth and eighteenth centuries of a bour-geois public space of politics, of commercial and intellectual exchange. Cor-neille's discomfort with the conventions of theatrical public space suggests a related development, the relegation of a feminized world of affect to the *toilette* and the increasingly privatized spaces of *maison, salle,* and *cabinet.*

CHAPTER SIX

Armchair Travel

Shopping in the London exchanges or at Paris's Galerie du Palais, women in early modern London and Paris encountered objects and commodities from distant places to which they could rarely expect to travel themselves; there they also bought books, including not only the texts to which Corneille alludes in his comedy but the romance novels that were best sellers among metropolitan audiences in Paris—and London—and which men and women read both aloud in company in urban salons and silently in the privacy of the *cabinet*. This chapter is concerned not with representations of urban life and landmarks, or with how movement though urban space was represented, but with what city readers read. In particular, it looks at women readers, but it begins by considering women's exclusion from certain kinds of spatial movement, from the travel so important to education, knowledge, and power in the seventeenth century, and argues that that exclusion contributed to the vogue for romance novels among metropolitan writers and readers.

Early in her study of seventeenth-century Parisian culture entitled *Cartesian Women*, Erica Harth delimits the gendered boundaries within which women of that period and place lived: "The demands of feminine modesty and the inaccessibility of the educational apparatus . . . formal schooling, voyages, materials, and equipment—kept even the most educated women well within the limits of orthodoxy."[1] By my own spatial vocabulary—delimits, boundaries, place—I mean to emphasize, in keeping with the theoretical preoccupations of this book, the spatial aspect of this exclusion: women were proscribed from the space of the school and the academies in which the new science so crucial to the Enlightenment was being constituted. A great deal of recent feminist work has been concerned with both school and academy, and there is interesting work to be done certainly on women's exclusion from materials and equipment, but in this chapter I want to explore women's exclusion from travel, from the voyages that, in the course of the seventeenth century, became a crucial form of knowledge identified increasingly with the newly developing empiricism. This claim requires, of course, important qualification: medieval and early modern Europe was inhabited primarily by, in the great French historian Jacques Le Goff's expression, sedentary beings, "des êtres sédentaires."[2] Few medieval and Renaissance men or women traveled at all. The travel of which I write in this chapter was not proscribed only to women, but materially to all but a few men as well. Nomadic travel from one palace or house to another characterized the habits of both the French and English aristocracies of the early modern period; young boys and girls often traveled to live in other households as part of their upbringing; demographic records show that all sorts of persons, both men and women, traveled to urban centers in search of work or preferment; and pilgrims, religious minorities, explorers, and mercantile adventurers traveled the globe. But the inter- and extracontinental travel associated with education with which I am concerned was ordinarily the privilege of a male elite.

Though much recent work in early modern studies has been interested in travel, it has primarily been concerned with the so-called age of discovery and with colonial expansion.[3] But in the seventeenth century, Europeans traveled in increasing numbers not only to colonize the so-called New World and bring back to European urban markets its commodities—gold, tobacco, sugar, hardwoods—but to accumulate cultural capital in what are already the early stages of the grand tour. Jonathan Dewald describes the appeal and significance of travel for the French male elite: young nobles traveled because contemporaries believed separation from home to be an important element in education. Such ideas touched all social classes.[4] Travel offered not only knowledge of newly discovered or visited lands and cities, peoples and things; travel became an important epistemological model for knowing. Here is Descartes in the *Discourse on Method* (1637):

> Sitôt que l'âge me permit de sortir de la sujétion de mes précepteurs, je quittai entièrement l'étude des lettres; et me résolvant de ne chercher plus d'autre science que celle qui se pourrait trouver en moi-même, ou bien dans le grand livre du monde, j'employai le reste de ma jeunesse à voyager, à voir des cours et des armées, à fréquenter des gens de diverses humeurs et conditions, à recueillir diverses expériences, à m'éprouver moi-même dans les rencontres que la fortune me proposait, et partout à faire telle réflexion sur les choses qui se présentaient que j'en pusse tirer quelque profit. Car il me semblait que je pourrais rencontrer beaucoup plus de vérité dans les raisonnements que chacun fait touchant les affaires qui lui importent, et dont l'événement le doit punir bientôt après s'il a mal jugé, que dans ceux que fait un homme de lettres dans son cabinet.

> As soon as I was old enough to escape the authority of my teachers, I gave up letters entirely and resolved not to pursue any study except that which I might find in myself, or really, in the great book of the world. I spent the rest of my youth traveling, seeing courts and armies, frequenting persons of varied types and conditions, gathering varied experiences, proving myself in the encounters that fortune dealt me, and everywhere reflecting on whatever came my way so that I was able to take some profit from it. It seemed to me that I would be able to meet much more of truth through the judgments each person exercises in his own affairs,

the consequences of which punish him soon after he has judged wrongly, than through those made by a scholar in his study. (trans. mine)[5]

Of interest here once more is the spatial dimension of knowledge: travel and what it teaches is opposed to what goes on in the *cabinet* or private study. *Method*, after all, derives from the Greek word *hodos* meaning route, road, or way. Descartes goes on, famously, to abandon travel as well as letters and to call for the study of self: "Après que j'eus employé quelques années à étudier ainsi dans le livre du monde, et à tâcher d'acquérir quelque expérience, je pris un jour résolution d'étudier aussi en moi-même, et d'employer toutes les forces de mon esprit à choisir les chemins que je devais suivre" [18] (After I had spent some years studying thus in the book of the world and applying myself to acquiring some experience, I resolved also to study myself, and to use all my mental powers to choose the ways / roads I ought to pursue / follow; trans. mine). Significantly, that self-study which is the only form of knowledge worth pursuing, the only knowledge that can lead to truth, is enabled through travel which has delivered the speaker, little by little, from the errors that beset reason. Not only does Descartes *not* forsake travel in this passage "one day I resolved also [*aussi*] to study myself," he says, but he can only describe self-study as travel: "I resolved to use all my mental powers to choose the paths / roads I ought to follow." As many commentators have noted, metaphors of the road or route abound in the *Discours de la méthode* and elsewhere in Descartes.[6] Nor does the philosopher forsake the language of travel after his famed retreat, when he formulates the cogito in his *Meditations*.

Like the French, the English also recognized the educational importance of travel. Much maligned by the sixteenth-century humanists, in the course of the seventeenth century travel's usefulness comes to be widely acknowledged. In his study of English travelers abroad, John Stoye illustrates how "travel by young men on the continent came to be accepted as an essential part of their education."[7] Here again is Samuel Purchas's uneasy defense of travel from *Hakluytus Posthumus, or Purchas his Pilgrimes* (1625), which I considered earlier in another context:

> As for Gentlemen, Travell is accounted an excellent Ornament to them; and therefore many of them comming to their Lands sooner than to their Wits, adventure themselves to see the Fashions of other Countries, where their soules and bodies find temptations to a twofold Whoredom, whence they see the World as *Adam* had *knowledge of good and evill*, with the losse or lessening of their estate in this *English* (and perhaps also in the heavenly) Paradise, and bring home a few smattering termes, flattering garbes, Apish crings, foppish fancies, foolish guises and disguises, the vanities of Neighbour Nations . . . without furthering of their knowledge of God, the World, or themselves. I speake not against Travell, so usefull to usefull men, I honour the industrious of the liberall and ingen-

uous in arts, bloud, education: and to prevent exorbitancies of the other, which cannot travell farre, or are in danger to travell from God and themselves, at no great charge I offer a World of Travellers to their domesticke entertainment.

Purchas's address to his reader looks backward, as we have seen, to the sixteenth-century fear of foreign travel as perilous to body and soul. He rehearses the antiquated and gendered English paranoia about travel and its temptations found in the early humanists, including Roger Ascham, who, it will be remembered, bemoaned the Circean dangers Italy posed young Englishmen. It is a prejudice still repeated in Stoye's *English Travellers Abroad 1604–1667: Their Influence on English Society and Politics*, which, though published in 1952 and revised in 1989, remains the only full-length study of seventeenth-century English travel in Europe. There Stoye laments the "wasting away of life in pleasant places on the continent, supported on rentals from English property" that he claims has been "common throughout a long period of English history."[8] In the passage cited from Purchas, who was himself a clergyman, he represents travel as a gendered allegory of the Fall. Travel offers knowledge of good and evil, its pursuit leads to whoredom, and its costs, like fashion with which it is linked, to the alienation of property: "the losse or lessening of their estate in this *English* Paradise." Purchas's dual message presents travel, on the one hand, as original sin and dangerous temptation, on the other, as ornament, fashion, vanity, but both are linked to femininity. We should appreciate the irony of that onus, since women, as we have seen, were in fact long proscribed from the educative and epistemologically enabling travel commended by thinkers, writers, diplomats, military men, here even by the Protestant clergy.

But finally Purchas's attack on travel is, of course, a canny argument on behalf of travel *writing* that eschews travel's pitfalls: expense and temptation to sin. As he puts it, "At no great charge I offer a World of Travellers to their domesticke entertainment." Purchas's pronoun *their* refers to the beginning of this passage: travel is accounted an excellent ornament of Gentlemen; looking forward, as we have pointed out, to the grand tour when travel was both the prerogative, and the prerequisite, of a gentleman's education, it also reminds us once again that women, with certain important exceptions, and those classes of men excluded from gentlemanly pursuits, were by and large excluded from the cultural capital travel proffered.[9]

The new spatial practices associated with travel were recorded in numerous new representational forms, including not only travel accounts but also, as we have seen, the survey, the guidebook, and books and pamphlets on the art or practice of travel. By the mid–seventeenth century, English apologies for travel no longer enumerate its dangers but instead extol its educational uses and advantages. As I have already pointed out in my discussion in chapter 1 of the survey and guidebook, the English traveler James Howell declares in his popular *Instructions for forreine travell* (1642) that "*Peregrination . . .* may be not improperly called a *moving Academy,* or the true *Peripatetique Schoole,*" an allusion to Aristotle's school named for the walk in the Lyceum where that philosopher taught.[10] Like Descartes, Howell defends travel as philosophical learning and argues for its educative and epistemological value.

As does virtually every travel writer of the seventeenth century, Howell claims to write from "experience," the locus classicus of travel writing. He emphasizes the importance of the traveler's movement through space as eyewitness, what might be termed a kind of scopic cogito (see the discussion of Howell in chapter 1). Howell's praise of the eye and the eyewitness, as I have argued, dramatizes the importance of a hegemonic subjectivity that depends on presence, but the seeing eye, interestingly and paradoxically, produces the "I" of writing. Howell's writing project undermines his claims on behalf of the eye, since his own eyewitness account can only be recorded in a book. Both Descartes in the *Discours* and Howell here resort, after all, to what both claim as a discredited writing. Subjectivity, then, is produced *not* by moving through city, state, or the "new world," but by the "I" that recounts those journeys. In both Descartes and Howell, the space of travel is denied in the very act of inscribing the graphic marks and spaces that make up writing. When Descartes writes of travel and the experience it provides, of course, his is an epistemological project, a metaphysics that exceeds the naive empiricism advertised by Howell and Purchas. They merely offer "travel" on the cheap to those aspiring or simply curious men, and of course women, who may not be able to afford travel but can manage the price of a book.

It is in that space—the space of the book, the space of writing and reading that proliferated in the urban markets of early modern London and Paris— in which I locate the seventeenth-century romance novel that notoriously travels the world over, through territories of emotion and relationship as well as exotic spaces and places, mapping fictional travel of the educative sort, travel as a source of social knowledge from which women were largely excluded but to which literate women at least traveled in the course of the century as avid writers and readers. This claim, like my earlier point about travelers, requires qualification: the avid readers and writers of which I write here represent a small number of privileged men and women as compared to the larger population (an average print run was about a thousand).[11] Nonetheless, the romance novel was the mobile genre par excellence, and it figures in interesting ways both the exclusions and the possibilities confronted by women in response to the new importance of travel as cultural capital in seventeenth-century Europe. It allowed them the possibility of travel in one of the few venues permitted them—as writers and readers.

Commentators have long opposed the romance novel and travel writing; they often quote a letter dated 1663 by the minor poet and academician Jean

Chapelain in which he observes that French reading habits were changing: "voyages," he opines, "are in vogue both at court and in town [Paris]," while novels have fallen out of favor.[12] But even in the course of asserting the fall of the novel—and it is worth remembering here that in both the French and English traditions, we are still some ways away from what modern critics have been willing to call a novel at all—Chapelain indicates its extraordinary popularity: travel writing, he asserts, is "an entertainment much wiser and more useful than that offered by these agreeable pleasantries that have so enchanted all the idlers, male and female, all about us, and from which our Italian, German, and Dutch neighbors have imbibed poison to their disadvantage and our shame" (trans. mine).[13] Chapelain rehearses the charge of frivolity, already familiar in the seventeenth century, against the romance novel and opposes it to the utility of travel writing, but he nonetheless admits the genre's extraordinary popularity.

Though Chapelain omits the English from those empoisoned by the French novel, we know the English were avid readers of the genre from Honoré d'Urfé's *L'Astrée* to Lady Mary Wroth's *Urania* to Madeleine de Scudéry's romance novels. Though the evidence of women's reading is at present scant and anecdotal, the references to Scudéry's *Artamène ou le Grand Cyrus*, perhaps best known through Molière's satiric portrayal of it as the favored reading matter of his provincial aspiring *précieuses* in their assault on the capital, are particularly interesting.[14] The Caroline court of Henrietta Maria is known to have emulated French models.[15] Somewhat later Dorothy Osborne's letters, for example, reveal that she was particularly fond of French romances; during her three-year courtship with William Temple, which was opposed by both their families, Osborne sends to him in London *Artamène* volume by volume in the early 1650s and, as Jacqueline Pearson has pointed out, "uses the situations of that novel to address their own situation and problems."[16] *Artaméne* appeared in the midst of the Fronde, between 1649 and 1653, the final volume appearing only in September of that year, which means that, despite the upheavals in Paris, amazingly, Scudéry's popular novel managed to reach its audience abroad immediately. Pepys, whose diary occasionally records conjugal reading, reports his wife reading *Artamène* sometime before his own scurrilous, one-handed perusal of the almost contemporaneous pornographic French novel *L'école des filles*. Both the bourgeois Katherine Philips and the aristocratic Margaret Cavendish are said to have admired Scudéry's romances.[17] Her novels, which remain today unavailable in any modern edition in French or English, were translated immediately after they appeared in Paris into Spanish, Italian, German, English, even, it is claimed, Arabic.[18] Aphra Behn's earliest endeavor with her pen, *The Young King*, was virtually a translation of the well-known author of romances La Calprenède, and she put her own hand to romance in her popular, if notorious, *Love Letters between a Nobleman and His Sister*.

As a major commentator on the seventeenth-century French novel observes, it is the genre at once most despised by critics but, despite occasional complaints about its length, mostly from critics rather than readers, most adored by the public.[19] That public, constituted and expanded by a burgeoning urban print culture, awaited the publication of a new volume with such anticipation that readers were willing to pay exorbitant prices for single sheets before an entire print run was completed.[20] In France we know that booksellers charged more for the romances than for other kinds of books—two, even three times as much as for books materially comparable.[21] Individual volumes of Scudéry's ten-tome *Clélie* seem to have been sold in even smaller gatherings to inflate profits; even the typography of Scudéry's novels witnesses the profit to be made from romance fiction: large type ensured multiple volumes for an avid market.

The opposition of *utile et dulce* alleged by Chapelain in distinguishing between travel writing and the novel is only one of many charges leveled against the romance novel. These texts were also criticized for *invraisemblance* and for what in French is termed *dépaysement*—for producing in their readers a sense of rootlessness or displacement, we might say; these romances are said to lack specificities of place and therefore to displace their readers in both time and space. Scudéry's three multivolumed novels published between 1640 and 1660, *Ibrahim, Artamène ou le Grand Cyrus* and *Clélie*, are set respectively in the Mediterranean from Monaco and Genoa to Constantinople, in Persia, and in the ancient Roman world. Long maligned for roving flagrantly through space, Scudéry's novels have been shown by recent commentators to demonstrate scholarly care and precision in their presentation of ancient history and place.[22] She never mistakes the situation of countries or cities, rivers or seas. No seacoast in Bohemia here, as in Shakespeare's *Winter's Tale*. The novels have been remembered primarily as romans à clef of the Fronde years, so the critique of placelessness is in part no doubt a response to the displacement of contemporary personages and events back in time and into other, often exotic places.[23] But the countless critical objections to the seventeenth-century romance novel are also due to their insistent idealism so contrary to the dominant realism on which arguments about the rise of "the" novel are founded.[24] Settings in and travel to exotic locales were both an appropriation of the experience of travel on the part of those denied its cultural and epistemological capital and an important marketing strategy aimed at metropolitan readers avid for such exotic curiosities.[25]

Scudéry's characters themselves recognize and assert the power of travel. In the first volume of *Artamène*, the hero of the title, sounding very much like Descartes, declares: "I want to educate myself by traveling, I want to prove myself through whatever befalls me, I want to know myself" (trans. mine).[26] In one of Scudéry's later published collections of conversations, *Entretiens de morale* (1692), in a discussion of travel, one Amintor remarks that there is

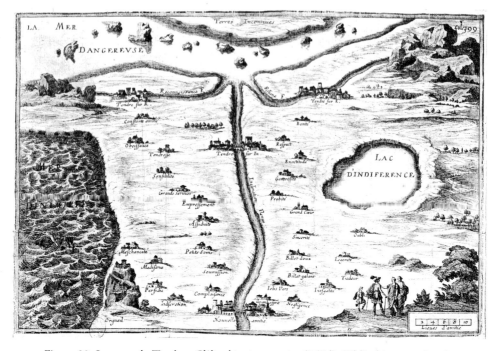

Figure 29. La carte de Tendre, *Clélie, histoire romaine* (1654). Bibliothèque nationale

"une autre manière de voyager sans changer de place" (another way of traveling, without even moving): reading.[27] The romance novel was, in Purchas's
phrase, *domestic* entertainment, but like the travel writing he hawks, it was
also a mode of travel for its sedentary readers, so often, we should remember,
said to be women; it offered them access to the new ways of knowing from
which they were so frequently materially excluded. The characters of these
novels are constantly on the move, not only through space but through feeling
and desire, mapped famously as travel through fictive space, as an emotional
and emotive geography with its own rivers, seas, cities, and towns, its terra
incognita, in the repeatedly reprinted, widely imitated, often ridiculed but
rarely seriously considered *carte de Tendre* (fig. 29).[28]

Scudéry's allegorical map seems to have come about as a *jeu d'esprit* amid
the *galante* conversation and collaborative cultural production of her famous
Saturdays, the name given to her regular gatherings of an urban elite we have
since termed the salon.[29] After having circulated apparently for sometime
among her circle in manuscript, it appears in print in the first volume of
Clélie. The map displaces courtship from the temporal world of the sonneteer
to the spatial world of the geographer; its presumed travelers are positioned
on a promontory above *Tendre*, a privileged position of territorial power and
appropriation.[30] In the novel, *amitié* is a problem of traversing space. At the
moment when the map is introduced, it is in response to the plea "Dittes moy

où j'en suis" (tell me *where* I am).[31] The development of feeling and emotion is presented not as a development in time but in spatial terms: as cities and towns along the rivers of Inclination, Esteem, and Gratitude or Recognition. Diectics—the linguistic forms that anchor the speaker or character in space and time—situate Scudéry's characters, but instead of the temporal diectic markers characteristic of the sonnet, Scudéry uses spatial diectics (where, here, there, far) and the language of movement through space (which way, place, lead, go, voyage, route). Herminius engages himself to undertake a voyage through *Tendre* "J'aimerois mieux l'avoir fait que d'avoir veû toute la Terre" (I would rather have made that voyage than to have seen the entire globe).[32] Scudéry uses terms employed by geographers: beyond tender *amitié*—a state stronger than friendship, but not yet dangerous desire—lie the *terres inconnues*, the unknown lands. The *carte de Tendre* inspired countless knockoffs, libertine versions, and parodies; it was written of in poems, pamphlets, and letters, reproduced in books and pamphlets, on fans, boxes, and firescreens. The *carte* with its obstacles and barriers, rivers and mountains, stops and layovers, models the narrative strategies of romance itself with its set pieces, so-called detours and digressions that thwart linear progress.[33]

Travel writing or writing of travel, whether in the romance, travelers' accounts, defenses and arts of travel, or Descartes's *Discours*, as I have argued, paradoxically depends on the homebody, that is, the reader with access to the book market. In short, in the seventeenth century before the development of lending libraries and organized serial publication, travel writing depended on a metropolitan consumer / reader in search of "domestique entertainment."[34] Such writing, particularly the seventeenth-century novel, appealed primarily to a metropolitan audience in London and Paris and served for its armchair recreation. In Paris, when it appeared during the years of the Fronde, Scudèry's romance novel *Artamène* may well have offered readerly escape from the troubles and hardships of civil war.

Since Molière's send-up of provincial would-be *salonniéres* in *Les precieuses ridicules*, literary historians have been fascinated by the seventeenth-century urban salon culture of men and women engaged in learned and witty conversation. Our evidence has been chiefly "cultural"—that is, reference and allusion in various literary sources. Historians have often been skeptical about such claims, but recently Annick Pardailhé-Galabrun in her fascinating study of things, *The Birth of Intimacy: Privacy and Domestic Life in Early Modern Paris*, has gathered with painstaking exactitude from Parisian testamentary inventories evidence that documents the enormous appeal of what we anachronistically call salon culture across status lines. What she finds is an extraordinary plethora of chairs, chairs that encumbered seventeenth-century Parisian interiors. Here are the names of only a few: *chaises à bras, tabourets, escabeaux, vertugadins, caquetoires, fauteuils, sièges.* "Chairs are omnipresent and encroaching" (Les chaises sont omniprésentes et envahissent), she declares, on average twelve chairs per household, always many more than there were occupants.[35] This evidence of an excess of chairs is presented in a section of her book devoted to sociability, but Pardailhé-Galabrun never interprets this evidence; she hazards no inferences or conclusions, no judgments or interpretations, nor does she cite any of the varied literary evidence that corroborates salon culture. She has done the archival work that documents this excess of chairs, but she eschews the work of interpreting the facts she has amassed.

Carolyn Lougée argued more than twenty years ago that the salons were first and foremost arenas of sociability that, though they promoted social mobility, actively discouraged women's learning and intellectual exchange. Women's roles were severely constrained, and *savante* was a term of derision assiduously eschewed by *salonnières*.[36] Scudéry certainly takes pains to distance herself from both the term and the role, most emphatically in the final volume of *Artamène*, book 10, in the so-called "Histoire de Sapho" in which Scudéry's namesake Sapho is distinguished from her ludicrous *savante* double Damophile.[37] The appeal of salon culture extended from the highest aristocratic circles to the *noblesse de robe* and down the social hierarchy. In a popular pamphlet from midcentury, *Le caquet de l'acouchée* (1622), which might be roughly translated *The New Mother's Chatroom* by borrowing from contemporary cybertalk, the ailing speaker seeks medical advice and is told to make her way "à la ruelle." *Ruelle* was the name given to the space of conversation, the alcove or area between bed or couch and wall where one of the earliest *salonnières*, Madame de Rambouillet, is said to have received her intimates. "That will rejuvenate you and return you to perfect health" (Cela vous fera rajeunir e remettre in vostre pristine santé), the speaker is told. She eventually makes her way to the home of a friend recently delivered where she encounters a host of other women, rich and poor, single and married, young and old, who "started to chat or talk" (commencerent à caqueter). The widely reprinted pamphlet is a generic amalgam, related on the one hand to the old popular form "when gossips get together," on the other a satiric send-up of plebeian aspiring *salonnières*.

Though the work of reconstructing salon culture in seventeenth-century London has only begun, there are tantalizing pieces of evidence from across the channel: the matchless Orinda and her circle whose Society of Friendship is said to be a "community much like the salons' female-centered world of love, writing and court politics"; Behn's coterie named in her poem "Our Cabal" with its pastoral pseudonyms after the style of Scudéry; and finally Hortense Mancini, Duchess of Mazarin, who fled husband and uncle in France to arrive in London in what seems, according to both the novel and contemporary accounts, the safest way for a woman to travel, dressed as a man. There she set up what one commentator has dubbed "a genuine French salon."[38]

Literary evidence, of course, poses difficulties for the historian, but inventories and accounts are, of course, hardly free from the conventions, generic constraints, rhetorical organization, even exceptionalism, of literary materials. As a literary historian, I also dig in the archives, tracking down the uncanonized, sometimes ephemeral writings of the early modern period, but the secondhand fact from outside the domain of the literary, the fact of an excess of chairs, is keenly interesting to my work as an interpreter of texts. Historians and literary critics alike, after all, are all dealing with the secondhand, with what the French term *brocante*, or, in the argot of a passing but lamented moment in literary history, the "always already." What did the denizens of seventeenth-century Paris do in all those chairs? From the limit cases of Seigneur de la Grange with his 173 *sièges* (seats) in a household of ten to a certain widow Ollivier whose one room in the rue d'Anjou where she lived alone contained ten chairs and five armchairs,[39] seventeenth-century Paris was apparently a city of conversation, of the salon culture in which, as literary historians have long supposed, women and men conversed, performed, collaborated and read aloud, made reputations and lost them, won preferment and failed to advance, all the while engaged in what I am calling armchair travel.

After volume 5 of Scudéry's *Artamène, ou le grand Cyrus*, heroic deeds and action give way to the depiction of contemporary life and persons, to characters from Scudéry's famed *samedis*. *Clélie*, said to have been the best-selling book of the seventeenth century, is made up primarily of conversations. When the vogue for romance faded later in the century, Scudéry published several volumes of "conversations," some taken from the earlier novels, some supposedly reconstructed from her *samedis*. Conversation, as Elizabeth Goldsmith points out at the outset of her book on salon culture entitled *Exclusive Conversations*, comes from the Latin "to frequent, or live with," that is, etymologically the word is imbued with *place*.[40] In the world outlined by Erica Harth with which this chapter began, in which women are excluded from places of institutionalized learning and from educative travel, conversation and the novel, so often read aloud in the salon, come to have enormous educative and even epistemological status. In conversation, the *salonnières* could travel to disallowed places, could speculate in the optative on all kinds of terrae incognitae—on the limits and disadvantages of marriage, on pleasure and desire, on higher math and the movement of the planets.[41] They could traverse the epistemological routes and byways Descartes urges on his readers, a way that led to the cogito and to the subject of modernity, not overland or by sea but in the urban spaces of early modern Paris.

Today in Paris, in the fifth arrondissement, behind the Pantheon in the rue Rollin, a stone plaque memorializes Descartes's own sojourn in Paris. Only a step or two away is the rue Descartes itself, which runs between the rue Montagne Ste. Geneviève and the rue Thouin, along the Lycée Henri IV. Rollin, Descartes, Geneviève, Thouin: the streets of Paris, as Walter Benjamin has observed, are haunted by the dead, the dead remembered as names that mark urban space.

CHAPTER SEVEN

Death, Name, and Number

Memorials are history unfinished, or the first or rough
draughts of history, and antiquities are history defaced,
or some remnants of history which have casually escaped
the shipwreck of time.

BACON, *The Advancement of Learning*

In Washington, D.C., at the far end of the Mall from the Capitol, beyond
the Washington Monument, and in the shadow of the Lincoln Memorial is
the Vietnam Veterans Memorial. Across from its long expanse of black granite
is a book that registers alphabetically all the dead whose names are there etched
in stone in the order in which they died. Visitors can look up the name of a
friend or relative, its location, and nearby even buy paper and crayon to make
a rubbing of the name, a memorial of the memorial itself; across the Mall in
south west, past the Smithsonian, L'Enfant Plaza, and Hawthorne High
School, at Raoul Wallenberg Place, is the United States Holocaust Memorial
Museum. Upon entering the museum, until recently visitors picked up an
assumed identity, a proper name and accompanying narrative through which
to trace Holocaust history. The museum walls, like the streets and monuments
of the city itself, are marked by the names of the dead.

City space is everywhere inscribed by death and memory—buildings, street
names, monuments, and landmarks are all marked by the dead: Brown University, Washington D.C., the Boulevard Haussmann, the Eiffel Tower, the
Hancock Building, the Sears Tower, Martin Luther King Boulevard, Leland
Stanford Jr. University. With the exception of monarchs and an occasional
commander in chief, toponymy is usually reserved for the dead. Whereas once
place-names were associated with natural features of landscape or situation
(Fenchurch, Moorgate, the Marais, rue du Rocher, River Road, Ocean Boulevard) or with religious orders and saints (Blackfriars, Saint Germain) or with
guilds, métiers, or markets (rue des Orfèvres, rue de la Bucherie, Carter Lane,
Market Street) in the seventeenth and eighteenth centuries they came increasingly to honor rulers, political authorities, military victories, philanthropy,
and finally cultural achievement—in short, elites of various sorts.[1] Such memorials are an often unremarked feature of urban space and cognitive mapping
such that our movement through any city is always in some sense retrospective, a function of memory—not only the memory of a given street or build-

ing, of a now-obscured feature of landscape or activity of daily life, but of the sedimentary memory of the dead.[2] Anthropologists, sociologists, and urban historians argue for the importance of death rituals and commemorative practices to the reproduction of social life.[3] Landmarks, monuments, street names, public squares, buildings, and universities commemorate certain persons and not others, certain kinds of actions and not others, and thereby both inscribe and reproduce social relations and particular political economies. They also make of the city, in Walter Benjamin's arresting formulation that insists on the textuality of names, a haunted "linguistic cosmos," in which "the cityscape is, like a language, haunted by an ancient and unfathomable history."[4]

The last ten years have witnessed a striking cultural preoccupation with memory: newly built monuments and museums shape cultural memory in the postindustrial nation-state at the same moment that ethnic and nationalist memory is manifested in arson, massacre, genocide, and the mass grave; books and conferences announce memory's return or alternatively claim its persistence; therapists specialize in its retrieval while lawyers contend to prove its truth or falsehood; not memory room or filing cabinet or megabyte, recent work in neurophysiology and neurobiology suggests the truism the literary has long known, that memory is of the past, but fashioned in the present. This cultural preoccupation with memory, nostalgia, trauma, and longing comes paradoxically on the heels of what has been termed the end of history, cultural amnesia, presentism, *posthistoire*.[5] The turn of the millennium produced an acceleration of this turn to memory marked by a proliferation of museums, archives, collections, monuments, local and oral histories, databases, the docudrama. In his powerful meditation on "Les lieux de mémoire," Pierre Nora relates this preoccupation to identity politics. Such forms defend what he calls a "refugee memory": they are the rituals of a society increasingly without ritual, of a fugitive sacredness in a culture of desacralization, of differentiation in societies that make of equality a fetish; they are the signs of recognition and belonging to a group, in a society that recognizes only individuals, equal and the same.[6] At the same moment, literary studies, cultural studies, and history are witnessing what some commentators have termed the end of the end of history, in the turn to anecdote, the *petit récit*, microhistory.[7] In the flight from master narratives, history has been reduced to the incidental, to accretion, recording, and storage.

In my epigraph taken from *The Advancement of Learning*, Bacon distinguishes forms of historical evidence by drawing a temporal distinction between memorials and antiquities; memorials are records, the data we might say, that which comes before, whereas antiquities come after, they are ruins, remainders, monuments defaced. History is the missing middle between the pre- and the post-, memorials and antiquities, both of which Bacon textualizes—rough drafts and remnants. But in elaborating on this distinction in the passage that follows, he contradicts his claim that antiquities "casually" escape the "shipwrack of time." His emphasis instead is on the industry and exactitude, "the scrupulous diligence and observation" required for the salvation of antiquities as history: "Antiquities or Remnants of History are, as was said, *tanquam tabula naufragii*, when industrious persons by an exact and scrupulous diligence and observation, out of monuments, names, words, proverbs, traditions, private records and evidences, fragments of stories, passages of books that concern not story, and the like, do save and recover somewhat from the deluge of time."[8] In this passage, Bacon's Latin tag is a complex pun. Though *tabula* is usually translated in modern editions as "board" or "plank," thus "like the planks of a shipwreck," *tabula* also means an offering against shipwreck. The word means both the remains left after such a calamity and that which would prevent it. But there is an additional network of meanings: *tabula* also denotes a writing tablet or slate, a list or schedule, an account book or ledger, a formal accusation, a statute, public records, state papers—in other words, all those historical antiquities Bacon enumerates.

John Stow exemplifies Bacon's "industrious person." Both his *Annals* and his *Survey of London* are marked throughout by reminders of his historical labors: in the preface he says that he has "seene sundry antiquities my selfe," made a "search of Records," and employed "divers written helpes": "I found recorded that," "I have seene an account made," it was "registered in the end of the booke of Remembrances, in the Guildhall of London," "Edward Hall notes," "I have read."[9] Stow has found out London's history through travail, archival work as we now call it, the sifting through of records of all sorts, a labor that has earned him recognition as a proper name in historiography.[10] In the *Survay*, Stow begins his record of the city's history in chronicle fashion by citing the names of English monarchs, "in the yeare 1378, the first of Richard the Second," "in the yeare 1463, the third of Edward the fourth," "in the yeare 1536, Queene Anne Bullein," "in 1539 the 30 of Henrie the 8," "in the yeare 1548 the second of King Edward"; the examples could be multiplied interminably. Stow would at first seem to rehearse political history with a vengeance—chronicle history that depends on the actions of great men and a few great women, his survey organized by the generic conventions of the *de claribus* tradition. This is particularly the case in the opening sections of the *Survay* in which Stow, as his full title demonstrates, *A survay of London Conteyning the Originall, Antiquity, Increase, Modern estate, and description of that City written in the yeare 1598, by John Stow Citizen of London*, presents accounts of the city's origins, its founders, conquerors, and rulers, and enumerates its antiquity.

I say enumerates because "antiquity" in Stow's title means not so much London in former times, its antic history, but what is generally understood from the plural or collective sense of the word—antiquities—the manners and matters, customs and precedents of former times as well as remains or monuments, the "remnants of history," as Bacon calls them. In early modern

English, antiquities in the collective sense was often expressed in the singular as well as the plural. Stow enumerates London's antiquity—its customs, monuments, and remains—the principal bridges, gates, and conduits, its walls, its sports and pastimes. Wrestling celebrated the feast of Saint Bartholomew, bonfires that of John the Baptist; such rites are always linked to the proper name of monarch, saint, or citizen which for Stow is their etiology, their origin or cause.

But as many commentators have noted, the *Survay* is a book in several parts; the movement from the origin and antiquity of London to its modern estate and description is marked by a shift in Stow's use of the proper name. Whereas the first section records hierarchies, landmarks, events, and their perpetrators, and is linked generically to older historical forms—annals and chronicles, to history in the temporal sense—the second section, some three-quarters of the whole, shifts to the topographic survey proper organized not by time but by space.[11] Stow declares he will distribute the city into parts, thereby claiming to "methodize" London in the Ramist sense, "to declare the antiquities noteworthy in every of the same; and how both the whole and parts have been from time to time ruled and governed." This is a peripatetic knowledge presented as a diurnal movement through city space: "I will begin at the east," he says, "and so proceed through the high and most principal street of the city to the west" (13^v).[12]

Stow famously records the city as a pedestrian moving through its streets and wards, but that perambulation through urban space lays no claim to the eyewitness account. The future tense, "I will begin at the east," produces the movement Stow traces as readerly, linked both to the spatial memorial practices Mary Carruthers has analyzed in medieval culture and to the newly configured urban spaces of early modern London.[13] With Stow, we read our way through London via the records, documents, and monuments he has consulted to write his *Survay.* Today, Stow's own monument is preserved in the church of Saint Andrew Undershaft; an engraving of it appears on the title page to John Strype's seventeenth-century biography and was eventually included in the 1720 edition of the *Survey* itself. Stow is represented seated writing, with books both open and closed in the surrounding ornament. For many years the London and Middlesex Archaeological Society sponsored an annual commemorative service, recently revived, attended by the Lord Mayor, who replaced the quill pen in Stow's hand with a new one. The city that still remembers John Stow and that we perambulate as we read his *Survay* is memorial, everywhere inscribed by the proper names that commemorate its citizens whose accumulated wealth was bequeathed on memorials of numerous kinds—almshouses, hospitals, dozens of free schools, colleges, chapels, monuments and brasses, granaries and their upkeep, bequests to the poor. Sir Thomas Gresham, the founder and principal investor of early modern London's first shopping mall, the Royal Exchange, on his death endowed a series

of lectureships, a bequest Stow records in detail: not only the lecture topics—
rhetoric, music, divinity, and so forth, but also the names of the lecturers and
how much they were paid. Though Stow complains repeatedly of a decline in
hospitality and, according to recent work on the wills of Londoners, underrep-
resents charitable giving to the poor, as he moves through a given ward, he
meticulously records memorials with variations on the following: "These were
the monuments in this church, Sir Robert Turke and Dame Alice his wife,
John Tirell Esquire, Simon Kempe Esq., James Manthorpe," on and on for
some forty names; in the later Middle Ages and early modern period, memorials were built and endowed by wealthy fishmongers, merchants, drapers, citizens of London, each named in his or her turn.[14]

In Anthony Munday's continuation of Stow published in 1618, with another edition in 1633, his additions consist largely of monumental inscriptions and accounts of various memorial benefactions such as that of Sir John
Pemberton, a Lord Mayor under James who, "among his many gifts," erected
and endowed a free school and gave money, as did many of his peers, to
Christ's Hospital. Munday includes memorial verses on Pemberton that insist
on the charitable power of capital:

> Marble nor Touch, nor Alabaster can
> Reveale the Worth of the long buried Man:
> For oft (we see) Mens Goods, when they are gone,
> Doe pious Deeds, when they themselves did none.
> Mine (while I liv'd) my Goodness did expresse,
> 'Tis not Inscriptions make them more or lesse:
> In Christ I hope to rise amongst the Just,
> Man is but grasse, all must to Wormes and Dust.[15]

Despite its conventional *contemptus mundi* close and its shift to the first-person singular, these lines insist that "Mens Goods . . . Doe," that property, not
monuments, has the power to secure memory. Pemberton's donations to
school and hospital enroll his name among London's worthies in Munday's
addenda to Stow. This relation between the name and charitable benefaction
is elsewhere emphasized in Munday's inclusion of an anecdote about a certain
William Jones, merchant, "free of the Worshipful Company of Haberdashers."
Among his many good works, Munday tells of his going among the poor as
a "liberall Benefactor" meanly disguised, giving "with his hands: yet not in
his owne name." A gloss in the margin reads "this man blew no trumpet of
his charitable actions." The suppression of the proper name in London's early
modern memorial culture was evidently uncommon, since both the anecdote
itself and the marginal note insist on Jones's anonymity as exceptional.[16]

What was once the province only of rulers, saints, and heroes becomes in
early modern London available to a host of persons undistinguished by birth,
faith, or valor. When this new preoccupation with memorials has been re-

marked at all, social historians and anthropologists of death, funeral ritual, and philanthropy attribute it to the development of bourgeois individualism. A psychologized, post-Enlightenment subject is called upon anachronistically to explain a historical shift from purgatorial prayer to material benefactions that predates individualism. Nineteenth-century interpreters of the Enlightenment notoriously produced the Renaissance as the discovery of man: Burckhardt writes of "the development of the individual" (Die Entwicklung des Individuums) and his preoccupation with *fama*; Weber understood the Protestant ethic as "a powerful unconsciously refined arrangement for the breeding of capitalist individuals."[17] For all his interest in institutions and social and economic change, individualism for Weber is the motor of both cultural achievement and capital accumulation. Though cultural commentators and historians claim to have abandoned Burckhardt and Weber, in fact many of their Enlightenment assumptions and conclusions continue to dominate cultural critique. The ongoing preoccupation with identity politics and the continuing cultural fixation on subjectivity belie the disavowal of individualism that has been the hallmark of recent cultural studies. Too frequently work on subjectivity and identity politics repeats the very moves and claims it would criticize. What David Simpson has recently termed the "as a" construction (I speak as a white gay man, as a Latina bourgeois feminist, as an African American heterosexual, etc.) appeals to categories and thereby seems to deny individualist, transcendental claims, but at the same time asserts for its user authority grounded in individualist epistemologies on which property, rights claims, and capital accumulation depend.[18]

Though social and economic historians have long challenged notions of a newly individualized self in accounting for the development of capitalism in early modern England and pointed instead to a variety of factors including changing agrarian practices, the increase in coinage, the rise of banking, and so forth to account for that development, recent studies of death and English philanthropy in early modern England nevertheless rely on psychologized individualist arguments. They claim that the dramatic rise in memorial benefactions reflects a new notion of the self. According to Claire Gittings, new forms of memorialization in early modern England witnessed increased anxiety about death "arising from a changing conception of the self and a heightened sense of individuality."[19] In Keith Thomas's words, the Reformation and abolition of the state of purgatory eventually meant that "every individual was now to keep his own balance sheet."[20] W. K. Jordan and David Owen, who both recognize and document the outpouring of private giving as a response to economic revolution, nevertheless open their studies of early modern English philanthropy with encomia to the "benefactions of Englishmen" and "their fashioning of an ethic of social responsibility which was to be the hall-mark of the liberal society."[21] "The mitigation of poverty, disease, infirmity and ignorance" is produced as a matter of individual agency shaped by Weberian notions of Protestant doctrine and teaching in the wake of the Reformation.[22] The seventeenth-century political economy of monopoly, speculation, enclosure, and colonial expansion which enabled the capital accumulation that endowed, and continues to endow, schools and hospitals, builds monuments and buildings, names streets and squares is presented as the fruit of individual labor. Instead of assimilating these new material forms of memorialization to a discourse of secularization, democratization, and liberal individualism, I want to consider such memorial donation not merely as individual achievement but as entailed by an economic system that enabled certain persons and not others to aid the unfortunate, that is, the *unnamed*, with the very profits extorted from them through mercantile and colonial accumulation, through what was dubbed in early modern England "commerce."

In his *Ancient Funeral Monuments* (1631), which surveys the monuments of the great, John Weever locates his project in relation to the work of John Leland and the chorographers who precede him; like Stow, he has extracted his material from "approved authors, infallible records, lieger books, charters, rolls, old manuscripts, and the collections of judicious antiquaries," but Weever has also traced his monuments through the space of early modern England, from church to churchyard, village to town, crossroads to city.[23] His project is in part a reclamation of what had been destroyed during the dissolution, and he quotes approvingly Elizabeth I's proclamation in the second year of her reign, a part of the Elizabethan Settlement, against the breaking and defacing of monuments.[24] But Weever's book is important as well because it marks that shift I have analyzed in Stow, from a history written through the names and actions of illustrious persons to a history of entrepreneurial success enabled by new forms of capital accumulation. Weever marks this shift in a preoccupation with status in the ritual surround of death: "Sepulchres should bee according to the qualitie and degree of the person deceased, that by the Tombe every one might bee discerned of what ranke hee was living" (B6ᵛ). "Stately monuments," he admonishes, "were not due nor allowed to every man that was of ability to erect the same," and "swelling titles, lofty inscriptions or epitaphs," he claims, were once "prohibited to be inscrib'd, insculpt, or engraven upon the sepulchres of men of meane desert." Such inscriptions are due only to men of valor, martial men, or eminent persons in government. Weever strenuously objects to the proliferation of memorials that attribute more honor "to a rich quondam Tradesman, or griping usurer, then is given to the greatest Potentate entombed in Westminster" (B7ʳ) (*quondam* should be understood as satiric, roughly translated as "to a rich once upon a time Tradesman"). Modern epitaphs, Weever opines, are all vanity and will provoke future generations to vice rather than virtue. The language he uses is familiar to any reader of Jacobean city comedy or popular pamphlets: such monuments and epitaphs threaten to make of the Temple of God "a Schoolehouse of the monstrous habits and attires of our presentage, wherein Taylors may finde out new fashions. And which is worse, they garnish their Tombes, now adayes, with the pictures of naked men and women; raising out of the dust, and bringing into the church, the memories of the heathen gods and goddesses, with all their whirligiggs" (B7ʳ). Once upon a time, men of mean rank kept their postmortem places; now money—riches—enables them even in death to compete with their betters; the proper name is not staying in its proper place. Leaving aside the important question of whether in fact there was ever an Edenic moment in the commemoration of death when riches could not overcome rank, Weever's book witnesses the same change I have remarked in Stow to the middling sort; the poor, however, are unnamed in both Stow and Weever.

Parish registers recording weddings, christenings, and burials were first mandated by Thomas Cromwell in 1538.[25] In the sixteenth and seventeenth centuries, the vast majority of those who died, whether rich, poor, or of the middling sort, even those in large suburban parishes, are named; the naming even of the poor in parish registers suggests familiarity and a detailed knowledge of neighbors and relationships not only in the country but in London as well. When names are unknown, the nameless are entered by their spatial relation at death to the urban topography or, frequently, to their propertied betters:

A man that died in the streete by the book shop (24 September 1581)
A Poore woman being a vagrant whose name was not knowne shee dyed in the striete under the seate before Mr. Christian Shipmans house called the Crowne
Christian A vagrant died at Mrs. Crews doore (11 July 1588)
A striplinge who dyed near the barens of broome upon the hill Right over against Jeames Eveure a baker . . . (29 September 1590)
A creple that died in the streete before John Awstens doore (15 November 1596)
A mayde a vagrant unknowen whoe died in the streete nere the posternes (23 July 1597)
A poore man who died in a stable whose name we could not learne (3 January 1610)[26]

The attempt to name and record witnesses the development of a demographic impulse and of record keeping itself, but the naming of the urban elite and middling sort comes about also because of increased accumulation, both the accumulation of persons and of goods, not because of some new attitude toward individual identity that prompted the quest for memorialization as Gittings, Owen, and Jordan suggest. Counting, recording, and dating—the accumulation of data—was one response to the chaotic growth especially of the poor and vagrant that so troubled early modern London, its rulers, administrators, and clerks. Memorial naming was the elite response to the urban demographic explosion, its assurance against anonymity. As Vanessa Harding shows in her fine study of death and burial in early modern Paris and London, death was "an important occasion for signaling differentiation and relation to privilege."[27] Newly accumulated capital and a burgeoning urban populace fostered memorial benefaction and post-Reformation commemorative practices among a broadly privileged urban sort.[28]

Weever's book discovers and describes the monuments and epitaphs of illustrious persons, but his view of memorialization is firmly lodged in a traditional humanist topos: that fame is conferred through writing: "above all remembrances (by which men have endeavored, even in despight of death to give unto their Fames eternitie) for worthinesses and continuance, books, or writings, have ever had the preheminence," a claim he supports with a humanist appeal to classical authority in the form of an elegiac couplet translated as:

The muses works stone monuments out last
Tis wit keepes life, all else death will down cast.

Perhaps no text better witnesses this claim than Sir Thomas Browne's meditation on death and its memorials, *Hydriotaphia / Urn-Burial*, which argues that no memorial outlasts death, but in its own longevity demonstrates the dictum captured in Weever's homely English, "Tis wit keepes life."[29] Published in 1658, *Hydriotaphia*, as its subtitle, *A Brief Discourse of the Sepulchral Urns lately found in Norfolk*, indicates, is an early ethnographic study of death customs, practices, and attitudes. As such, and written as it is by a practicing provincial doctor imbued with the humanist classical past, it might seem an odd choice for the topic of this essay, the inscription of capital in urban space by the proper name. Renaissance critics, still writing in the shadow of Michelet and Burckhardt, have generally read Browne's text as a meditation on "human identity and the quest for its immortal retention."[30] Commentators praise its "extraordinary imaginative height" as somehow "preternatural" and preserve its Christian assumptions about the afterlife in their own rhetoric by remarking its "haunting themes."[31] Those critics who forgo grand humanist narratives of mortality and address Browne's style do so in terms of a formal authorial achievement fully congruent with such humanist rhetoric. It is termed "wonder" or alternatively "a virtuoso performance"; Browne is "the laureate of the forgotten dead." Stanley Fish insists that the reader attends to Browne's prose "not because of any real interest or concern, but because we wonder where [he] will go next and how he will get there," spurred on by an idle curiosity Fish calls epistemological.[32]

But Browne's *Urn-Burial* is remarkable for its metaphoric insistence not only on an inexorable mortality but on memorialization as commerce. It is everywhere an ethnographic allegory, his own culture's political economy writ large. This is particularly true toward the end of the essay, which critics generally privilege as the locus of Brown's own reflections on mortality, identity, and the longing to be remembered, its motivations and vanity. Everywhere his rhetorical prose, sometimes described in terms of release into "wonder," in fact relies on commercial comparison, on a vocabulary of exchange, arithmetic, telling, and accounting. Consider this passage, for example, in which he reflects on those who so fear death that they never escape worrying the moment of its coming: "How many pulses made up the life of *Methuselah*, were work for *Archimedes*: Common Counters summe up the life of *Moses* his man. Our days become considerable like petty sums by minute accumulations; where numerous fractions make up but small round numbers; and our dayes of a span long make not one little finger."[33] How many, counters, sum and petty sums, accumulations, fractions numerous, round numbers: the language of life measured, we might say memorialized, since merchants' day books were in fact sometimes known as "memorials," by urban commercial practices. Numeracy is the mode for inscribing death; number is called upon to control anxiety about the moment of death and its inevitability, what Kant will later term the mathematical sublime in which number witnesses a failure in understanding, our bewilderment before that moment that can never be known but only registered in enumeration. Here that failure is marked by a typical humanist syncretic appeal to both the ancients and scripture—Methuselah, Archimedes, and Moses. Methuselah was and remains proverbial for his long life (Genesis 5:27); the allusion to Moses, the man of God, is to Psalm 90, a prayer in which the Lord for whom a thousand years "are but as yesterday" is juxtaposed with the petty span of a man's life, "threescore and ten," perhaps fourscore. Archimedes was known in the period for his calculation of the incalculable, the number of grains of sand in the universe represented by means of a notational system he devised for expressing enormously large numbers. Names, italicized throughout the printed text, stand in for an opposition between the incalculable and the numerable.

Later in his musings on the vanity of "restlesse inquietude for the diuturnity of our memories" (166), Browne points out the irony of memorializing a name when "Who knows whether the best of men be known? or whether there be not more remarkable persons forgot, than any that stand remembered in the known account of time? Without the favour of the everlasting Register, the first man had been as unknown as the last. . . . Oblivion is not to be hired: The greater part must be content to be as though they had not been, to be found in the Register of God, not in the record of man" (167).[34] Browne here points out the noncongruence between remembered name and remarkable person. "Every houre," he says, "addes unto that current Arithmetique." Account, register (a register was not only a book or volume in which regular entry was made but particularly some record or book having public or commercial importance), add, arithmetic, hire, record. Browne's often-remarked parallelism itself depends on a logic of equation and accumulation, not subordination: "The Egyptian mummies which Cambyses or time hath spared, avarice now consumeth. Mummy is become merchandise"; "In vain do individuals

Figure 30. Deat[hs] Dance through London, 1625. Magdalene College, Cambridge

hope for immortality, or any patent from oblivion" (168).[35] Browne's language of commerce marks the memorial not simply as, in George Williamson's words, "a meditation of man's attempts to subsist after death, to conquer time, to preserve his identity," what Williamson terms "The Purple of *Urn Burial*," but as an instance of mercantile endeavor, a memorial calculus in which the merchant puts up a caution or security against the accumulating debt of time.[36]

In his broad-ranging survey of the religious and philosophical sources of the self, Charles Taylor complains of what he terms "over-simple or reductive variants of Marxism" that propose "diachronic-causal explanations" for the rise of capitalism and the self/identity associated with that rise, but ignore what gave that new identity its appeal: "What drew people to it? Indeed, what draws them today? What gave it its spiritual power?"[37] Taylor disclaims "ambitious" historical explanation in favor of "moral ideals, understandings of the human predicament, concepts of the self," precisely those aspects of identity commentators consistently remark in Browne. And though Taylor acknowledges that "these two orders of question can't be entirely separated," in fact his book eschews historical explanation in favor of the history of ideas. Browne's *Hydriotaphia* demonstrates on the one hand the limits exacted by Taylor's demurral and on the other the importance of attempting to articulate so-called idealist and materialist inquiry. Commerce, money, numeracy are, in Lucien Febvre's words, like other social facts, not "'things' but ideas, representations, human judgments on 'things'" as certainly as the religious and philosophic ideas Taylor surveys.[38] Browne's essay and early modern memorials trace not simply an individualized self but also the displacement of mercantile operations within a culture of conspicuous consumption played out in funereal customs, monuments, and memorial benefactions, even in ballads and in the traditional imagery of the dance of death (fig. 30), where death visits the rich and wealthy at Saint Paul's and the Royal Exchange.[39] Such memorials witness an economy of accumulation and display, not a modern psychologized consciousness.

That death should be an important arena of differentiation in the early modern city is not surprising given its ubiquity and scale. Annual death tolls in London in the late sixteenth century ranged between three and four thousand persons; the toll in Paris is thought to have been even higher. During times of plague, London lost between 10 and 20 percent of its entire population, and the population of Paris declined during the wars of religion, perhaps as much as one-third during the siege. Both cities were recording some twenty thousand deaths per year in the 1670s. As Harding points out, the dimensions of mortality were enormous and posed a host of problems and challenges to authorities and to urban dwellers themselves.[40] Even as a country doctor, Browne himself would have had considerable experience of death, its rituals and monuments.

In surveying the funereal customs of ancient civilizations—Greek, Roman, and Semitic, those of the European and English past, even the American and Chinese, Browne, like Stow and Weever, everywhere relies on the proper name. His authorities witness not the annals of English history but the humanist's digestion of the classical past and Christian scripture. Virtually no ancient writer, ruler, or hero goes unmentioned, and the ancients are rivaled only by biblical names. But these names are memorable not so much for the persons and histories they record but because of the wit Browne employs to endow them with fame and memory. They are made memorable not for their individual lives and histories but through Browne's metaphysical conceits, odd juxtapositions, and puns. Though we might expect proper names, linked as rigid designators to historical places and persons, to resist such linguistic play, Browne's names are notoriously errant. Cremation urns are found— guess where—in the *Burnham* villages; an authority on burial sites and remains in Norway and Denmark is named *Wormius*. Chapter 2 ends with a succession of paronomastically allusive proper names: "To what Nation or person belonged that large Urne found at *Ashburie*. . . . What those large Urnes found at little *Massingham*, or why the *Anglesea* Urnes are placed with their mouths downward, remains yet undiscovered" (147). An urn of bones and ashes is found at *Ashbury*; "large urns" are discovered in "*little Massingham*"; the urns strangely positioned at an angle are at *Anglesea*.[41] In *Urn-Burial*, Tacitus is silent, and the "large discourses of Caesar" which tell us nothing of the forms of burial among the ancient Britons might have been augmented by none other than Scribonius Largus (145). Browne empties the name of its specificity, marks it only as a place of longing, a unit or trace without psychological consciousness or being. Names in Browne's prose become commodified; he uses names to his own commodity, his convenience or occasion; he deals in names. Whereas one might expect Wormius to mean Olaus Worm, as the standard anglicized gloss makes him, author of *Monumenta Danica* (1643), Wormius becomes instead, through a corrosive paronomasia, the worms of decomposition, the very bodily decay the memorial is imagined to forestall.

Puns corrode, like death itself, the power of the name to mark and specify; they empty it of pathos. The proper name in Browne's usage is improper in its insistence on what Derrida observes as the originary "erasure and the imposition of the letter . . . the proper name has never been, as the unique appellation reserved for the presence of a unique being, anything but the original myth of a transparent legibility."[42] The proper name is what might be termed, from the later perspective of capitalism, the fetish of individualism; its words mark, paradoxically, anxiety about the lack of the very memory the inscription of the proper name on memorials is supposed to ensure. In Browne's essay, mortality is not only the subject of meditation and rumination, it is paradoxically the work of the proper name that fails in its expected specificity and individual distinctiveness.

What makes the proper name seem so powerful an index of individual identity? In the first chapter of *Capital*, Marx famously writes a series of equations to define and explain the relative form of value and the logic of the commodity, a logic that has since been analyzed in relation to a proliferating series of symbolic economies.[43] For Marx, gold is the universal equivalent, the money form, universally exchangeable, its fetish character a result of a covering over of the social relations of labor, and of a fantasy of inherent value. The proper name is the fetishized "individual" equivalent, imagined to mark the particular. The proper name is the commodity fetish of individualism, presumed indexical and historical. But the proper name of memorials marks instead the accumulation of cultural and material capital; it speaks the memorial calculus of early modern London's rising bourgeoisie and its determination to mark the populous space of the city with its names in death, the quondam what's his name tradesman whose memorials figure not individualism but the early modern urban acceleration of capital accumulation.[44]

In Browne's *Urn-Burial* as in Stow's *Survey*, memorialization depends on accumulation and marks a shift from the authority of names to the authority of numbers. In early modern England, *memorial* meant not only commemoration of the dead as monument, custom, or ritual act but also a host of written genres including the memorandum, the chronicle or memoir, informal state and diplomatic papers, and, as I have already pointed out, a merchant's day book, the record of daily transactions that included the type and quantity of merchandise, money amounts, terms of payment, and the names of the parties involved.[45] To memorialize means not only to remember the dead but to keep an account—like the body count recorded on the Vietnam Veterans Memorial, or the memorial objects left at the wall beneath a remembered name and subsequently displayed at the Smithsonian, or the piles of shoes and other objects called upon to witness the Holocaust, modest vestiges enshrined to record the unspeakable, a kind of virtual memory of the past marked by accumulation itself. Memory has come to depend on the register, the memorial account, the archive, the database, on accumulation in space, what Pierre Nora terms the "matérialisation de la mémoire," a distended accumulation that may also be history, but may be something else, or may have displaced history altogether.[46] Perhaps the much remarked contemporary turn to history in literary and cultural studies—the accumulation of stories, facts, anecdotes, minor autobiographies, especially our own—marks not a turn to history but the substitution of deposits of cultural capital for argument and the analysis of economic, social, and rhetorical systems.

CHAPTER EIGHT

Sex in the City

We must hear the words that were never spoken. . . .
We must make the silences of history speak. . . . Only
then do the dead accept the sepulcher.
—MICHELET

What do archives have to tell us? Why have they come to occupy a privileged place in the study of letters and culture? What kind of knowledge do they offer, or rather, do we produce from them? In the case of such materials as depositions and law cases, even wills and inventories, what is their status in relation to so-called literary texts? Why have those of us working in early modern studies particularly, though not exclusively, and I count myself among them, come down with, in Derrida's translator's catchy phrase, "archive fever"? This chapter explores these questions by way of London's brothels and the Bridewell courtbooks that are the principal archival sources about them, by reading Thomas Nashe's notorious poem, *A Choise of Valentines*, and ends by turning briefly to the other side of the channel, to the notorious Parisian criminal den known as the Cour des Miracles.

My epigraph from Michelet raises the related theoretical issue with which this chapter is concerned and which has dogged social history, women's history, and literary history: what of those who cannot, in Marx's oft-cited formulation, represent themselves, the poor and vagrant, the prostitutes and petty criminals who as we have seen are effaced from the guidebooks and surveys of early modern Paris and London?[1] Almost two decades ago, early work in women's history initiated the governing metaphor for this problem: "becoming visible." The historian's work is to "recover" the traces of those who left no textual traces of their own.[2] The implication of the metaphor, of course, is that we can mine the depths, that we can uncover, unmask, expose, bring to light, discern, excavate lost lives. The sources for this hermeneutic endeavor are archives of various kinds waiting for our interpretive pickax, for the mask to be ripped away, to come out of hiding, so that such lives can become visible. As my diction and irony suggest, such an endeavor raises doubts, as does the opposition of the hidden and the visible, of inside and outside, on which it depends.

The rapid growth of both London and Paris during the late sixteenth and seventeenth centuries, in terms of both population and the development of large-scale markets, fostered, as we have seen, an unprecedented accumulation of both financial and cultural capital and promoted distinctive urban behaviors. Commercial sex was one such behavior. Prostitution would seem to be an urban phenomenon. To be sure, sexual acts for all sorts of favors—food, shelter, clothing, even money—occurred in the countryside beneath its proverbial hedgerows, but prostitution in the organized sense of sex for money that took place in brothels, or what were termed "bawdys" in early modern London, and involving bawds and procurers as well as prostitutes themselves, was a market phenomenon associated with town and, increasingly, city life.[3] The courtbooks, as do pamphlets, plays, and poems, insist on the commercial character of prostitution in early modern London: it is "trade," "custom," or "traffic," prostitutes are "ware," "hackneis to lett-out to hire," and "merchandise" whose bodies were for "use," "a bargaine for any buyer." Intercourse and a woman's genitals were termed "the commodity," pimps were termed "brokers," and clients had to "deal" with prostitute or bawd.[4] Marriage, by contrast, is conventionally imagined as eccentric to urban locales and markets, as Edenic or pastoral; even adulterous love is sometimes situated or linked metaphorically to an idyllic open air, from walled garden to forest floor.

But commercial sex is city sex. "How happy . . . were cities if they had no suburbs," exclaims Thomas Dekker in one of his many pamphlets detailing the evils of London life. In early modern London, however, though both royal edict and city authorities repeatedly banished prostitutes and brothels from within the City, both Ian Archer and Paul Griffiths, in his interesting and useful study "The Structure of Prostitution in Elizabethan London," have shown a startling number of such establishments within the City—a historical fact confirmed in numerous city comedies and contemporary pamphlets that recount prostitution taking place within the City's precincts.[5] Following the shutdown of the Bankside stews in 1546, prostitution seems to have intensified in the City. In Dekker's *News from Hell* (1606), the speaker complains that "Bawdes . . . now sit no longer upon the skirtes of the Cittie, but iett up and downe, even in the cloake of the cittie, and give more rent for a house, then the proudest London occupier of them all."[6]

Archer, Griffiths, and others have shown that there was a crackdown on sexual crimes, including prostitution, in the 1570s and early 1580s directed not only against organized brothels and so-called casual prostitution—the expression used by historians to distinguish streetwalking from the more organized sort—but also against adultery, fornication, and women termed "bawds" for harboring pregnant single women, and finally, and most unusually, the pursuit not only of prostitutes themselves but of their clients, a state of affairs that provides a tantalizing background to Shakespeare's *Measure for Measure*.[7] Repeatedly the crackdown on brothels and prostitution is justified by the city authorities because brothels were said to harbor all sorts of petty criminals—thieves and crooks, counterfeiters, and offenders of all sorts—and thus posed a threat to public order.[8]

The Bridewell courtbooks are the principal archival source for historians, including Archer and Griffiths, working on prostitution in early modern London. The courtbooks considered here record the depositions of numerous prostitutes, bawds, and pimps and paint a suggestive picture of London's sexual underworld. Though not complete, the courtbooks extend from 1559 until 1642, and into the modern period.[9] Bridewell, built as a royal palace begun in 1515 between Fleet Street and the Thames, was given to the city and granted its charter in 1553, one of four London hospitals founded in the mid–sixteenth century to manage the problem of the urban poor.[10] From these courtbooks, historians have produced a picture or profile of prostitution in early modern London. Commercial sex was loosely organized and widespread. The largest recorded brothel housed nine women, though others harbored no more than two or three. Fees varied, but averaged between four and five shillings, more than most women made in a week.[11] Prostitutes paid room and sometimes board of some four to six shillings a week, as well as handing over approximately half their earnings to the bawd or keeper.[12] Records show evidence of organized cooperation among the brothel keepers, with women being carried from one house to another when a large group of clients was expected or simply turned up.

According to Archer, many brothel keepers paid subsidies—taxes, we might say—in the top third of those levied, which put them in the ranks of, in his words, "relatively prosperous craftsmen and petty retailers" (215). Archer goes on to say that prostitution was a "service industry directed toward the gentry and visitors" and was thus often protected by the authorities, but Griffiths has shown that for the small sample of some 219 clients whose status can be identified, apprentices and servants made up the largest segment, about 39 percent.[13] Brothel clients, however, included aristocrats, gentry, foreign emissaries and businessmen, Inns of Court men, pages, city citizens, servants, and apprentices. The Bridewell courtbooks even record the deposition of one Katherine Jones who apparently counted among her clients the son of one of the Bridewell governors. The prostitutes themselves were, and here I quote Griffiths, "mostly single young women . . . [a] high proportion of whom were given the significant age titles 'maid' or 'servant.' "[14]

As this outline suggests, historians who study the Bridewell courtbooks use them to produce a set of facts and numbers about prostitution—how it was organized and administered, where it took place, how much it cost, who were the prostitutes, who the clients—even if they admit, as does Griffiths, the fragmentary nature of the evidence and claim only to show patterns. Rarely do they consider questions of language, affect, dress, motivation, desire, or performance. When motives are considered, it is usually those of the authorities, rarely the prostitutes themselves. The city fathers worried about public order, crime, the breakdown of households, and public morality. Griffiths rightly observes that this focus reduces "mere personal matters of motivation to an incidental footnote." He goes on: "However, in their own narratives the women often place a telling emphasis upon procurement, which may well have been a strategy, for by shifting the blame they could emerge as victims" (49). Repeatedly, he notes, women recount being brought by a particular man, or occasionally woman, to a brothel where a man then had "the use of her body"; they tell of being tricked by false promises of marriage or by a master or mistress, or occasionally, of having been driven to prostitution by poverty and want.

The etiological mode is so ubiquitous as to suggest that such origin stories, rather than merely a strategy for shifting blame, as Griffiths suggests, may have been solicited in response to some judicial version of the age-old question, "How did a girl like you end up in a place like this?" In *Dust*, her wonderful book about archives, Carolyn Steedman looks at similar records of magistrates in the nineteenth century that she shows are constructed by "the legally required questions."[15] In these written accounts produced by questioning, the interlocutor has been removed in transcription, but Steedman nevertheless goes on to argue that "apart from not being written down by the liver of the life presented, these brief narratives fulfil the criteria for autobiographical narration" (48). Similarly, Griffiths assumes that, though written down by recorders, what we find in the archives are, in his words, "their own narratives," the women's voices and lives we are searching for. Though he recognizes the courtbooks are mediated, nevertheless he asserts that "as we read the depositions . . . we are perhaps closer to the authentic voice of the bawd and prostitute" than we are in the fictive works of Dekker, Greene, Nashe, and the rest: "pamphlet, ballad and play," he declares, "must adopt a supporting role to the courtbook."[16] In other words, despite the obligatory acknowledgment of fiction in the archives, as his words suggest, Griffith assumes the courtbooks represent a level of truth the literary cannot. According to him, the literary documents concerned with prostitution "are pervaded with a profound didacticism and a preoccupation with the conventional pattern of authority and social relations."[17]

But from the perspective of literary studies, both claims are suspect. First, the so-called literary texts often fail at their wonted didacticism, a point to which I shall return when we turn to Nashe's poem; and second, the Bridewell courtbooks themselves, read *rhetorically* or *literarily*, tell a somewhat different story, certainly not one of women's "own narratives" and of "authentic voice." The Bridewell records are judicial; that is, they are concerned with law and punishment and offer only traces of other aspects of prostitution found in the literary record. Each of the courtbooks begins with pages and pages of lists of names—the names of all those deposed. Both men's and women's names, since persons were committed to Bridewell for many reasons, not just sexual crimes—for vagabondage, theft, and other petty offenses. The records are written in a succession of secretary hands, some open and expansive, even slapdash, others crabbed, neat, and precise. Reading these records, one is struck not with a sense of the personal narratives of those arraigned but of their formulaic character—in the double sense of character—and then of the mannerisms, rhetoric, and diction, in short, the personal style, of the various scribes and recorders themselves. They are written in the third person and always begin with the name of the person arraigned. We learn where the accused was apprehended, that he or she was brought before the governors or "into this house" on a particular date, and often at the commandment of some particular person, and sometimes there is a deposition of the accused.

Almost invariably the name of the accused is followed by an identifying phrase to place him or her in the urban social hierarchy—apprentice of, draper journeyman, wife of, daughter of, tapster, goldsmith, shoemaker, waterman, but also common harlot, common bawd, common beggar, common drunkard, plain vagabond, and naughty vagabond. The ubiquitous *common* insists on the preoccupation with status and degree, with hierarchy, that characterized early modern social relations.

Each scribe has different formulas for describing prostitution. In the early books that are preserved from 1559 to 1562, following each name, the recorder begins almost every entry concerned with commercial sex "a lewd harlot," a "common harlot," "a common bawd," "a lewd woman." The usual length is seven or eight lines, though one later scribe—and here, we ask, is the instigator the scribe or the governors themselves—tends to record longer depositions, though there are occasional lengthy accounts throughout. The telling or titillating detail is rare indeed, and its citation by social historians or literary critics may tell us more about the narratives we are writing than about the general character of early modern prostitution. Several scribes use the expression "the use of her body," but others employ the phrase "committed whoredom." Prostitutes are rarely termed "whores," which, as Laura Gowing has observed, is a common term of derision that rarely means prostitute;[18] instead, they use "harlot," and in the seventeenth-century books, "strumpet" and the ambiguous "nightwalker." Reading the courtbooks, one is hard put to imagine the voice of any of the deponents; women who may have described the sexual acts for which they were detained and brought to Bridewell with that repeated phrase, "the use of my body," used a semilegal formula. In fact, the phrase seems more likely to have been the recorder's term of art, if you will, to cover the multitude of ways women must have admitted to the sexual acts for which they were being paid and arraigned. And interestingly, despite the prominence such information takes in historians' accounts of prostitution, economic references to payment of any kind are relatively few. In other words, the facts and patterns we draw from archives and texts of all kinds depend, of course, on the questions we pose. And though that lesson may seem an old one, long since learned and commonly acknowledged, the temptation to seek the marginal voice or lost women's speech, to read records as conveying the real the literary cannot, frequently overcomes better judgment.

On the one hand, Thomas Nashe's *Choise of Valentines* corroborates much of what we learn from the Bridewell courtbooks and other evidence about prostitution in early modern London. But it also offers a strikingly different view of the sex trade and early modern sexual practices and desire. As many commentators have noted, *A Choise of Valentines* begins with a pseudo-Chaucerian opening:

> It was the merie moneth of Februarie
>   When yong-men in their iollie roguerie
> Rose earelie in the morne fore breake of daie
>   To seeke them valentines so trimme and gaie;
> With whom they maie consorte in summer sheene,
>   And dance the heidgeies on our toune-greene.[19]

The young man of the poem, one Tomalin, leaves the countryside in which the poem opens for the city where he seeks and finds his valentine, one Francis, working in an urban brothel. Their initial attempt at sex is apparently foiled by Tomalin's premature ejaculation, which is quickly followed by a successful but, unhappily for Francis, short-lived coupling that disappoints his lady, who fortunately is prepared to satisfy herself with a handy dildo. Nashe makes use not only of Chaucer but also of Ovid's then popular *Amores* just translated by Marlowe, and the *louche* ovidianism popular among young writers and readers in the 1580s and 1590s, one that provoked numerous erotic poems sometimes marked by bold, even grotesque comedy.[20] Nevertheless, modern readers of Nashe's poem have been preoccupied with its psychosexual effects, with Francis's resort to the dildo with its presumed impact on male subjectivity or the male ego.[21]

The poem circulated only in manuscript in Nashe's lifetime, though the controversy it generated with Gabriel Harvey, and references to the poem in print by others, suggest it may have been widely known and read in literate circles.[22] The poem seems to have been first printed only in 1899 and, then, "privately printed for subscribers only."[23] Its nineteenth-century editor opines that it would not be "accorded the dignity of print" but "that the world cannot afford to lose any 'document' (a word that first editor puts in scare quotes) whatsoever which bears, or *may* bear, in the slightest degree . . . on the reconstruction . . . of the life and times of the immortal bard of Avon" (vii). In other words, we ostensibly owe the preservation in print and Victorian publication of this piece of Elizabethan pornography to Shakespeare and bardolatry. Ronald McKerrow, who edited Nashe's works at the beginning of the twentieth century, did not include *A Choise of Valentines* in his edition, but F. P. Wilson added it to his reedition of McKerrow in the 1960s. The poem is prefaced by a dedicatory poem "To the right Honorable the lord S" long assumed to be the Earl of Southampton whose taste for witty, Ovidian erotic verse prompted a host of such efforts in the 1590s, but Wilson argues that Lord S is Fernandino Stanley, Lord Strange, fifth Earl of Derby, poet himself and patron to whom Nashe also dedicated *Pierce Penniless*. Recent commentators have accepted that attribution.[24]

Tomalin, who is the poem's initial speaker, represents his quest for Francis as a religious pilgrimage: "Euen on the hallowes of that blessed Saint / That doeth true lovers with those ioyes acquaint," he, a "poore pilgrim" goes "to my ladies shrine, / To see if she would be my valentine." He discovers that she has been driven from the village by "Good Justice Dudgeon-haft" and has "shifted to an upper ground" and "house of veneric." Both Wilson and the Penguin editor, J. B. Steane, note that "upper ground" refers to Upper Ground Street in London, "a street of low repute in Southwark" that ran (and runs) parallel to the river between the notorious Paris Garden and the Bankside, an area rife with brothels and other seamy urban commerce and activities.[25] There Tomalin meets a bawd and asks if she has "hackneis to lett-out to hire." The poem spins out the initial comparison of brothel to shrine: Tomalin can enter the "Oratorie" only after he has paid his "offertorie." Disappointed in the bawd's initial offerings, he demands "fresher ware" and "gentle mistris Francis," for whom the bawd demands a higher price in gold.

Francis's shift to London offers another perspective on "betterment" migration, as it has been called, from the country to the city, a perspective perhaps best expressed in the bawd's lines from Dekker's *The Honest Whore, Part II*: "We want tooles, Gentlemen, to furnish the trade: they weare out day and night, they weare out till no mettle bee left in their backe; wee heare of two or three new Wenches are come up with a carrier, and your old Goshawke here is flying at them" (3.3.4–7).[26] Dekker emphasizes prostitution as a trade with prostitutes as its tools; the aptly named Goshawke preys upon the unsuspecting, newly arrived immigrants to the city. Nashe takes a different tack in that Francis seems to have been already practicing her trade informally in the village, which prompts the village authorities to chase her away. When Francis finally appears, her appearance "in her velvet goune's, / And ruffs, and periwigs as fresh as Maye," witnesses a feature of prostitution in early modern London traces of which appear in the Bridewell courtbook depositions, but which historians seldom remark. Prostitutes are repeatedly associated with sartorial extravagance, with transgressing sumptuary laws and dressing beyond both their appropriate social and financial means, in silks and velvets, ruffs and white holland smocks, wigs and jewels. In fact, such costumes, and I use that word intentionally, would seem to be linked in both literary and archival sources to affect and desire. Here is Nashe on Francis's entrance:

Sweeping she coms, as she would brush the ground,
  Hir ratling silke's my sences doe confound.

Oh, I am ravish't: voide the chamber streight,
For I must neede's upon hir with my weight. (77–80)

Here in the boldly rhymed couplet we find the bold, comic effects that characterize the poem. Tomalin is aroused by the sound of Francis's rustling silk gown; her silks, in fact, seem to be potent—they have the power to "ravish." Francis's extravagant dress endows her with sexual power and makes her both more expensive and more desirable, a state of affairs common to much writing about prostitution in the period. In Greene's contemporary pamphlet printed in 1592, the date usually given for Nashe's poem, *A Disputation between a Hee-Conny-Catcher, and a Shee-Conny-Catcher, whether a Theefe or a whoore, is most hurtful in Cousonage to the Commonwelath,* in the section entitled "The Conversion of an English Courtesan," a young woman recounts her fall from a good family and initial seduction into a brothel and prostitution by saying simply "As my apparel was costly, so I grew to be licentious." In Nashe's own contemporaneous *Christs Teares over Jerusalem* in which he lambastes prostitution instead of presenting it, as in *A Choise,* as a titillating and amusing joke, the speaker asserts that "the ende of gorgeous attyre, (both in men and women,) is but more fully to enkindle fleshly concupiscence, to assist the devil in lustful temptation."[27] In Thomas Cranley's *Amanda: or the Reformed Whore* (1635), Amanda's gowns, jewels, ruffs and muffs, fans, and perfume are part of her prostitute's paraphernalia, which the speaker sees in her chamber; at her conversion, she says to him, "Take my clothes and sell them all away," and having detailed them once again at length, for the reader's pleasure of course, she ends, "They are for Ladies, and for wives of Earles."[28] Prostitutes not only wore the clothes of gentlewomen; like Moll Flanders, they apparently disguised themselves "Proteus-like" and went, according to the reformed Amanda, "in black, as chambermaid, as country wench, neat habit of a citizen, [and] Lady" (F2ʳ). Such "severall formes, and shapes" served both as disguises when on the run and also, as with Eliza Haywood's heroine Fantomina, to provoke, enhance, or reawaken desire.

But such costumes did not always serve. From the Bridewell courtbooks, 17 February 1599, we find another Frances, Frances (Lat. franc, free) apparently being a common name for prostitutes, one Frances Baker, working in the house of a Mistress Holland, who is sent for to another house, that of Mistress Hibbens, where two gentlemen "had the use of her body," but one refused to pay her because Mistress Hibbens had promised him a gentlewoman:

Mistress Hibbens did cause this examinant to put off all her own apparel and put on one suit of apparel or other either silk, or silk rashe or stuff gowns . . . and put on a white holland smock with a durance petticoat of two or three yards of velvet, and the cause why the gentleman aforesaid would give this examinant no money was because he knew the apparel which this examinant had on her back when he used her body to be the

apparel of the said Mistress Hibbens. And further this examinant saith
that the said Mistress Hibbens hath always lying in her house ready of
her own divers suits of apparels for women viz. silk gowns of several
colors. . . .when any other sorts of people do come to her house, she will
array such wenches for them as she thinketh they will be in liberalitie
towards her.[29]

Similarly, a deposition of 21 January 1578 concerning a brothel in Clerken-
well tells of one Marye Donnelley, who had "a silke gowne & was ther
abused & kept especially by gentlement & welthye men with velvett
gaskins & such apparell & not for the common sorte." In the words of another deposition, prostitutes had to be trimmed "wth swete water & calles &
cotes & thyngs for the purpose fitt for the degree of them that use them."[30]
The courtbook depositions offer occasional glimpses of the link among dress,
sexuality, and degree; sometimes clothing served merely to identify the depo-
nent, but at others, to enhance the market transaction, to match or meet the
desire or status of a given client, and to articulate significant currents of social
desire. The frisson of transvestism in early modern England would seem to
be not a crossing of gender boundaries but a status masquerade, a flaunting
not so much of femininity as of what we now call class. The prostitute does
not adopt the sexuality of the other but simulates a sexually charged status or
degree.[31]

In Nashe's poem, the speaker is driven wild by Francis's "ratling silks" and
"sweet lyning," or linen, which he personifies, asking its permission to raise
it to reveal first her legs, then her knees, and finally her "mannely thigh."[32]
"Smock, climbe a-pace," he cries in an exaggerated anthropomorphism reminiscent of Ovid. Francis's ravishing silks and manly thigh have been read
as gender reversals that threaten Tomalin's masculinity, and certainly they
foreshadow her willingness to take her pleasure into her own hands, but there
is little sense at this point in the poem of sexual anxiety. When her sexual
parts are revealed, Tomalin says the sight surpasses heaven and paradise alike
and offers a conventional pastoral description:

> A prettie rysing wombe without a weame,
>   That shone as bright as anie silver streame;
> And bare out lyke the bending of an hill,
>   At whose decline a fountaine dwelleth still,
> That hath his mouth besett with uglie bryers
>   Resembling much a duskie nett of wyres. (109–14)

This final couplet is arguably the only negative allusion to women's sexuality
in the poem. As mentioned earlier, Tomalin's member "dye[s] ere it hath seene
Jerusalem," a state of affairs brought on not, however, by his sight of her "uglie

bryers" like a "duskie nett of wyres," but quite explicitly by his excitement at grasping her "loftie buttock barred with azure veine's."

When after her ministrations Tomalin is aroused again, the poem engages in a long description of their intercourse in which Nashe plays with Petrarchan rhetoric and with rhythm—the lovers keep "crochet-time, / And euerie stroake in order lyke a chyme" (185–86). Each time Tomalin is about to reach orgasm, Francis exhorts him to "Togeather lett our equall motions stir / Togeather let us liue and dye my deere." Tomalin, again nearing the little death, Francis begs him to hold out but an hour, but half an hour, nay but a quarter—in short, what Francis desires is to prolong their *joint* pleasure, and as my quotations suggest, the poem is at comic pains to emphasize their shared efforts toward that goal. When Tomalin does come, Francis laments, "Adieu faint-hearted instrument of lust / That falselie hast betrayde our *equale* trust" (italics mine). She turns instead to her "little dilldo ... / That bendeth not," and goes on to detail the pleasure that instrument will supply.

"Dildo," the *OED* tells us, is a "word of obscure origin, used in the refrains of ballads"; the dictionary attributes the word's first usage meaning "artificial penis" to Nashe's poem. The second usage cited is from Florio's Italian-English dictionary, where a "pastinaca muranese" or a "murano parsnip" is defined as "a dildoe of glasse." In Nashe's *Choise of Valentines*, the dildo is described at length; it is hollow, can be filled with hot water or milk to simulate ejaculation, is made of glass, and is said to work by means of "forraine artes." Recent critics have emphasized that it represents a socially censured, threatening, nonreproductive sexuality and a bid for female agency whether represented in positive or negative terms.[33] But perhaps more significant is the dildo as a marker of a certain urban and mercantile sophistication. Dildos would have been known to Nashe and his contemporaries literarily through Aretino's dialogues, and though these sexual prostheses of glass, as opposed to leather, may have been a fantasy of pornographic writing, they may well have been available locally, not merely via literary allusion.

We know that Murano glass objects were imported to England as early as the fourteenth century. In 1549 a group of Muranese glassmakers settled in London and produced Venetian glass for several years, and in 1571, a Muranese glassmaker named Jacapo Verzelini emigrated from Antwerp, where he had worked for many years; he received a royal patent to produce Murano glass, brought additional recruits from Italy, and manufactured Venetian glass in London for at least fifteen years—his work survives, dating from 1577 until the 1590s.[34]

In Nashe's poem the dildo is associated with foreign parts and stands for foreign pleasures, what Ascham earlier in the century in warning young men from traveling in Italy called the enchantments of Circe. The Italian dildo blown from Venetian glass, perhaps manufactured in London, illustrates the xenophobic English view of exotic and commercial sexual practices and their fruits. For London writers of the late sixteenth and seventeenth centuries, not only sexual prosthetics but prostitutes themselves were frequently from somewhere else—they were Dutch courtesans and bawds, Welsh whores, and, closer to home but still eccentric to the City proper, Hackneys and Westminster whores. Similarly, lust is Dutch, and places of sexual resort were associated with the foreign: Paris Garden and Holland's Leaguer, and the pox, of course, was French. At the end of Nashe's poem, Tomalin asks for exotic, unaffordable "Druggs and Electuaries of Indian soile, / That strengthen wearie members in their toile,"[35] and in *Christs Teares*, Nashe complains of "veneriall machavielisme." And despite his own poem which gives the lie to his claim about Italian venery, he maintains that the English "have not words to unfold" what goes on in the stews: "Positions and instructions have they [the Italians] to make their whores a hundred times more whorish . . . waters and receipts, to enable a man after he is spent."[36] Italian, French, Dutch, Indian—all these displacements seek to distance, if not save, the English from sexual pollution.[37]

Jonathan Crewe first remarked the confusion of pronoun reference in Nashe's poem that sometimes makes it difficult to determine who is speaking.[38] At line 245, Tomalin apparently begins to speak again and to complain "how he [the dildo] usurps in bed and bowre." The dildo is personified, first by Francis and then by Tomalin, who calls him "my Mistris page," "this womans secretarie" and "a ladies chamberlaine," all labels out of context for the country Tomalin and his only-just-arrived-in-the-city female companion. They signal the poet's intervention toward the end of the poem with conventional stereotypes about higher-status women's use of their male servants— page, secretary, chamberlain—for sexual purposes.

Rather than emphasize, as have other recent critics, the poem's psychosexual thematics, which assume a reader's identification with Tomalin's initial sexual difficulties and fear of Francis's sexual aggressiveness,[39] the end of the poem calls attention to the author's distanced control over its entertaining eroticism and the ways in which the prostitute's body and her pleasure are displayed as a cultural production, as a poetic performance with erotic effects for its readers. Masculine sexual limitation is safely confined to the comical rube Tomalin, whose country origins, crude lust, and naïveté inhibit identification with the sophisticated, knowing, possibly mostly male audience to which the poem is pitched. The last seventy-five lines move away from the narrative and appeal more directly to the poem's readers and their assumed salacious enjoyment of the dildo's action, which is said to "alter [its] pace," "For, who in pathe's unknownen, one gate can keepe?" The poet operates the dildo for the reader's entertainment and as a reminder of labile, sexual possibility rather than anxiety about male sexual performance.[40]

In its last two quatrains, the poem segues from Tomalin's account of paying the bawd and leaving the brothel, to the poet's reflections on its reception:

What can be added more to my renowne?
    She lyeth breathlesse, I am taken doune,
The waues doe swell, the tydes climbe or'e the banks,
    Iudge gentlemen if I deserue not thanks,
And so good night unto you eue'rie one,
    For loe, our threed is spunne, our plaie is donne. (311–16)

The poem would seem to end, then, with Nashe's bravura assertion of the powerful erotic effects of what Pepys was later to term "one handed reading." Judge, gentlemen, if I deserve not thanks, he says, as the waves swell and the tides climb o'er the banks. Interestingly, in one of the manuscript copies at the Bodleian (Rawlinson MS. Poet. 216, fols. 96–106), the "gentlemen" of line 314 reads "gentleweomen" and thus posits a female readership, or instead perhaps seeks to enhance the poem's sensational appeal to men.[41]

Nashe's poem, then, safely distances its elite readers from sexual anxiety whether about male performance or female sexuality. The commercial world of prostitution is packaged for an elite urban readership that can enjoy Nashe's literary tumbling act from his parodic religious diction to his hyperbolic Petrarchism to his imitation of Ovid. Though there is a great deal more to be said about this poem, which ends with a short epilogue in which Nashe claims Ovid as his poetic precursor and promises more serious praise of his patron now that his "mynde [is] purg'd of such lascivious witt," I want to turn instead briefly to a similar appropriation of urban crime for the delectation of a Parisian elite before returning to the question of archives with which this chapter began.

Like London's Southwark suburbs where prostitutes and all kinds of petty criminals sought refuge, Paris too had its criminal quarter, the so-called Cour des Miracles. Literally, *cour* refers to a dead end or cul-de-sac, and the *cour des miracles* where urban poor, beggars, criminals, and prostitutes lived. In seventeenth-century Paris, the Cour des Miracles was located between the rue Montorgueil, the convent of the Filles-Dieu, and the rue Neuve-Saint-Sauveur. There, according to the late seventeenth-century memoirist and antiquarian Henri Sauval, in a square of considerable size that he described as stinking, muddy, and unpaved, all the criminals of Paris were gathered in another world with their own laws, vocational training, religious practice, customs, and behaviors.[42] Young boys were said to be initiated into the fraternity of pickpockets and cutpurses, girls and women "les moins laides se prostituoient pour deux liards les autres pour un double, la plupart pour rien" (the least ugly prostituted themselves for two liards, others for a double, but most for nothing at all). Of particular interest to Sauval and other chroniclers of the *cour des miracles* were the stories of simulated injury, sickness, and poverty—con men and women were said to pretend to be blind, deaf, crippled, ill while they plied their trade, but to return to the *cour* at night, transformed in an instant, healed, as Sauval ironically notes, without recourse to miracles.[43]

As in London, such tales of an urban counterculture, a world turned upside down with its own laws, its own language, its own government, were popular. Such legends allowed the better-off to forgo charity and inspired Louis XIV to establish the Hôpital Général in which to incarcerate paupers and criminals.[44]

Stories of the Cour des Miracles and the metamorphoses that took place there were so fashionable that ballets were presented at court for the king in 1653 and 1655 with courtiers playing the parts of the "Concierge & les Locataires de la Cour de miracles" (concierge and inhabitants of the court of miracles). The ballet begins by representing a scene of elite consumption in which gallants and coquettes alight from coaches to buy ribbons and jam, reminiscent of Corneille's *Galerie du Palais*, then shifts to an episode in which two bourgeois de Paris are attacked by "filous" or thieves, as in Berthaud's poem *Paris burlesque*, and finally a scene set in the Cour des Miracles itself, where beggars, cripples, and amputees are miraculously healed to dance a *gaillarde* and sing a serenade.[45] The spectators seem to have judged it a huge success. The king's ballet aestheticizes the fear the elite felt in response to urban crime summed up in a passage from the bourgeois Pierre de l'Estoile's diary in his description of the new year in January 1606:

> Force meurtres, assassinates, voleries, excés, paillardises, et toutes sortes de vices et impieties, régnèrent en ceste saison extraordinairement. Insolences de laquais à Paris jusques aux meurtres, dont il y en eust de pendus; faux monnoyeurs pris et descouverts; deux assassins qui avoient voulu assassiner le baron d'Aubeterre en sa maison, roués tous vifs en Grève; ung soldat des Gardes pendu pour avoir tué son hoste, afin de lui voler dix francs qu'il avoit; ung merchant venant à la Foire, tué d'un coup de cousteau qu'on lui qu'on lui laissa dans la gorge, trouvé en cest estat le long des trenchées des fauxbourgs Saint Germain: sans dix neuf autres qu'on trouve avoir esté tués et assassins, en ce seul mois, par les rue de Paris don't on n'a pu descouvrir encore les meurtriers. Pauvre commencement d'année, nous menassant de pire fin.

> So many murders, assassinations, robberies, excesses, debaucheries, and all sorts of vices and impieties reign in this extraordinary season. The insolence of lackeys in Paris, even to murders for which they have been hanged; counterfeiters arrested and discovered; two killers, who had wanted to assassinate Baron d'Aubeterre in his own house, set on the wheel alive in the Place de Grève; a soldier of the Guards hanged for having murdered his host to steal ten francs from him; a merchant coming to the Fair killed by one stab of a knife they left in his throat, found like that in the ditches just outside St. Germain: and that doesn't even take into account nineteen others killed or assassinated, in this one month, *by the streets of Paris*, in which you may still find the murderers. A poor beginning to the year which threatens us with an even worse end. (trans. and italics mine)[46]

De l'Estoile's journal entry records the fears of an urban elite in the face of seemingly uncontrolled crime. The aristocracy and the bourgeosie under attack, murderous lackeys above the law, loyalty and hospitality transgressed, merchants unable even to reach the foire Saint-Germain to conduct their business, killed in cold blood and left in a ditch, acts perpetrated by the "the streets of Paris" in which the killers still roam free, and worse to come. De l'Estoile goes on, in time-honored fashion, to blame the times. No one fears God any longer, and today He is no longer to be found among men. By making the streets of Paris the perpetrator of the many crimes that take place in the city, de l'Estoile reveals the panic produced by the mix of persons that was an important feature of the urban environment. The court ballets featuring imagined scenes in the *cour des miracles* demonstrate at one and the same time the fear and fascination provoked by the spatial assembly of the poor, the vagrant, of prostitutes and cutpurses, in Paris.

The archive fever that has taken hold in literary studies threatens the study of literature with a renewed historicism of a distinctly old rather than new type. Both historians and literary scholars claim to have learned Natalie Davis's lesson concerning fiction in the archives, but as Griffiths's willingness on the one hand to allot a truth value to the Bridewell courtbooks and the so-called voices they record, and on the other to reject so-called literary evidence demonstrates, archives remain a privileged repository, a place of facts from which truth can be teased out. Literary historians and critics have increasingly found sanctuary in the archives, relieved to leave "theory" behind; we have taken refuge in paper remains in the name of scholarship, and the desire to claim for ourselves the privilege and authority of truth and science. The stories of women who left no textual remains of their own and whose stories Griffiths calls "their own narratives" and their "authentic voice" are to be "recovered" from archives, emancipated somehow from the dark confines of interpretation. But this chapter has endeavored to show how the depositions and cases, records and statutes, fears about public order, even the topography of the urban brothels join *with* plays and pamphlets, poems and fictions, ballets and masques, in a hermeneutic flood that enables us to constitute meaning through the act of writing.[47] We claim to know archives are shaped by genre, custom, and trope, by ideology and hierarchy, habit and authority, but we remain reluctant to accept that the meanings they give up are not self-evident, but the result of reading and interpretation as surely as any literary text.

Paperwork

Footnotes historicize what scholars do. They remind us and our readers that writing is "a concrete series of acts carried out under particular circumstances . . . against the ideologies that tempt us out of time."[1] The preceding chapters are filled with notes to myriad historical studies on early modern London and Paris: on bridges and landmarks, on urban demography and migration, on streets and transport, trade and consumption, pollution and sewage, travel and reading, sex and death. Though my notes inevitably call upon the authority of such studies, the purpose of this book is the reading of literary and cultural texts: street literature, the poetry of Isabella Whitney, Nashe, Donne, and Boileau, the drama of Shakespeare, Jonson, Middleton, and Corneille, topographies, guidebooks and pamphlets, the novels of Scudéry and Furetière. Presumably, the endnotes on the history of London and Paris, which far outnumber those to a particular edition or critical essay on the texts I analyze, allow us to judge the literary and cultural artifacts that are my subject against the "real events" or "facts" of history, or, as Natalie Zemon Davis insists, "their fidelity to 'real events,' or at least to the same events as recounted by others."[2] The "others who recount" are not only various contemporary accounts preserved in archival sources but the versions of those events produced and published by both recent historians and literary scholars.

This problem of the relation between "fact" and "fiction" has particularly dogged studies of urban writing that have focused on what we might term, anachronistically, "realist" texts, texts that purport to represent everyday urban life and social relations. A case in point is the recent handbook, Blackwell's *Companion to English Renaissance Literature and Culture*, which, as its title declares, claims to be a reader's guide to early modern literature and culture. The chapter entitled "The Literature of the Metropolis" offers a curious view of urban writing.[3] It begins by noting the vast demographic shifts from country to city that made London a metropolis. Whereas the court defined itself through the masque, the author observes, the ruling city elite did so through the Lord Mayor's inaugural pageants. He goes on, still in his opening paragraph, to note in a sentence or two that numerous genres represented London's development as a metropolis. The article ends ten pages later where a reader might have expected it to begin, with a brief discussion of John Stow. But the bulk of the entry purporting to survey the literature of the metropolis for both students and scholars is devoted entirely to the London underworld and to debates about the status of historical evidence and literary and cultural texts on that topic. A student or reader unacquainted with the multiple genres associated with urban writing would imagine that London was represented only as a city of crime, "a threatening unofficial realm inhabited by tricksters, parasites, and rogues of all kinds."[4] There is no mention of English city comedy, nor of satire or urban/e poetry; there are no ballads or broadsides, no popular narratives such as Nashe's *Unfortunate Traveler*—in short, the manual article presents a skewed account of metropolitan literature. Its slant reflects current critical and popular preoccupations with subcultures and the outlaw, with poverty and the dispossessed, preoccupations to be found in the work of various disciplines at the present moment, from anthropology to social and urban history.[5] In the preceding chapters I have tried to present a broader perspective of "metropolitan literature" that encompasses the multiple genres and forms of writing that represented both early modern Paris and London.

Instead of the kind of broad survey appropriate to the demands of a handbook or manual,[6] John Twyning's article focuses almost exclusively on conycatching pamphlets, which he uses to rehearse the debates that have dogged the literature of London's underworld for the last century: are cony-catching pamphlets and other representations of London crime "factual accounts"? Do they offer an authentic "contemporary view of crime in Tudor England"? Twyning takes a balanced view shared by most critics currently writing under the broad rubric of new historicism or cultural materialism: because "urban fact and literature correspond . . . does not mean we should simply read such texts as straightforward evidence. Despite the correspondence between fact and fiction, they should not be collapsed into one another. . . . The cony-catching pamphlet was both an authentic description of a social fiction and a fictive account of a cultural fact."[7] More interesting for my purposes than the narrow focus on the London underworld, or than the debate itself, however interesting, are the seemingly inescapable terms within which the debate is cast: the eternal binary fact/fiction and the seemingly inevitable chiasmus: authentic description/fictive account: social fiction/cultural fact. Both the binary and the chiasmus *are* powerful and inescapable, for me as for others; but the preceding chapters have sought at least to trouble those oppositions by focusing on the rhetorical operations and tropes that structure our reading and interpretation.

In the United States, New Criticism, and specifically the work of its best-known proponents, John Crowe Ransom, Allen Tate, and Robert Penn Warren, was a reaction against scientific positivism and narrowly conceived philological study that suppressed the materiality and productivity of language.[8] Similarly, poststructuralism challenged the positivist emphasis on rational meaning and, famously for some, notoriously for others, insisted on textuality, on the play of language and the signifier. The recent, trumpeted return to history does not reinstate a long-lost history ignored by empty formalisms,

as is sometimes alleged, for neither New Criticism nor poststructuralism, as
practiced by its best proponents, ignored or forgot history. Instead, all too
often the turn to history over the last twenty-five years has been, as Tate noted
with regard to historical method long ago in his essay "Miss Emily and the
Bibliographer," an attempt on the part of literary studies to imitate the scientific method. Too much recent work in literary studies has embraced the descriptive and the instrumental, as comfortable as an old shoe, and turned away
from the work of reading.

In his elegant meditation on history writing and its inevitable literariness,
Les noms d'histoire, or *The Names of History*, Jacques Rancière writes of the
paradox of our having found the "other"—women, the poor and dispossessed,
the queer, the colonized—at the very moment history has turned away from
the proper name. Within the French context, he analyzes the shift represented
by the *annales* school in which not only the proper name is lost, sunk, drowned
in the *longue durée*, but even papers and archives, with their anecdotes and
details, their idioms and rhetorics, are refuted, displaced in the name of economic and social history represented instead by graphs, charts, grids, tables,
diagrams, maps, and numbers.[9] At the very moment that the discipline of
history turns its back on papers as lies, as fictions in the archive, we in literature, and I emphatically include myself, embrace that very morass of paper—
what Rancière ironically terms *paperasse*, always a pejorative term in French
that means bureaucratic paperwork, what deserves the dustbin, musty piles of
useless files and papers. Literary critics and commentators feverishly scour the
records of kings and princes, of diplomats and clerics, of guilds and hospitals,
to claim a sciencity history itself no longer accords such archives.

My readings of city texts have attempted to demonstrate that a history of
urban subjectivity, of feeling and affect, motivation and ethics, is not to be
found in statistics on marriages or births, or in the analysis of wills or courtbooks. What we can know "authentically" and with certainty about crime,
beggary, and prostitution, and the women, and no doubt men who were its
practitioners, is not to be found any more in depositions or records than in
other sorts of texts. We decipher hands, transcribe them, read microfilms, go
blind, so we can recover a paralepsis, that which is omitted, those who, in
Marx's time-honored formulation, "cannot represent themselves." Thus my
epigraph for chapter 8 from Michelet's journal: "We must hear the words that
were never spoken. . . . We must make the silences of history speak. . . . Only
then do the dead accept the sepulcher."[10] Rancière reminds us with irony of
the hubris of such claims: "Their speech is full of meaning, but they know
nothing of that meaning—the role of the historian is to deliver this voice" in
a kind of necrophiliac fantasy (63). There is history, as Rancière puts it, "because there is an absence of things in words," "a twofold absence—of the thing
itself, and the more fearful absence of truth in language—its metaphoricity, its
literariness, which the counting and tables and numbers and charts seek to

avoid," from which too often not only historians, but literary and cultural critics as well, turn away in our own recourse to archives. What must be avoided is merely reversing the lesson—fiction in the archives—by saying there is history in our fictions. We need to use the operations of reading—of language, figure, and rhetoric—to tell different stories. Otherwise we occupy the merely "subaltern role of explaining residual phenomena" (81).

"The production of the *hidden* is a poetic operation," says Rancière, "essential to the constitution of knowledge in historical study" (52). This study has attempted to address Rancière's observation in the context of literary studies. However old the lesson, even the truism for those several generations trained as new critics or formalists in close reading and deconstruction, that the production of knowledge is always a poetic operation, it bears repeating precisely because it is so difficult to enact. We may know and agree that language is at once a bearer of truth and of lies; the problem comes about as we work to perform that knowledge in the context of writing cultural criticism. *Archives*, as Derrida reminds us, is etymologically related to authority—the *arkhē* was the place where high magistrates lived; and the *archontes* were both the guardians of the official documents deposed there and their interpreters.[11] The archive is, in his resonant phrase, the "prosthesis of memory," our own handy dildo to satisfy unfulfilled desire.

In Derrida's consideration of the archive he locates "mal d'archive," or archive fever, as the English translator renders his title, in a moment in Freud in which the good doctor wonders—in writing, of course—if the publication of his papers, their archivization, is pointless, a worthless, wasted effort. Derrida reads in this speculation, in this modesty topos, a manifest resistance to psychoanalysis on Freud's part.[12] At the moment of its archival institution is resistance, repudiation, the death wish, for without the Freudian archive, Freud and psychoanalysis would not exist. Our appeal to the archive and its fantasies of fact represents a manifest resistance on our part to writing and its insistent assertion of the impossibility of ever providing "just the facts."

INTRODUCTION

1. For other early comparisons of London and Paris, see Thomas Gainsford, *The Glory of England* (1618), James Howell's *Londinopolis* (1657), and *Gallus Castratus* (1659), a response to John Evelyn's *Character of England*, which compares the "republican" architectural style of London to the "monarchical" style of Paris. On the making of the English metropolis, see the essays in A. L. Beier and Roger Finlay, eds., *London 1500–1700: The Making of the Metropolis* (London: Longmans, 1986). Also on early modern London, see, among others, Valerie Pearl, *London and the Outbreak of the Puritan Revolution* (London: Oxford University Press, 1961), as well as her many articles; Jeremy Boulton, *Neighborhood and Society: A London Suburb in the Seventeenth Century* (Cambridge: Cambridge University Press, 1987); Steve Rappaport, *Worlds within Worlds: The Structures of Life in Sixteenth-Century London* (Cambridge: Cambridge University Press, 1989); Ian Archer, *The Pursuit of Stability: Social Relations in Elizabethan London* (Cambridge: Cambridge University Press, 1991); and, more recently, Joseph P. Ward, *Metropolitan Communities: Trade Guilds, Identity, and Change in Early Modern London* (Stanford, CA: Stanford University Press, 1997). The literature on nineteenth-century Paris is immense: see Jean Favier's *Paris, deux mille ans d'histoire* (Paris: Fayard, 1997) and the multivolumed *Nouvelle Histoire de Paris*, particularly Jean-Pierre Babelon, *Paris au XVIe siècle* (Paris: Diffusion Hachette, 1986), René Pillorget, *Paris sous les premiers bourbons, 1594–1661* (Paris: Diffusion Hachette, 1988); G. Detham, *Paris au temps de Louis XIV* (Paris: Diffusion Hachette, 1990), and Pierre Lavedan, *Histoire de l'urbanisme à Paris*, 2nd ed. (Paris: Diffusion Hachette, 1993).

2. On cultural capital, see Pierre Bourdieu, *Distinction: A Social Critique of the Judgment of Taste*, trans. Richard Nice (Cambridge, MA: Harvard University Press, 1984).

3. On urban demography and its effects, see Kingsley Davis's classic study, "The Urbanization of the Human Population," which first appeared in *Scientific American* (1965) and is reprinted in *The City Reader*, ed. Richard T. LeGates and Frederic Stout (London and New York: Routledge, 1996), 2–11.

4. Ibid., 2. H. J. Dyos argues that the statistics Kingsley adduces are in some respects ahead of the qualitative changes involved in the process of transposing and modifying agrarian institutions to an urban setting. *Exploring the Urban Past: Essays in Urban History*, ed. David Cannadine and David Reeder (Cambridge: Cambridge University Press, 1982), 69.

5. See Jan de Vries, *European Urbanization 1500–1800* (Cambridge, MA: Harvard University Press, 1984); on the larger processes of urbanization and the importance of networks or systems of cities, see also H. J. Dyos, "Agenda for Urban Historians," in *The Study of Urban History*, ed. H. J. Dyos (London: Edward Arnold, 1968), and,

more recently, Christopher Friedrichs, *The Early Modern City 1450–1750* (London: Longmans, 1995).

6. De Vries, *European Urbanization*, 96.

7. On the English population explosion in this period, see E. A. Wrigley and R. S. Schofield, *Population History of England 1541–1871: A Reconstruction* (Cambridge, MA: Harvard University Press, 1981), who estimate an increase in population of some 66 percent, from three million to just over five million between 1550 and 1650; and Roger Finlay, *Population and Metropolis: The Demography of London 1580–1650* (Cambridge: Cambridge University Press, 1981). But see Vanessa Harding, "The Population of London, 1550–1700: A Review of the Published Evidence," *London Journal* 15 (1990): 111–28.

8. On the demography of Paris, see the *Nouvelle Histoire de Paris,* cited earlier; Philip Benedict, *Cities and Social Change* (London: Unwin Hyman, 1989), which draws on unpublished material provided by Jean-Noël Biraben; many books and articles by Roland Mousnier; and Barbara Diefendorf's discussion in *Beneath the Cross: Catholics and Huguenots in Sixteenth-Century Paris* (New York: Oxford University Press, 1991).

9. For the major proponents of the "crisis" argument, see Eric Hobsbawm's and Hugh Trevor Roper's articles in *Crisis in Europe, 1560–1600,* ed. Trevor Aston (London: Routledge and Kegan Paul, 1965); and David Maland, *Europe in the Seventeenth Century* (London: Macmillan, 1966).

10. See Theodore K. Rabb, *The Struggle for Stability in Early Modern Europe* (New York: Oxford University Press, 1975).

11. See especially L. Wirth, "Urbanism as a Way of Life," *American Journal of Sociology* 44 (1938): 1–24; and R. E. Pahl, ed., *Readings in Urban Sociology* (Oxford: Pergamon Press, 1968).

12. John Patten, *English Towns, 1500–1700* (Folkestone: Dawson, 1978). John Schofield and others point out that England was no more urbanized in 1600 than in 1300, but that the population was much more densely located in London by the beginning of the seventeenth century; "The Topography of London, ca. 1600: An Archaeological Survey," in *Material London ca. 1600,* ed. Lena Cowen Orlin (Philadelphia: University of Pennsylvania Press, 2000), 296–321. Derek Keene argues that the explosive growth of the sixteenth century returns London to the levels of the thirteenth century and that London remains peripheral to Europe, dominated first by Antwerp, then Amsterdam, until the second half of the seventeenth century; "Material London in Time and Space," in *Material London,* 57.

13. See Charles Tilly's longer definition in *The Vendée* (Cambridge, MA: Harvard University Press, 1964), 16–20; Wirth, "Urbanism as a Way of Life"; and Pahl, *Readings in Urban Sociology.* Concerning water, H. J. Dyos points out that a continuous supply of water was unattainable in London before 1900; *Exploring the Urban Past,* 70. On water in Paris, see Roland Mousnier, *Paris: Capitale au temps de Richelieu et du Mazarin* (Paris: A. Pedone, 1978), 129–31. On the social and economic repercussions of demographic growth, see the classic studies of F. J. Fisher, *London and the English Economy, 1500–1700,* ed. P. J. Corfield and N. B. Harte (London: Hambledon Press, 1990); and E. A. Wrigley, "A Simple Model of London's Importance in Changing English Society and Economy, 1650–1750," *Past & Present* 37 (1967): 44–70. On English trade, see Theodore Rabb, "Investment in English Overseas Enterprise, 1575–

1630," *Economic History Review*, n.s., 19 (1966): 70–81, in which he points out that "in the history of British expansion, [there is] no more active period than the first thirty years of the seventeenth century" (70). On France, see Françoise Bayard and Philippe Giugnet, *L'économie française aux XVIᵉ, XVIIᵉ, XVIIIᵉ siècles* (Paris: Ophrys, 1991), who show that geographic extension particularly characterized the French economy of the seventeenth century in which there was extraordinary growth in the production and availability of *nouveautés* in the capital, including silk, mirrors, fur, cocoa, tobacco, and cane sugar.

14. Though the full effects of the so-called financial revolution in England will not be felt until the late seventeenth and eighteenth centuries, after the period of this book's focus, there was already a *concentration* of financial capital in London and Paris. See P. G. M. Dickson, *The Financial Revolution in England: A Study in the Development of Public Credit 1688–1756* (London: Macmillan, 1967); and Larry Neal, *The Rise of Financial Capitalism: International Capital Markets in the Age of Reason* (Cambridge: Cambridge University Press, 1990).

15. Amsterdam grew from some thirty thousand in 1578 to about two hundred thousand in 1675 and became what van Zanden terms the "first modern urban industrial area in the world"; *The Rise and Decline of Holland's Economy: Merchant Capitalism and the Labour Market* (Manchester, UK: Manchester University Press, 1993), 31; though its rate of growth was comparable to London's, it never achieved the overall population of London or Paris. See David Ormrod, *The Rise of Commercial Empires: England and the Netherlands in the Age of Mercantilism, 1650–1770* (Cambridge: Cambridge University Press, 2003); Jan de Vries and Ad van der Woude, *The First Modern Economy: Success, Failure and Perseverance of the Dutch Economy, 1500–1815* (Cambridge: Cambridge University Press, 1997); and Patrick O'Brien, Derek Keene, Marjolein 't Hart, and Herman van der Wee, eds., *Urban Achievement in Early Modern Europe: Golden Ages in Antwerp, Amsterdam and London* (Cambridge: Cambridge University Press, 2001). See also Fernand Braudel, *Afterthoughts on Capitalism and Material Civilization* (Baltimore: Johns Hopkins University Press, 1977), 85–86.

16. See Simon Schama, *The Embarrassment of Riches: An Interpretation of Dutch Culture in the Golden Age* (Berkeley: University of California Press, 1988), 285.

17. See De Vries, *European Urbanization*, for a challenge to this view and a review of such claims, 1–10.

18. Raymond Williams, *Keywords* (New York: Oxford University Press, 1976), 47. Jean-Pierre Babelon compares the changes in seventeenth-century Paris with Haussmannization in *Demeures Parisiennes sous Henri IV et Louis XIII* (Paris: Le Temps, 1965).

19. See, among others, Susan Buck-Morss, *The Dialectics of Seeing: Walter Benjamin and the Arcades Project* (Cambridge, MA: MIT Press, 1989); essays in William Sharpe and Leonard Wallock, eds., *Visions of the Modern City* (Baltimore: Johns Hopkins University Press, 1987); and Mary Ann Caws, ed., *City Images: Perspectives from Literature, Philosophy, and Film* (New York: Gordon and Breach, 1991). On the industrial city's challenge to patriarchal structures, see Elizabeth Wilson, *The Sphinx in the City: Urban Life, the Control of Disorder and Women* (Berkeley: University of California Press, 1991); and Laura Gowing's essay showing that this process is already at work in early modern London, "'The Freedom of the Streets': Women and Social Space, 1560–1640," in *Londinopolis: Essays in the Cultural and Social History of Early Modern*

London, ed. Paul Griffiths and Mark S. R. Jenner (Manchester, UK: Manchester University Press, 2000), 130–51.

20. "Paris, the Capital of the Nineteenth Century" (1935) and "Paris, Capital of the Nineteenth Century" (1939), in *The Arcades Project*, trans. Howard Eiland and Kevin McLaughlin (Cambridge, MA: Harvard University Press, 1999). The literature on nineteenth-century Paris is immense; see Jean Favier's *Paris, deux mille ans d'histoire*, cited earlier, which presents the development of the city from its origins, as the title indicates, but nevertheless devotes itself primarily to nineteenth- and twentieth-century Paris in both its text and bibliography. On modernity and the nineteenth century, see Marshall Berman, *All That Is Solid Melts into Air* (New York: Simon and Schuster, 1982).

21. Georg Simmel, "The Metropolis and Mental Life," in *The Sociology of Georg Simmel*, ed. Kurt Wolff, trans. H. H. Gerth with C. Wright Mills (New York: Macmillan, 1950). Commentators have challenged Simmel's claims on behalf of individual agency and autonomy. See, for example, Frederic Jameson, *Postmodernism, or, the Cultural Logic of Late Capitalism* (Durham, NC: Duke University Press, 1991); and Elizabeth Grosz, "Bodies-Cities," in *Sexuality & Space*, ed. Beatriz Colomina (Princeton, NJ: Princeton Papers on Architecture, 1992), 241–54. On Simmel's continued importance in the study of urbanism, see Dietmar Jazbinsek, "The Metropolis and the Mental Life of Georg Simmel: On the History of an Antipathy," *Journal of Urban History* 30 (2003): 102–25.

22. Miles Ogborn, *Spaces of Modernity: London's Geographies, 1680–1780* (London: Guilford Press, 1998), 3. Ogborn's first chapter offers a useful review of the literature on modernity; subsequent chapters locate various geographies of modernity in eighteenth-century London, including the Magdalen Hospital, the London streets, the Vauxhall Gardens, the Excise, and the Universal Register Office.

23. Quoted in ibid., 3.

24. Bruno Latour, *We Have Never Been Modern* (Hemel Hempstead, UK: Harvester Wheatsheaf, 1993), 41.

25. See Robert Mandrou's *Introduction à la France moderne: Essai de psychologie historique 1500–1640*, 3rd ed. (Paris: Albin Michel, 1998), 18–20.

26. In *The Condition of Postmodernity: An Enquiry into the Origins of Cultural Change* (London: Blackwell, 1989), David Harvey claims that the appeal of the past is a psychological response to the bombardment of stimuli (Simmel), which has provoked the current interest in mementos, museums, ruins, the retro style (286); on the organization of urban space, see the quite different approaches of Lewis Mumford, *The City in History* (New York: Harcourt, Brace and World, 1961), and Jane Jacobs, *The Death and Life of Great American Cities* (New York: Vintage, 1961).

27. See Paul Zumthor, *La mesure du monde* (Paris: Seuil, 1993), and "Lieux et espaces au moyen âge," *Dalhousie French Studies* 30 (1995): 3–10.

28. Zumthor, "Lieux et espaces," 4.

29. See, for example, Derek Gregory, *Geographical Imaginations* (Oxford: Blackwell, 1994); Tom Conley, *The Self-Made Map: Cartographic Writing in Early Modern France* (Minneapolis: University of Minneapolis Press, 1996); Jeremy Black, *Maps and Politics* (London: Reaktion, 1997); and Black, *Literature, Mapping, and the Politics of Space in Early Modern Britain*, ed. Andrew Gordon and Bernhard Klein (Cambridge: Cambridge University Press, 2001).

30. Harvey, *The Condition of Postmodernity*, 205.

31. Michel Foucault, *The Order of Things: An Archaeology of the Human Sciences* (New York: Vintage, 1973). The English translation renders precisely the French text: "progrés," "espace d'ordre," "champ épistémologique," "espace du savoir," "histoire," "archéologie." *Les mots et les choses* (Paris: Gallimard, 1966), 13. In addition, the English translation of "sur fond" as "basis" de-emphasizes the spatial dimension of the French idiom.

32. Michel Foucault, "Questions on Geography," in *Power/Knowledge*, ed. Colin Gordon (New York: Pantheon, 1980), 70.

33. See, for example, Jameson, *Postmodernism*; Edward Soja, *Postmodern Geographies: The Reassertion of Space in Critical Social Theory* (London and New York: Verso, 1989); Mike Davis, *City of Quartz: Excavating the Future in Los Angeles* (London and New York: Verso, 1990); Homi Bhabha, *Nation and Narration* (London and New York: Routledge, 1990); Saskia Sassen, *Cities in a World Economy* (Thousand Oaks, CA: Pine Forge Press, 1994); Anthony Vidler, *Art, Architecture, and Anxiety in Modern Culture* (Cambridge, MA: MIT Press, 2000); and David Harvey, *Paris: Capital of Modernity* (London and New York: Routledge, 2003).

34. John Agnew, "Representing Space: Space, Scale and Culture in Social Science," in *Place/Culture/Representation*, ed. James Duncan and David Ley (London and New York: Routledge, 1993), 251–71.

35. See Edward Casey, "How to Get from Space to Place in a Fairly Short Stretch of Time," *Senses of Place*, ed. Steven Feld and Keith H. Basso (Santa Fe, NM: School of American Research Press, 1996), 13–52. On the impact of the digital age on urban life and the way in which an "aristocracy of talent [can] live where they want to and dictate a geography of wealth" emancipated from industrial cities, outer boroughs, and less desirable core and periphery areas, see Joel Kotkin, "Grass-roots Business: Why Wall Street Is Losing Out to 40 Acres and a Modem," *New York Times*, 28 December 1998, sec. 3, p. 7. See also his book *The New Geography: How the Digital Revolution Is Reshaping the American Landscape* (New York: Random House, 2000).

36. Casey, "How to Get from Space to Place," 14–15, quoting Fred R. Myers, *Pintupi Country, Pintupi Self: Sentiment, Place and Politics among Western Desert Aborigines* (Berkeley: University of California Press, 1991).

37. See Soja, *Postmodern Geographies*, and his *Postmetropolis* (Oxford: Blackwell, 2000).

38. See Tim Hall and Phil Hubbard, eds., *The Entrepreneurial City: Geographies of Politics, Regime and Representation* (Chichester and New York: Wiley, 1998).

39. David Harvey, "From Managerialism to Entrepreneurialism: The Transformation of Governance in Late Capitalism," *Geografiska Annaler* 71 (1989): 7.

40. See Raphael Samuel's "On the Methods of History Workshop: A Reply," *History Workshop Journal* 9 (1980): 162–76; and Carolyn Steedman's discussion of his work in *Dust: The Archive and Cultural History* (New Brunswick, NJ: Rutgers University Press, 2001).

41. See James Chandler's extended discussion of Fredric Jameson's characterization of new historicism as homological and "detailism" or "localism" in his *England in 1819: The Politics of Literary Culture and the Case of Romantic Historicism* (Chicago: University of Chicago Press, 1998), particularly chapter 1 and pp. 156–66. Chandler's review of the problem of historical specificity in Sartre, Lévi-Strauss, Jameson, and

Kenneth Burke, among others, is useful. On Jameson, homology, and the new historicism, see chapter 3.

42.On antinationalism and world literature, see Franco Moretti, "Conjectures on World Literature," *New Left Review*, n.s., 1 (2000): 54–68. For a fine historical and theoretical account of global comparative literature, see Emily Apter, "Global *Translatio*: The 'Invention' of Comparative Literature, Istanbul, 1933," *Critical Inquiry* 29 (2003): 253–81.

CHAPTER ONE
EARLY MODERN LONDON AND PARIS

1. Mazarin had first attempted to lure Bernini to Paris in 1645; there followed a hiatus of more than a decade—the Fronde years—before Louis again attempted to bring Bernini to Paris in 1662. The negotiations took some time: on 18 April, Bernini received permission for the trip from the pope; he began the trip on the twenty-ninth of that month. His arrival in Paris was of sufficient public interest to warrant an announcement in the *Gazette de France*, which included in its notice the sum Bernini was to be paid by the king.

2. Paul Fréart de Chantelou, *Journal de voyage du Cavalier Bernin en France*, ed. Milovan Stanić (Saint-Jean-de-Braye: Macula L'insulaire, 2001); all references in the text are to this edition. In English, *Diary of the Cavaliere Bernini's Visit to France*, ed. Anthony Blunt, trans. Margery Corbett, and annotated by George C. Bauer (Princeton, NJ: Princeton University Press, 1985), 3.

3. The *Journal* was first published by Ludovic Lalanne in the *Gazette des Beaux-Arts* between 1877 and 1884, and subsequently in a single volume in 1885. That edition was based on a manuscript discovered in the library of the Institut de France.

4. Compare Bernini's view of Paris with a contemporary account of London by a Dutch diplomatic attendant, Lodewijck Huygens, who notes the superb panorama of London he sees from the tower of Windsor Castle that included the London smoke that had obscured his view when he had earlier climbed to the top of Saint Paul's. Noted in Mark S. R. Jenner, "The Politics of London Air: John Evelyn's *Fumifugium* and the Restoration," *Historical Journal* 38 (1995): 539.

5. On the urban skyline, see Spiro Kostof, *The City Shaped* (Boston: Little, Brown, 1991), 279–87.

6. See Kevin Lynch, *The Image of the City* (Cambridge, MA: MIT Press, 1960; repr., Cambridge, MA: MIT Press, 1986).

7. See Spiro Kostof, *The City Shaped* (Boston: Little, Brown, 1991); and Renzo Dubbini, *Geography of the Gaze in Early Modern Europe*, trans. Lydia Cochrane (Chicago: University of Chicago Press, 2002).

8. Georg Braun and Frans Hogenberg, *Civitates orbis terrarum 1572–1618*, ed. R. A. Skelton (Cleveland: World, 1966).

9. For a discussion of the"voyeur-god," a translation of the perspectival *sub specie aeternitatis*, and the city panorama, see de Certeau, *The Practice of Everyday Life*, trans. Steven F. Rendell (Berkeley: University of California Press, 1984), 92–93.

10. Robert Burton, *The Anatomy of Melancholy* (Kila, MT: Kessinger, 1998), based on the 1651 edition, 437, 456. Sir Thomas Elyot similarly observes that one might

"in one houre to beholde those realmes, cities, sees, ryvers, and mountaynes, that uneth in an olde mans life can nat be iournaide and pursued . . . I can nat tell what more pleasure shulde happen to a gentil witte than to beholde in his owne house euery thynge that wit hin the worlde is contained"; *The Boke Named the Gouernour* (1531), Early English Books Online.

11. De Certeau, *Practice of Everyday Life*, 93.

12. On the size of Rome, see "Roma," *Enciclopedia Italiana* 39 (1949). As Wolfgang Braunfels notes in his *Urban Design in Western Europe: Regime and Architecture, 900–1900*, trans. Kenneth J. Northcott (Chicago: University of Chicago Press, 1988), as early as Diderot's *Encyclopédie*, the article on Rome stresses that Paris was six times and London seven times the size of Rome (390). See also Rose Marie San Juan's splendid book on Rome, its tourists, spaces, and guidebooks; *Rome: A City Out of Print* (Minneapolis: University of Minnesota Press, 2001).

13. On the multiple forms of notation and writing in early modern culture, see Juliet Fleming, *Graffiti and the Writing Arts of Early Modern England* (Philadelphia: University of Pennsylvania Press, 2001).

14. See Marcel Poëte, *La promenade à Paris au XVIIe siècle* (Paris: Librairie, 1913); Poëte, *Paris. La vie et son cadre. Au jardin des Tuileries. L'art du jardin. La promenade publique* (Paris, 1924).

15. In 1601, for example, the *prévôt* of the Parisian merchants tells Henry IV that "les grand villes, les rois et [les] princes avoient de coustume de donner des lieux spatieux et places publiques, des portiques et pourmenoirs faictz et enrichis exprès pour recevoir les habitans et prendre leurs plaisirs" (large cities, kings and princes usually provide spacious places, public squares, porticoes and walks made and embellished expressly for their inhabitants and their pleasures), quoted in Marcel Poëte, *Paris durant la Grande Epoque classique* (Paris, 1911).

16. Quoted in de Certeau, *Practice of Everyday Life*, 97.

17. Chantelou reports Colbert's view of Bernini's expectations: "qu'on ne mettait pas le monde sur le pavé de jour à l'autre, qu'il ne savait comme l'on en usait à Rome, mais que ce n'était pas l'usage en France" (we don't put people out on the streets from one day to the next—he didn't know what they did in Rome, but it was not what was done in France).

18. For the debate on the middling sort, see *The Middling Sort of People: Culture, Society and Politics in England, 1550–1800*, ed. Jonathan Barry and Christopher Brooks (New York: St. Martin's Press, 1994).

19. De Certeau, *Practice of Everyday Life*, 93.

20. See Steven Rappaport, *Worlds within Worlds: The Structures of Life in Sixteenth-Century London* (Cambridge: Cambridge University Press, 1989), 76–77; A. L. Beier and Roger Finlay, eds., *London 1500–1700: The Making of the Metropolis* (London: Longmans, 1986), 9–10; and E. A. Wrigley, "A Simple Model of London's Importance in Changing English Society and Economy, 1650–1750," *Past & Present* 37 (1967): 44–70. On Paris, see Philip Benedict, ed., *Cities and Social Change* (London: Unwin Hyman, 1989); and Barbara Diefendorf, *Beneath the Cross: Catholics and Hugenots in Sixteenth-Century Paris* (New York: Oxford, 1991).

21. On the impact of spatial practices and performances "from below" on maps, views, and prospects, see Andrew Gordon, "Performing London: The Map and the City in Ceremony," in *Literature, Mapping and the Politics of Space in Early Modern*

Britain, ed. Andrew Gordon and Bernhard Klein (Cambridge: Cambridge University Press, 2001), 69–88.

22. The major ballad collections are W. Chappell, ed., *The Roxburghe Ballads* (Hertford, 1869–99; repr., New York: AMS Press, 1966), 9 vols.; and H. E. Rollins, ed., *The Pepys Ballads* (Cambridge, MA: 1929–32), 8 vols. See also Tessa Watt, *Cheap Print and Popular Piety 1550–1640* (Cambridge: Cambridge University Press, 1991); and Natascha Würzbach, *The Rise of the English Street Ballad 1550–1650*, trans. Gayna Walls (Cambridge: Cambridge University Press, 1990). On ballads of London, see Peter Lake, "From Troynovant to Heliogabulus's Rome and Back: 'Order' and Its Others in the London of John Stow," in *Imagining Early Modern London: Perceptions and Portrayals of the City from Stow to Strype 1598–1720*, ed. J. F. Merritt (Cambridge: Cambridge University Press, 2001).

On pamphlet literature, see also Mihoko Suzuki, *Subordinate Subjects: Gender, the Political Nation, and Literary Form, 1588–1688* (Burlington, VT: Ashgate, 2003); Alexandra Halasz, *The Marketplace of Print: Pamphlets and the Public Sphere in Early Modern England* (Cambridge: Cambridge University Press, 1997); Laura Caroline Stevenson, *Praise and Paradox: Merchants and Craftsmen in Elizabethan Popular Literature* (Cambridge: Cambridge University Press: 1984). On rogues, cony-catching pamphlets, and the Elizabethan underworld, see *The Elizabethan Underworld*, ed. A. V. Judges (New York: Dutton, 1930); Arthur F. Kinney, *Rogues, Vagabonds and Sturdy Beggars* (Amherst: University of Massachusetts Press, 1990); William C. Carroll, *Fat King, Lean Beggar: Representations of Poverty in the Age of Shakespeare* (Ithaca, NY: Cornell University Press, 1996); Linda Woodbridge, *Vagrancy, Homelessness, and English Renaissance Literature* (Urbana: University of Illinois Press, 2001); essays by Lee Beier, Patricia Fumerton, and Linda Woodbridge in *ELR* 33 (2003); and Craig Dionne and Steve Mentz, eds., *Rogues and Early Modern English Culture* (Ann Arbor: University of Michigan Press, 2004). For Paris, see *La bibliothèque bleue: Littérature populaire en France du XVIIᵉ au XIXᵉ siécle* (Paris: Juillard, 1971); *La bibliothèque impériale: Catalogue de l'histoire de France* (Paris, 1855–1932), 23 vols.; *Oeuvres complètes de Tabarin*, ed. Gustave Aventin (Paris: Jannet, 1858), 2 vols.; Alain Mercier, *La littérature facétieuse sous Louis XIII* (Geneva: Droz, 1991); Hubert Carrier, *Les mazarinades: La conquête de l'opinion* (Geneva: Droz, 1989); and Christian Jouhaud, *Mazarinades: La Fronde des Mots* (Paris: Auber, 1985).

23. On the problem of the binary "popular" and "elite" and the mixed readership of cheap print, see Watt, *Cheap Print and Popular Piety.*

24. "Urban ballad-writers wrote to be heard, not read"; Frederick O. Waage, "Social Themes in Urban Broadsides of Renaissance England," *Journal of Popular Culture* 11 (1977): 732.

25. Bob Scribner, "Is a History of Popular Culture Possible?" *History of European Ideas* 10 (1989): 177. Roger Chartier addresses this issue by arguing that cultural consumption should be understood as a form of production. See also Watt, *Cheap Print and Popular Piety*, who considers how the "collective responses of cheap print 'consumers' influenced what was printed and reprinted" (4).

26. John Selden as quoted in *Samuel Pepys's Penny Merriments*, ed. Roger Thompson (New York: Columbia University Press, 1977), 12.

27. See Peter Clark and D. Souden, eds., *Migration and Society in Early Modern England* (1987), and note 20 above.

28. Ian W. Archer, "Material Londoners?" in *Material London, ca. 1600*, ed. Lena Cowen Orlin (Philadelphia: University of Pennsylvania Press, 2000), 176.

29. On the idealization of prosperity and the mercantile cultural ideal, see Stevenson, *Praise and Paradox*, 30–31; on the related demonization of the vagabond, see Craig Dionne, "Fashioning Outlaws, the Early Modern Rogue and Urban Culture," in *Rogues and Early Modern English Culture*, 41.

30. On the historical Richard Whittington, see Caroline M. Barron, "Richard Whittington: The Man behind the Myth," in *Studies in London History Presented to Philip Edmund Jones*, ed. A. E. J. Hollaender and William Kellaway (London: Hodder and Stoughton, 1969), 197–248. Barron hypothesizes that Whittington's benefactions kept his name alive and promoted the legends and ballads about him. Interestingly, Whittington was somewhat anomalous for his time in not aspiring to a gentry model by investing in land; rather, he lent to the Crown and invested in civic improvement. On Whittington's career and the historical practices surrounding the London freedom, see James Robertson, "The Adventures of Dick Whittington and the Social Construction of Elizabethan London," in *Guilds, Society and Economy in London 1450–1800*, ed. Ian Anders Gadd and Patrick Wallis (London: Centre for Metropolitan History, 2002), 51–66. On apprenticeship in London, see Ian Archer, *The Pursuit of Stability* (Cambridge: Cambridge University Press, 1997); and J. P. Ward, *Metropolitan Communities* (Stanford, CA: Stanford University Press, 1997).

31. Quoted in *Samuel Pepys's Penny Merriments*, 55.

32. Whittington was initially appointed to serve out the term of the deceased incumbent and was subsequently elected Lord Mayor three times; there is no evidence of his having had a cat, and Barron, "Richard Whittington," points out that his wealth derived from his career as a mercer, wool exporter, and royal financier.

33. On the discrepancies between visual and printed accounts of such civic pageants emphasizing their elaborate allegories and hierarchical pageantry and various recorded accounts by others, including foreigners and dignitaries, see Malcolm Smuts, "Public Ceremony and Royal Charisma: The English Royal Entry in London, 1485–1642," in *The First Modern Society*, ed. A. L. Beier, David Carradine, and James M. Rosenheim (Cambridge, Cambridge University Press, 1989), 65–93.

34. On the Lord Mayor's pageants, see David M. Bergeron, *English Civic Pageantry 1558–1642* (London: Edward Arnold, 1971); and Jonathan Barry, "Civility and Civic Culture in Early Modern England: The Meaning of Urban Freedom," in *Civil Histories, Essays Presented to Sir Keith Thomas*, ed. Peter Burke, Brian Harrison, and Paul Slack (Oxford: Oxford University Press, 2000), 181–96. On the dressing-up of the city streets and its crowds, see Rhonda Sanford, "Playing in the Street: Civic Pageantry in Early Modern London," *Selected Papers from the West Virginia Shakespeare and Renaissance Association* 25 (2002): 35–50. See also Janette Dillon, *Theatre, Court and City, 1595–1610* (Cambridge: Cambridge University Press, 2000).

35. Jean Howard makes this argument about Eyre's wealth in "Material Shakespeare / Materialist Shakespeare," in *Shakespeare Matters: History, Teaching, Performance*, ed. Lloyd Davis (Newark: University of Delaware Press, 2003). On the historical rather than legendary sources of Whittington's wealth, see note 30.

36. On the difficulties young women faced in the capital, see Merry Wiesner, *Women and Gender in Early Modern Europe* (Cambridge: Cambridge University Press, 1993); and Ann Rosalind Jones, "Maidservants of London, Sisterhoods of Kinship and

Labor," in *Maids, Mistresses, Cousins and Queens*, ed. Susan Frye and Karen Robertson (Oxford: Oxford University Press, 1999), 21–32.

37. Fitz Stephen's panegyric first saw print in the 1603 edition of Stow's *Survay of London*.

38. See Ian Gadd and Alexandra Gillespie, eds., *John Stow (1525–1605) and the Making of the English Past* (London: British Library, 2004).

39. For a recent survey of these arguments, see David Harvey, "Cartographic Identities: Geographical Knowledges under Globalization," in *Spaces of Capital: Toward a Critical Geography* (New York: Routledge, 2001).

40. See Richard Helgerson, "The Land Speaks: Cartography, Chorography and Subversion in Renaissance England," *Representations* 16 (1986): 51–85, also in *Forms of Nationhood* (Chicago: University of Chicago Press, 1992); and the work of J. B. Harley, including "Maps, Knowledge, and Power," in *The Iconography of Landscape*, ed. Denis Cosgrove and Stephen Daniels (Cambridge: Cambridge University Press, 1988), and "Deconstructing the Map," *Cartographica* 26 (1989): 277–312.

41. For a thoughtful critique of topography as "science" and of the problems of geographic representation, see James Duncan and David Ley's introduction to their collection, *Place/Culture/Representation* (London and New York: Routledge, 1993), 1–21.

42. Lawrence Manley, "From Matron to Monster: Tudor-Stuart London and the Languages of Urban Description," in *The Historical Renaissance: New Essays in Tudor and Stuart Literary Culture*, ed. Heather Dubrow and Richard Strier (Chicago: University of Chicago Press, 1988), 351.

43. Though not published until 1572, Braun and Hogenberg's map is usually dated 1560. Though concerned with eighteenth-century taste and the perception of landscape, see John Barrell's "The Public Prospect and the Private View: The Politics of Taste in Eighteenth-Century Britain," in *Projecting the Landscape*, ed. J. C. Eade, *Australia National University Humanities Research Centre Monograph* 4 (1987): 15–35. Barrell argues that the appreciation of landscape was a means of legitimating political authority, since only the man of independent means, released from private interests, could grasp the larger good (15–16).

44. For a review of such representations of London, see Paul Slack, "Perceptions of the Metropolis in Seventeenth-Century England," in *Civil Histories: Essays Presented to Sir Keith Thomas*, ed. Peter Burke, Brian Harrison, and Paul Slack (Oxford: Oxford University Press, 2000), 161–80.

45. On London's increasing dominance of overseas English trade at the expense of provincial ports and towns and the entrepreneurial gentry, see Robert Brenner, *Merchants and Revolution: Commercial Change, Political Conflict, and London's Overseas Traders, 1550–1653* (Princeton, NJ: Princeton University Press, 1993).

46. See Manley, "From Matron to Monster." London was personified not only as a mother but also as a whore as in Thomas Dekker's *Seven Deadly Sins of London* (1606).

47. H. J. Dyos, *Exploring the Urban Past: Essays in Urban History*, ed. David Cannadine and David Reeder (Cambridge: Cambridge University Press, 1982), 191.

48. On London's expansion, see Norman G. Brett-James, ed., *The Growth of Stuart London* (London: George Allen and Unwin, 1935); Beier and Finlay, *London 1500–1700*; and John Schofield, *The Building of London from the Conquest to the Great Fire* (London: British Museum Publications, 1984). On early modern perceptions of

London's growth, both positive and negative, see Slack, "Perceptions." On James's efforts to regulate building and "clean up" London in response to its rapid growth, see Slack's *From Reformation to Improvement: Public Welfare in Early Modern England* (Oxford: Oxford University Press, 1999).

49. J. F. Merritt dubs Howell's *Londinopolis* a *Reader's Digest* of Stow; "The Reshaping of Stow's 'Survey': Munday, Strype and the Protestant City," in Merritt, *Imagining Early Modern London*, 67.

50. On the generic variety of urban description and the shift from personification to the authority of observation, see Lawrence Manley, "From Matron to Monster." Manley is concerned in the main with the characteristic feminine personification of London and modes of writing about the city; I am indebted to his thoughtful essay. An expanded version of the essay also appears in his *Literature and Culture in Early Modern London* (Cambridge: Cambridge University Press, 1995).

51. Steven Mullaney, *The Place of the Stage* (Chicago: University of Chicago Press, 1988), 17. Mullaney describes Stow's survey with the Foucauldian term *archaeology* of London that locates "by means of a quite substantial memory as well as by archives, chronicles, and oral accounts, the traces of a past whose outlines were daily growing more tenuous" (16). On Stow's nostalgia, see also Ian Archer, "The Nostalgia of John Stow," in *The Theatrical City: Culture, Theatre and Politics in London, 1576–1649*, ed. David L. Smith, Richard Strier, and David Bevington (Cambridge: Cambridge University Press, 1995), 17–34; Lawrence Manley's *Literature and Culture in Early Modern London*, 162–67; Patrick Collinson, "John Stow and Nostalgic Antiquarianism," in Merritt, *Imagining Early Modern London*; and Merritt's own essay, "The Reshaping of Stow's 'Survey': Munday, Strype and the Protestant City," 52–88, in which he demonstrates the gradual appropriation and adaptation of Stow by the Protestant mainstream.

52. John Stow, *The Survey of London*, reprinted from the text of 1603, ed. Charles L. Kingsford (Oxford: Clarendon Press, 1908; repr., Oxford: Clarendon Press, 1971), 117. All references are to the 1971 edition.

53. On the influence of method and Ramism on the *Survay's* organization, see Manley, "From Matron to Monster," 353–54.

54. Ibid., 359. Though Manley's claim is justified in the main, Stow does in fact refer to citizens, neighbors, passengers, the youths of the city and their sisters, and pastimes in which "every man" took part. See Stow, *The Survey of London,* ed. Kingsford, 1:95, 98, 101, 104, 126–27.

55. Manley, "From Matron to Monster," 351.

56. Collinson, "John Stow and Nostalgic Antiquarianism," shows that Fitz Stephen is often the source of Stow's nostalgia, not his memories, and argues that Stow's opposition to urban change is due in part to his closet Catholicism.

57. Manley, "From Matron to Monster," 349. Michel Foucault, "Questions on Geography," in *Power/Knowledge*, ed. Colin Gordon (New York: Pantheon, 1980), 69–70.

58. On Stow's social model, see Manley, "From Matron to Monster," 359; on place marketing and the missing poor, see John Rennie Short and Yeong-Hyun Kim, "Urban Crises/Urban Representations: Selling the City in Difficult Times," in *The Entrepreneurial City, Geographies of Politics, Regime and Representation*, ed. Tim Hall and Phil Hubbard (Chichester and New York: Wiley, 1998).

59. See Barrell, "The Public Prospect," 21, on the eighteenth-century panoramic ideal and the view.

60. See Helgerson, "The Land Speaks," and Manley, "From Matron to Monster."

61. On the development of Stow's text, see Merritt, "The Reshaping of Stow's 'Survey.' "

62. Vanessa Harding, "City, Capital, and Metropolis: The Changing Shape of Seventeenth-Century London," in Merritt, *Imagining Early Modern London*, 117.

63. On such manuals and guides for merchants, see P. Jeannin, "Guides de voyages et manuels pour marchands," in *Voyager à la Renaissance, Actes du colloque de Tours 1983*, ed. J. Céard and Jean-Claude Margolin (Paris: Maisonneuve et Larose, 1987). Paul Slack, "Perceptions," attributes *The Post of the World* to Richard Rowlands (Richard Verstegan).

64. See Harvey, "Cartographic Identitites," 227.

65. Donald Lupton, *London and the countrey carbonadoed and quartered into several characters* (1632), Early English Books On Line.

66. On perceptions of London and its suburbs, see Joseph P. Ward, "Imagining the Metropolis in Elizabethan and Stuart London," in *The Country and the City Revisited: England and the Politics of Culture, 1550–1850*, ed. Gerald M. MacLean, Donna Landry, and Joseph P. Ward (Cambridge: Cambridge University Press, 1999), 24–40.

67. On the early guides to Paris, see Maurice Dumolin, "Notes sur les vieux guides de Paris," *Mémoire de la Société de l'histoire de Paris et de l'île de France* 47 (1924): 209–85.

68. Since these additions do not appear in subsequent editions of Corrozet's text, commentators have generally attributed them to the bookseller Pierre Sargent, who brought out the 1543 edition.

69. The Bonfons printing family augmented and reprinted Du Breul; see also Pierre D'avity, *La prevosté de Paris et l'isle de France* (Paris, 1619, 1883); Thomas Platter, *Description de Paris par Thomas Platter le Jeune de Bale* (1599), trans. L. Sieber (Paris, 1896), among others.

70. Du Breul also published a substantially revised edition of Corrozet's *Antiquités* in 1608.

71. James Howell, *Instructions for forreine travell*, ed. Edward Arber for the English Reprint Series (London, 1869).

72. For a wide-ranging and comprehensive survey of the epistemological significance of seeing and its contested role in contemporary theory and intellectual history, see Martin Jay, *Downcast Eyes: The Denigration of Vision in Twentieth-Century French Thought* (Berkeley: University of California Press, 1994).

73. This brief discussion of print culture in London and Paris will be well known to specialists; it is designed simply as an overview for readers who may not be acquainted with both.

74. On the lengths to which the authorities would go to punish the authors and printers of illicit texts, see H. S. Bennett, *English Books and Readers, 1558–1603* (Cambridge: Cambridge University Press, 1965), 81–86; on the difficulties of administering the licensing system, see Watt, *Cheap Print and Popular Piety*, especially 43–50.

75. On literary patronage in England, see John Buxton, *Sir Philip Sidney and the English Renaissance* (London: Macmillan, 1954); Michael Brennan, *Literary Patronage in the English Renaissance: The Pembroke Family* (London: Routledge, 1988); and Rich-

ard Helgerson, *Forms of Nationhood: The Elizabethan Writing of England* (Chicago: University of Chicago Press, 1992).

76. Though Caxton's press was initially located in Westminster outside the City near his elite clientele, as the book trade expanded, it was increasingly centralized in London. Oxford and Cambridge played a role in English book production, particularly after the establishment of the university presses in the 1580s, but London was the center of the English book trade. See *The Cambridge History of the Book in Britain*, vol. 3, *1400–1557*, ed. Lotte Hellinga and J. B. Trapp (Cambridge: Cambridge University Press, 1999).

77. On the variety of written materials that continued to be preserved and circulated in manuscript, see D. F. McKenzie, "Speech-Manuscript-Print," in *New Directions in Textual Studies*, ed. Dave Oliphant and Robin Bradford (Austin: Harry Ransom Humanities Research Center, University of Texas, 1990); Harold Love, *Scribal Publication in Seventeenth-Century England* (Oxford: Clarendon Press, 1993); Peter Beal, *In Praise of Scribes: Manuscripts and Their Makers in Seventeenth-Century England* (Oxford: Oxford University Press, 1998); Margaret J. M. Ezell, *Social Authority and the Advent of Print* (Baltimore: Johns Hopkins University Press, 1999); and David McKitterick, *Print, Manuscript and the Search for Order 1450–1830* (Cambridge: Cambridge University Press, 2003). On Donne, see Arthur Marotti, *Manuscript, Print and the English Renaissance Lyric* (Ithaca, NY: Cornell University Press, 1995); on Sidney, see Henry Woudhuysen, *Sir Philip Sidney and the Circulation of Manuscripts, 1558–1640* (Oxford: Oxford University Press, 1996).

78. See J. W. Saunders, "The Stigma of Print: A Note on the Social Bases of Tudor Poetry," *Essays in Criticism* 1 (1951): 139–64; Steven W. May's reconsideration, "Tudor Aristocrats and the Mythical 'Stigma of Print,'" *Renaissance Papers* (1980): 11–18; and Wendy Wall, *The Imprint of Gender, Authorship and Publication in the English Renaissance* (Ithaca, NY: Cornell University Press, 1993).

79. One well-known example is Ralegh's "The Lie." See Michael Rudick, ed., *The Poems of Sir Walter Ralegh: An Historical Edition* (Tempe, AZ: Renaissance English Text Society, 1999), xlii–xlvii.

80. See Douglas A. Brooks, *From Playhouse to Printing House: Drama and Authorship in Early Modern England* (Cambridge: Cambridge University Press, 2000).

81. On quarto publication, see Peter W. M. Blayney, "The Publication of Playbooks," in *The New History of Early English Drama*, ed. John D. Cox and David Scott Kastan (New York: Columbia University Press, 1997); and Paul Werstine, "Narratives about Printed Shakespeare Texts: 'Foul Papers' and 'Bad Quartos,'" in *Shakespeare: An Anthology of Criticism and Theory 1945–2000*, ed. Russ McDonald (Oxford: Blackwell, 2004), 296–317.

82. Anonymous, from *Wits Recreations* (London, 1640), sig. G3ᵛ, quoted in David Scott Kastan, "Print, Literary Culture and the Book Trade," in *The Cambridge History of the Book in Britain*, 3:115.

83. See Peter W. M. Blayney, *The First Folio of Shakespeare* (Washington, D.C.: Folger Library Publications, 1991); and David Scott Kastan, *Shakespeare and the Book* (Cambridge: Cambridge University Press, 2001).

84. On the pamphlets of the Fronde, see Carrier, *Les mazarinades*; and Henri-Jean Martin, *Livre, pouvoirs et société à Paris au XVIIᵉ siècle* (1598–1701), 2 vols. (Geneva: Droz, 1969; repr., Geneva: Droz, 1984).

85. On the *bibliothèque bleue*, see Geneviève Bollème, *La bibliothèque bleue: Littérature populaire en France du XVIIe au XIXe* (Paris: Julliard, 1971); Robert Mandrou, *De la culture populaire au XVIIe et XVIIIe siècles: La bibliothèque bleue de Troyes* (Paris: Stock, 1964); and Roger Chartier, *The Cultural Uses of Print in Early Modern France*, trans. Lydia C. Cochrane (Princeton, NJ: Princeton University Press, 1987).

86. On printing and the French book trade, see Lucien Febvre and Henri-Jean Martin, *L'apparition du livre* (Paris: Albin-Michel, 1958; repr., Paris: Albin-Michel, 1971), and the several volumes of *Histoire de l'édition française*, ed. Roger Chartier (Paris: Promodis, 1982–85).

87. On manuscript and print in France, see Jeanne Veyrin-Forrer, *Le lettre et le texte* (Paris: École normale supérieure de jeunes filles, 1987).

88. I will have more to say about the gendering of travel in this passage in chapter 6.

89. See John Stoye, *English Travellers Abroad 1604–1667* (London, 1952; reprinted and revised, New Haven, CT: Yale University Press, 1989). For a wide-ranging and compendious study of travel literature, see E. G. Cox, *A Guide to the Literature of Travel, Including Voyages, Geographical Descriptions, Adventures, Shipwrecks and Expeditions*, 3 vols. (Seattle: University of Washington, 1935–49).

90. On the importance of travel to the education of the French aristocracy, see Jonathan Dewald, *Aristocratic Experience and the Origins of Modern Culture, France, 1570–1715* (Berkeley: University of California Press, 1993), from whom this quotation from 1637 is taken.

91. On immigrants, see Laura Hunt Yungblut, *Strangers Settled Here amongst Us: Policies, Perceptions and the Presence of Aliens in Elizabethan England* (London and New York: Routledge, 1996).

92. Chantelou, *Journal du voyage du Cavalier Bernin en France*, 100; Blunt, *Diary of the Cavaliere Bernini's Visit to France*, 94.

CHAPTER TWO
TOWARD A TOPOGRAPHIC IMAGINARY

1. On the development of Paris, particularly useful are Jean-Pierre Babelon, *Paris au XVIe siècle: Nouvelle histoire de Paris* (Paris: Hachette, 1986); René Pillorget, *Paris sous les premiers Bourbons: Nouvelle histoire de Paris* (Paris: Hachette, 1988); Hilary Ballon, *The Paris of Henry IV* (Cambridge, MA: MIT Press, 1991); and Roger Chartier, "Power, Space and Investments in Paris," in *Edo and Paris*, ed. James L. McLain, John M. Merriman, and Ugawa Kaoru (Ithaca, NY: Cornell University Press, 1994), 132–52.

2. Quoted in Jacques-Thomas de Castelnau, *Le Paris de Louis XIII, 1610–1643* (Paris: Hachette, 1928).

3. Prompted by royal and aristocratic patronage, the Louvre, the Tuileries, and many of the new *hôtels particuliers* being built in Paris in the course of the seventeenth century were frequently represented in contemporary engraving. Though it extends beyond the limits of this study and into the eighteenth century, the 1997 exhibit "Paris et les parisiennes au temps du Roi-Soleil" at the Musée Carnavalet documents pictorially the urbanization of early modern Paris.

4. Germain Brice, *A New Description of Paris* (London: Henry Bonwicke, 1987), H10ᵛ–H11ʳ.

5. Jacques Du Breul, *Le Théâtre des antiquitez de Paris* (Paris, 1612), Hhiiiiᵛ.

6. On the rationalization and organization of urban space and capital accumulation, see David Harvey, *The Condition of Postmodernity: An Enquiry into the Origins of Cultural Change* (London: Blackwell, 1989), pt. 3.

7. On the problems of traffic in seventeenth-century Paris, see de Castelnau, *Le Paris de Louis XIII.*

8. Pierre de l'Estoile, *Mémoires-journaux* (Paris: Librairie des Bibliophiles, 1880), 8:83–84.

9. Du Breul reports that Henry "employe les plus ingenieuses & hardie inventions qui e sont offertes," Hhiiiiʳ.

10. Malherbe to Peiresc, quoted in François Boucher, *Le pont Neuf* (Paris: Le Goupy, 1925–26), 126.

11. On the debate, see Laure Beaumont-Maillet, *L'eau à Paris* (Milan: Hazan, 1991). On water in Paris, see Daniel Roche, "Le temps de l'eau rare du moyen-âge à l'époque moderne," *Annales ESC* 39 (1984): 383–99; and J.-P. Goubert, *The Conquest of Water* (Princeton, NJ: Princeton University Press, 1989).

12. On clocks, time, and urban life, see Georg Simmel, "The Metropolis and Mental Life," in *The Sociology of Georg Simmel*, ed. Kurt Wolff, trans. H. H. Gerth with C. Wright Mills (New York: Macmillan, 1950); and Alfred W. Crosby, *The Measure of Reality, Quantification and Western Society 1250–1600* (Cambridge: Cambridge University Press, 1997).

13. Brice, *A New Description of Paris*, H11ᵛ.

14. See Frédéric Lachèvre, *Les recueils collectifs de poésies libres et satiriques publiés depuis 1600 jusqu'à la mort de Théophile* (Geneva: Slatkine, 1968); and Alain Mercier, *La littérature facétieuse sous Louis XIII* (Geneva: Droz, 1991).

15. See the nineteenth-century collection *Oeuvres complètes de Tabarin*, 2 vols., ed. Gustave Aventin (Paris: Jannet, 1858); Georges Mongrédien, *Bibliographie Tabarinique* (Chartres: Durand, 1929); Michel Selimonte, *Le Pont Neuf et ses charlatans* (Paris: Plasma, 1980); and, more recently, Jonathan Marks, "The Charlatans of the Pont-Neuf," *Theatre Journal International* 23 (1998): 133–41. Mongrédien points out that though this literature pretends to be oral and popular, for the most part such claims are "purement fictif" (269).

16. *Seconde harangue du Mireilifique crocheteur de Paris, assis sur la cloche de la Samaritaine du Pont Neuf, à ses specatateurs* (1611).

17. *Lettre du Roy Henry IV en Bronze, du Pont neuf, a son fils Louis XIII de la Place Royale* (Paris, 1649).

18. Quoted in Hubert Carrier, *Les mazarinades: La conquête de l'opinion* (Geneva: Droz, 1989), 2:177. On the Pont Neuf as the library of Paris, see also the eighteenth-century antiquarian Henri Sauval, *Histoire et recherches des antiquités de la ville de Paris* (Geneva: Minkoff, 1973), 237; and C. Moreau, *Bibliographie des mazarinades* (Paris: Renouard, 1851).

19. Christian Jouhaud, *Mazarinades: La Fronde des Mots* (Paris: Aubier, 1985), 238.

20. J. P. Seguin, *L'information en France avant le périodique: 517 canards imprimés entre 1529 et 1631* (Paris: Maisonneuve et Larose, 1964), 254.

21. Henri-Jean Martin, *Livre, pouvoirs et société à Paris au XVIIe siècle* (Geneva: Droz, 1969).

22. See particularly Hubert Carrier, *La presse de la Fronde (1648–1653)* and *Les mazarinades: La conquête de l'opinion*. See also the pamphlet *Requête des marchands-libraires du Pont Neuf,* which represents "Ces pauures gens chaque matin / Sur l'espoir d'un petit butin / Avecque toute[s] leurs familles, / Garçons, apprentifs, femmes, filles, / Chargez leurs cols et plein leurs bras."

23. On cognitive mapping and city space, see Kevin Lynch, *The Image of the City* (Cambridge, MA: MIT Press, 1960; repr., Cambridge, MA: MIT Press, 1986).

24. Simmel, "The Metropolis and Mental Life." On the progressive polarization of aristocratic and bourgeois spheres as a result of urbanization, see Jouhaud, *Mazarinades*, 241–44.

25. Jürgen Habermas, *The Structural Transformation of the Public Sphere: An Inquiry into a Category of Bourgeois Society*, trans. Thomas Berger with Frederick Lawrence (Cambridge, MA: MIT Press, 1989).

26. Fredric Jameson, *Postmodernism, or the Cultural Logic of Late Capitalism* (London: Verso, 1991).

27. See, for example, the collection edited by Marc Fumaroli and Jean Mesnard, *Critique et création littéraires en France au XVIIe siècle* (Paris: CNRS, 1977); Gordon Pocock, *Boileau and the Nature of Neo-classisicm* (Cambridge: Cambridge University Press, 1980); Bernard Bray, "Le classicisme de Boileau: Les personnages et leur fonction poétique dans les satires," *Dix-septième Siècle* 143 (1984): 107–18.

28. Critics have recently begun to consider Boileau's presentation of Paris in Satire VI as "farce" or "absurde avant la lettre," but not in terms of contemporary Paris. See Pocock, *Boileau and the Nature of Neo-classicism*, and Simone Ackerman, "Les satires de Boileau: Un théâtre de l'absurde avant la lettre," in *Ordre et contestation au temps des classiques*, ed. Roger Duchêne and Pierre Ronzeaud (Paris: Papers on French Seventeenth-Century Literature, 1992); on Boileau's presentation of Paris, see Robert R. Corum, "Paris as Barrier: Boileau's Satire VI," *Papers on Seventeenth-Century French Literature* 19, no. 17 (1982): 627–39.

29. "La ville de Paris en vers burlesques," in *Paris ridicule et burlesque au dix-septième siècle*, ed. P. L. Jacob (Paris: Adolphe Delahays, 1859). There were many editions as well as other versions of this poem, which even seems to have inspired a subgenre, for example, "La ville de Lyon en vers burlesque" (Lyon, 1683).

30. Nicolas Boileau, *Oeuvres*, ed. G. Mongrédien (Paris: Garnier, 1961).

31. Peter Stallybrass, "Shakespeare, the Individual, and the Text," in *Cultural Studies*, ed. Larry Grossberg, Cary Nelson, and Paula Treichler (New York and London: Routledge, 1992), 593–612; Lawrence Manley, *Literature and Culture in Early Modern London* (Cambridge: Cambridge University Press, 1995), 216.

32. See particularly Stuart Hall, "The Toad in the Garden: Thatcherism among the Terrorists," in *Marxism and the Interpretation of Cultures*, ed. Cary Nelson and Lawrence Grossberg (Urbana: University of Illinois Press, 1988), 35–57.

33. See Ernest Jones, *The Life and Work of Sigmund Freud* (New York: Basic Books, 1953), vol. 1, chap. 10.

34. Ibid., 119.

35. The complete letters of Martha Bernays from which Jones quotes remain closed subject to strict covenants; a few have appeared piecemeal, and a full edition is now

under way (personal communication, Harold Blum, M.D., executive director, the Sigmund Freud Archives, Inc.). Whether Jones reports the letters reliably must await the appearance of this edition.

36. Jones, *The Life and Work of Sigmund Freud,* 1:118.

37. On topophobias, see Anthony Vidler, "Psychopathologies of Modern Space: Metropolitan Fear from Agoraphobia to Estrangement," in *Rediscovering History,* ed. Michael J. Roth (Stanford, CA: Stanford University Press, 1994); on topolatry, see Yi Hu Tuan, *Topophilia: A Study of Environmental Perception, Attitudes and Values* (Englewood Cliffs, NJ: Prentice Hall, 1974). For a different reading of Freud's relation to urban life, see Jonathan Crary's epilogue, "1907: Spellbound in Rome," in *Suspensions of Perception, Attention, Spectacle, and Modern Culture* (Cambridge, MA: MIT Press, 2000).

38. On Shakespeare's putative indictment of rebellion, see E. M. W. Tillyard, *The Elizabethan World Picture* (Harmondsworth: Penguin, 1963); and Richard Wilson, "'A Mingled Yarn': Shakespeare and the Cloth Workers," *Literature and History* 12 (1986): 168; see also Stephen Greenblatt in "Murdering Peasants: Status, Genre and the Representation of Rebellion," *Representations* 1 (1983): 23; on the other side, see Michael Hattaway, "Rebellion, Class Consciousness, and Shakespeare's *2 Henry VI,*" *Cahiers Elisabéthains* 33 (1988): 13–22; Annabel Patterson, *Shakespeare and the Popular Voice* (Oxford: Basil Blackwell, 1989), chap. 2; and Thomas Cartelli, in "Jack Cade in the Garden: Class Consciousness and Class Conflict in *2 Henry VI,*" in *Enclosure Acts: Sexuality, Property, and Culture in Early Modern England,* ed. Richard Burt and John Michael Archer (Ithaca, NY: Cornell University Press, 1994), 48–67; and Ellen C. Caldwell's thoughtful and balanced argument in "Jack Cade and Shakespeare's *Henry VI, 2,*" *Studies in Philology* 92 (1995): 18–79.

39. William Carroll, *Fat King, Lean Beggar: Representations of Poverty in the Age of Shakespeare* (Ithaca, NY: Cornell University Press, 1996), 156.

40. See, among others, Charles Hobday, "Clouted Shoon and Leather Aprons: Shakespeare and the Egalitarian Tradition," *Renaissance and Early Modern Studies* 23 (1979): 63–78.

41. Roger B. Manning, *Village Revolts: Social Protest and Popular Disturbances in England, 1509–1640* (Oxford: Oxford University Press, 1988), 187. On Cade and the urban context, see also Carroll, *Fat King, Lean Beggar,* 140–45.

42. Manning, *Village Revolts,* 187.

43. Shakespeare, *The Second Part of King Henry VI,* ed. Andrew Cairncross (Cambridge, MA: Harvard University Press, 1957; repr., Cambridge, MA: Harvard University Press, 1962), 4.2.61–66. All references in the text are to this edition.

44. I am grateful to Vanessa Harding for her advice about the dating of London place-names.

45. As David Scott Kastan points out in "Print, Literary Culture and the Book Trade," in *The Cambridge History of Early Modern English Literature,* ed. David Loewenstein and Janel Mueller (Cambridge: Cambridge University Press, 2002), "Caxton would not in fact set up the first printing press in England until 1476, some twenty-six years after the encounter the play represents, and still another twenty years would pass before John Tate would establish the first paper mill on English soil" (81). For an important perspective on literacy and rebellion, see Steven Justice, *Writing and Rebellion: England in 1381* (Berkeley: University of California Press, 1994).

46. See Caldwell, "Jack Cade and Shakespeare's *Henry VI, 2*," 59. Cade's attack seeks to arrest "the recording of arrears and the registration of property so that it could be controlled and alienated by the state and its (in this case often corrupt) agents" (59).

47. Gordon Home, *Old London Bridge* (London: John Lane, 1931), 191. On royal entries and their impact on popular opinion in Tudor and Stuart England, see Malcolm Smuts, "Public Ceremony and Royal Charisma: The English Royal Entry in London, 1485–1642," in *The First Modern Society*, ed. A. L. Beier, David Carradine, and James M. Rosenheim (Cambridge: Cambridge University Press, 1989), 65–93.

48. From a letter of the Spanish ambassador, Bernardino de Mendoza, in the *Calendar of Letters and State Papers, Elizabeth, 1568–1579*, ed. Martin A. S. Hume (London: Eyre and Spottiswoode, 1894), 2:641.

49. Vanessa Harding, "Metropolitan Crossings" and "Maintaining London Bridge, c. 1380–1550: Costs and Resources," in *I Ponti: Forma e costruzione dall'antico all'architettura del ferro*, ed. Donatella Calabi and Claudia Conforti (Milan: Documenti di architettura, 2001), 2.

50. On early modern London, see, among others, Valerie Pearl, *London and the Outbreak of the Puritan Revolution* (London: Oxford University Press, 1961), as well as her many articles on London; Jeremy Boulton, *Neighborhood and Society: A London Suburb in the Seventeenth Century* (Cambridge: Cambridge University Press, 1987); Steve Rappaport, *Worlds within Worlds* (Cambridge: Cambridge University Press, 1989); Ian Archer, *The Pursuit of Stability: Social Relations in Elizabethan London* (Cambridge: Cambridge University Press, 1991); and, most recently, Joseph P. Ward, *Metropolitan Communities: Trade Guilds, Identity, and Change in Early Modern London* (Stanford, CA: Stanford University Press, 1997).

51. See Steven Mullaney, *The Place of the Stage* (Chicago: University of Chicago Press, 1988); and David J. Johnson, *Southwark and the City* (London: Oxford University Press, 1969).

52. See Harding, "Metropolitan Crossings," 1–12.

53. Water mills were installed under the bridge's northernmost arch in 1581 but seem to have functioned only at certain tides. In 1613, Sir Hugh Middleton established the New River Company that brought water by means of canals from Ware and Hertfordshire. It provided water and used a pump and tower built to provide sufficient pressure to circulate water to nearby houses. See Craig Spence, *London in the 1690s: A Social Atlas* (London: Centre for Metropolitan History, 2000), 26–28. See also Mark S. R. Jenner, "From Conduit Community to Commercial Network: Water in London 1500–1720," in *Londinopolis: Essays in the Cultural and Social History of Early Modern London*, ed. Paul Griffiths and Mark S. R. Jenner (Manchester, UK: Manchester University Press, 2000), 250–72.

54. J. G. White, *A Short History of London Bridge* (London: privately printed, 1900).

55. Sir John Froissart, *Chronicles of England, France, Spain and the Adjoining Countries*, trans. Thomas Johnes (London: Henry G. Bohn, 1862), vol. 2, 695.

56. Frederic Gerchow, "Diary of the Journey of Philip Juilius, Duke of Stettin-Pomerania, through England in the Year 1602," ed. Gottfried von Bülow, *Transactions of the Royal Historical Society*, n.s., 6 (1892): 59. See also Peter Jackson, *London Bridge* (London: Cassell, 1971).

57. Quoted in de Certeau, *Practice of Everyday Life*, 97.

58. Stephen Anderson and Edward Keenan, "Deixis," in *Grammatical Categories and the Lexicon*, vol. 3 of *Language Typology and Syntactic Description*, ed. Timothy Shopen (Cambridge: Cambridge University Press, 1985), 1.

CHAPTER THREE
WALKING CAPITALS

1. See particularly Michèle Venard, *La foire entre en scène* (Paris: Librairie théâtrale, 1985); for literature about or performed at the fair, see the eighteenth-century collection *Le théâtre de la Foire* (Paris, 1737); Florent Carton Dancourt, *La foire Saint-Germain* (1696), *Société des textes français modernes*, ed. André Blanc (Paris: Librairie Nizet, 1985); Paul Scarron's "La foire Saint-Germain en vers burlesques," and François Colletet, "Le tracas de Paris," which purports to be a continuation of "La ville de Paris en vers burlesques" set at the fair.

2. John Taylor, "Bartholomew Faire," in *Old Book Collector's Miscellany*, ed. Charles Hindley (London, 1641). On the mix of persons in Paul's Walk, see Dekker's *A Guls Horne-booke*: "For at one time, in one and the same ranke, yea, foote by foot, and elbow by elbow, shall you see walking, the Knight, the Gull, the Gallant, the Upstart, the Gentleman, the Clown, the Captaine, the Appel-squire, the Lawyer, the Usurer, the Cittizen, the Bankrout, the Scholler, the Begger, the Doctor, the Ideot, the Ruffian, the Cheater, the Puritan, the Cut-throat, the Hye-men, the Low-men, the True-man, and the Thiefe: of all trades and professions, of all Countreyes some; quoted in John Twyning, *London Dispossessed: Literature and Social Space in the Early Modern City* (New York: St. Martin's Press, 1998), 124.

3. On London, see Laura Williams, " 'To recreate and refresh their dulled spirites in the sweet and wholesome ayre': Green Space and the Growth of the City," in *Imagining Early Modern London: Perceptions and Portrayals of the City from Stow to Strype 1598–1720*, ed. J. F. Merritt (Cambridge: Cambridge University Press, 2001), 185–213.

4. On walking and urban experience, see Deborah Nord, *Walking the Victorian Streets* (Ithaca, NY: Cornell University Press, 1995).

5. On the gaze that seeks to hold objects of the urban environment in a particular relation to the subject's desires as opposed to the glance that picks up what the gaze excludes and "restores the primacy of the ever-changing surface over the illusion of depth," see Christopher Prendergast, "Framing the City: Two Parisian Windows," in *City Images: Perspectives from Literature, Philosophy, and Film*, ed. Mary Ann Caws (New York: Gordon and Breach, 1991), 191.

6. R. C. Bald, *John Donne: A Life* (Oxford: Clarendon Press, 1970); see also Arthur Marotti, *John Donne, Coterie Poet* (Madison: University of Wisconsin Press, 1986).

7. See Vanessa Harding, "City, Capital, and Metropolis: The Changing Shape of Seventeenth-Century London," in Merritt, *Imagining Early Modern London*, 131.

8. On the inns, see Bald, *John Donne*; Phillip Finklepearl, *John Marston of the Middle Temple: An Elizabethan Dramatist in His Social Setting* (Cambridge, MA: Harvard University Press, 1969); and Wilfred Prest, *The Inns of Court under Elizabeth I and the Early Stuarts 1590–1640* (London: Longmans, 1972).

9. See Bald, *John Donne*; and Ronald J. Corthell, ' "Coscus onely breeds my just offence': A Note on Donne's 'Satire II' and the Inns of Court," *John Donne Journal* 6 (1987): 25–31. In reading Satyre I, J. B. Leishman wonders whether the poem presents the revolt of University and Inns of Court men against what was fashionable at court; *The Monarch of Wit* (London: Hutchinson, 1962), 110.

10. All references are to W. Milgate's edition, *The Satires, Epigrams and Verse Letters* (Oxford: Clarendon Press, 1967).

11. Bald remarks that members' rooms "were small cells."

12. On tobacco in early modern London, see Jeffrey Knapp, *An Empire Nowhere: England, America, and Literature from Utopia to The Tempest* (Berkeley: University of California Press, 1992), 134–74.

13. Allusions in the drama are too numerous to be enumerated; on this practice and contemporary examples, see my *Fashioning Femininity and English Renaissance Drama* (Chicago: University of Chicago Press, 1991), 122.

14. See, among others, John R. Lauritsen, "Donne's Satyres: The Drama of Self-Discovery," *Studies in English Literature* 16 (1976): 120; and John T. Shawcross, " 'All Attest His Writs Canonical': The Texts, Meaning and Evaluation of Donne's Satires," in *Just So Much Honor*, ed. Peter Amadeus Fiore (University Park: Pennsylvania State University Press, 1972). Thomas Doherty claims the humorist is perhaps "an aspect of the speaker's divided personality" and the satire an example of "Donnean 'dialogue of one' "; *John Donne, Undone* (London: Methuen, 1986), 111.

15. Y. Shikany Eddy and Daniel P. Jaeckle, "Donne's 'Satyre I': The Influence of Persius's 'Satire III,' " *Studies in English Literature* 21 (1981): 111.

16. Milgate, *The Satires, Epigrams and Verse Letters*, xviii.

17. On the moral discourse surrounding luxury goods, see Joan Thirsk, *Economic Policy and Projects: Economic Thought and Ideology* (Oxford: Oxford University Press, 1978); and Lorna Hutson, *Thomas Nashe in Context* (Oxford: Clarendon Press, 1989). I am grateful to Joel Altman for suggesting the relevance of the antiluxury discourse to Donne's satire.

18. Lawrence Manley, *Literature and Culture in Early Modern London* (Cambridge: Cambridge University Press, 1995), 379.

19. M. Thomas Hester, *Kinde Pitty and Brave Scorn: John Donne's Satyres* (Durham, NC: Duke University Press, 1982), 21; and Manley, *Literature and Culture in Early Modern London*, 397.

20. Manley, *Literature and Culture in Early Modern London*, 379.

21. Manley points out in passing that the satirist's companion is "a mirror of the speaker" and cites Donne's humorist as a prime example (ibid., 379).

22. "Changeling" appears in four manuscripts; Milgate gives "fondling" instead on the authority of what he terms "the reading of Donne's final version" (117).

23. John Donne, *Devotions* (Ann Arbor: University of Michigan Press, 1978), xxxiv.

24. Fredric Jameson, *Postmodernism, or, the Cultural Logic of Late Capitalism* (Durham, NC: Duke University Press, 1992), 359. On the impact of urbanization on populations, see Kingsley Davis, "The Urbanization of the Human Population," which first appeared in *Scientific American* (1956), reprinted in *The City Reader*, ed. Richard T. LeGates and Frederic Stout (London and New York: Routledge, 1996), 2–11.

25. Frances Ferguson, "Malthus, Godwin, Wordsworth, and the Spirit of Solitude," in *Literature and the Body*, ed. Elaine Scarry (Baltimore: Johns Hopkins University Press, 1988), 106.

26. On the breakdown of distinction and increasing availability of *civilité*, see Norbert Elias, *The Civilizing Process*, trans. Edmund Jephcott (New York: Pantheon, 1978).

27. Peter Stallybrass, "Shakespeare, the Individual, and the Text," in *Cultural Studies*, ed. Lawrence Grossberg, Cary Nelson, and Paula Treichler (New York and London: Routledge, 1992), 593.

28. See Betty Travitsky, " 'The Wyll and Testament' of Isabella Whitney," *ELR* 10 (1980): 76–94.

29. See Laura Gowing, " 'The freedom of the streets': Women and Social Space, 1560–1640," in *Londinopolis: Essays in the Cultural and Social History of Early Modern London*, ed. Paul Griffiths and Mark S. R. Jenner (Manchester, UK: Manchester University Press, 2000), 138, on the extensive circuits around the city demanded by servants' daily work.

30. Ibid., 130.

31. See Ann Rosalind Jones, "Maidservants of London, Sisterhoods of Kinship and Labor," in *Maids and Mistresses, Cousins and Queens*, ed. Susan Frye and Karen Robertson (Oxford: Oxford University Press, 1999), 21–32. On the irony of the impoverished speaker bequeathing goods throughout the city, see Wendy Wall, "Isabella Whitney and the Female Legacy," *English Literary History* 58 (1991): 35–62.

32. See Ann Rosalind Jones, "Apostrophes to Cities: Urban Rhetorics in Isabella Whitney and Moderata Fonte," in *Attending to Early Modern Women*, ed. Susan D. Amussen and Adele Seeff (Newark: University of Delaware Press, 1998), 159.

33. Lawrence Manley, ed., *London in the Age of Shakespeare: An Anthology* (University Park: Pennsylvania State University Press, 1986), 51. It is hard to imagine how this poem of loss and desire could be characterized as a "shopping list."

34. Jones, "Apostrophes to Cities," 160.

35. On the discrepancies between Dick's story and success in early modern London, see James Robertson, "The Adventures of Dick Whittington and the Social Construction of Elizabethan London," in *Guilds, Society and Economy in London 1450–1800*, ed. Ian Anders Gadd and Patrick Wallis (London: Centre for Metropolitan History, 2002), 51–66.

36. See Jones, "Maidservants of London, Sisterhoods of Kinship and Labor."

37. Though it addresses a somewhat later period, Robert Shoemaker's essay "Gendered Spaces: Patterns of Mobility and Perceptions of London's Geography, 1660–1750" nevertheless provides a useful perspective in *Imagining Early Modern London*, 144–66.

38. See Susan Hanson and Geraldine Pratt, *Gender, Work and Space* (New York: Routledge, 1995), 19.

39. On the development of the street as "a public space for the flow of traffic," see Wolfgang Schivelbusch, "The Policing of Street Lighting," in *Everyday Life*, ed. Alice Kaplan and Kristin Ross, a special issue of *Yale French Studies* 73 (1987); see also Jean Favier, *Paris, deux mille ans d'histoire* (Paris: Fayard, 1997), 631–38. On early attempts to regulate the flow of traffic in London, see Craig Spence, *London in the 1690s: A Social Atlas* (London: Centre for Metropolitan History, 2000), 32; and Chris R. Kyle,

"Parliament and the Politics of Carting in Early Stuart London," *London Journal* 27 (2002): 1–11. On the rise of hackney coaches, see Mark S. R. Jenner, "Circulation and Disorder: London Streets and Hackney Coaches, c. 1640–c.1740," in *The Streets of London: From the Great Fire to the Great Stink*, ed. Tim Hitchcock and Heather Shore (London: Rivers Oram Press, 2003), 40–53.

40. Joan Parkes, *Travel in England in the Seventeenth Century* (Oxford: Oxford University Press, 1925), 66.

41. For these statistics and stories of bankruptcy and ruin to make a figure in a carriage or coach, see *Advis aux bourgeois de Paris, sur la réformation des carrosses* (n.d.).

42. *A View of Paris, and Places adjoining with an Account of the Court of France . . .* (London: 1701), B4ʳ.

43. Henry Peacham, *Coach and Sedan, Pleasantly Disputing for Place and Precedence* (London, 1636), E1ʳ. On "promiscuous sociability," see Gillian Swanson, " 'Drunk with the Glitter': Consuming Spaces and Sexual Geographies," in *Postmodern Cities and Spaces*, ed. Sophie Watson and Katherine Gibson (Oxford and Cambridge, MA: Blackwell, 1995), 82). Though for the period immediately following the parameters of this study, see Susan Whyman, *Sociability and Power in Late-Stuart England: The Cultural World of the Verneys, 1660–1720* (Oxford: Oxford University Press, 1999), chap. 4, on coaches as a central feature of sociability among the elite.

44. Quoted in Manley, *Literature and Culture in Early Modern London*, 507.

45. *Les lois de la galanterie*, in Roger Duchêne, *Les Précieuses ou comment l'esprit vint aux femmes* (Paris: Fayard, 2001), 314.

46. Quoted in Andrew Gurr, *Playgoing in Shakespeare's London*, 2nd ed. (Cambridge: Cambridge University Press, 1996), 36. Nehemiah Wallington's diary records the dangers posed by coaches in the narrow London streets; see Paul S. Seaver, *Wallington's World: A Puritan Artisan in Seventeenth-Century London* (Stanford, CA: Stanford University Press, 1985), 65.

47. Quoted in Parkes, *Travel in England in the Seventeenth Century*, 67.

48. Collected in John Gutch, *Collectanea curiosa; or miscellaneous tracts, relating to the history and antiquities of England* (1781), 1:222.

49. In her essay " 'Drunk with the Glitter,' " Gillian Swanson argues that new modes of encountering objects—what she terms "modern forms of perception"—were produced by the wandering of the *flâneur* and by new forms of mobility characteristic of the nineteenth-century city (Swanson, " 'Drunk with Glitter,' " 80–98).

50. For this characterization of London, see the extended title of James Howell's *Londinopolis; an Historicall Discourse or Perlustration of the City of London, the Imperial Chamber, and chief Emporium of Great Britain . . .* (London, 1657).

CHAPTER FOUR
"Filth, Stench, Noise"

1. Algernon Charles Swinburne, *A Study of Ben Jonson*, ed. Howard B. Norland (1889; repr., Lincoln: University of Nebraska Press, 1993), 95. An exception is Andrew McRae's excellent essay " 'On the Famous Voyage': Ben Jonson and Civic Space," *Early Modern Studies* 8, special issue 3 (1998): 1–31, which quotes Swinburne and contextualizes Jonson's poem "within the physical and cultural environment of early

modern London." See also Katherine Duncan-Jones, "City Limits: Nashe's *Choise of Valentines* and Jonson's *Famous Voyage*," *Review of English Studies* 56 (2005): 247–62.

2. Though see Ivan Illich, *H₂O and the Waters of Forgetfulness* (London: Marion Boyars, 1986); the pioneering work of French historians Alain Corbin and Robert Mandrou; and most recently in England the work of Mark S. R. Jenner, cited below. On smoke pollution in London, with evidence predominantly from the late seventeenth century, see Jenner, "The Politics of London Air: John Evelyn's *Fumifugium* and the Restoration," *Historical Journal* 38 (1995): 535–51.

3. See Dietmar Jazbinsek, "The Metropolis and the Mental Life of Georg Simmel: On the History of an Antipathy," *Journal of Urban History* 30 (2003): 107.

4. Ibid., 108.

5. *Exploring the Urban Past: Essays in Urban History by H. J. Dyos*, ed. David Cannadine and David Reeder (Cambridge: Cambridge University Press, 1982), 69.

6. It would, perhaps, be worthwhile to investigate the possibility of such physical remains, the Paris sewers, for example, or in archaeological explorations of garbage, and so forth. My argument is concerned with how sensory phenomena are evoked textually.

7. Alain Corbin, *The Foul and the Fragrant: Odor and the French Social Imagination* (Cambridge, MA: Harvard University Press, 1986).

8. Mark S. J. Jenner, "Civilization and Deodorization? Smell in Early Modern English Culture," in *Civil Histories: Essays Presented to Sir Keith Thomas*, ed. Peter Burke, Brian Harrison, and Paul Slack (Oxford: Oxford University Press, 2000), 128. See also his "Early Modern Conceptions of 'Cleanliness' and 'Dirt' as Reflected in the Environmental Legislation of London, c. 1530–c.1700" (Ph.D. thesis, Oxford University, 1992).

9. Quoted in Corbin, *The Foul and the Fragrant*, 58. Jenner provides an amusing counterexample in the account of two London apprentices who flee to Paris during the English civil war. One relieves himself in the room of the inn in which he is staying and prompts his shocked landlord to complain bitterly that he "did anoy his howse & would bring the plague" (131).

10. On parks and gardens as "playgrounds for the wealthy, idle and dissolute [which] can simultaneously embody what they are imagined to counter," see Laura Williams, " 'To recreate and refresh their dulled spirites in the sweet and wholesome ayre': Green Space and the Growth of the City," in *Imagining Early Modern London: Perceptions and Portrayals of the City from Stow to Strype 1598–1720*, ed. J. F. Merritt (Cambridge: Cambridge University Press, 2001), 211.

11. On the use of fields and green space for sexual encounters by the nonelite, see Laura Gowing, " 'The freedom of the streets': Women and Social Space, 1560–1640," in *Londinopolis: Essays in the Cultural and Social History of Early Modern London*, ed. Paul Griffiths and Mark S. R. Jenner (Manchester, UK: Manchester University Press, 2000), 144.

12. *Les lois de la galanterie*, in Roger Duchêne, *Les précieuses ou comment l'esprit vint aux femmes* (Paris: Fayard, 2001), 314.

13. Antoine Furetière, *Le roman bourgeois*, ed. Marine Roy-Garibal (Paris: Flammarion, 2001), 73. All references are to this edition.

14. Ibid., 102.

15. On changing aristocratic and bourgeois codes of *civilité*, and particularly bodily codes, see Norbert Elias, *The Civilizing Process*, trans. Edmund Jephcott (New York: Pantheon, 1978).

16. *Récit de Fr. Greg. d'Ierni*, quoted in Henri-Jean Martin, *Livre, pouvoirs et société à Paris au XVIIᵉ 1598–1701* (Geneva: Droz, 1969), 34.

17. On the use of aromatics to counter stench, see Jenner, "Civilization and Deodorization," 133.

18. See Edward Chaney, *The Evolution of the Grand Tour* (London: Frank Cass, 1998).

19. James Howell, *Instructions for forreine travell*, ed. Edward Arber for the English Reprint Series (London: 1869).

20. There is considerable debate about the time of composition of Howell's letters. Some scholars claim Howell composed them for publication while in prison long after his travels.

21. James Howell, *Epistolæ Ho-Elianæ: The familiar letters of James Howell*, ed. Joseph Jacobs (London: David Nutt, 1892), book 1 (xx), 42. All references are to this edition.

22. From the diary of Orazio Busino, chaplain to the Venetian ambassador Pietro Contarini (1617–18), in *The Journals of Two Travelers in Elizabethan and Early Stuart England* (London: Caliban Books, 1995), 114–16.

23. Robert Chamberlain, *A Newe booke of Mistakes* (1637), quoted in Lawrence Manley, ed. *London in the Age of Shakespeare: An Anthology* (University Park: Pennsylvania State University Press, 1986), 133–34.

24. Karl Marx, *Economic and Philosophic Manuscripts of 1844*, in Karl Marx and Frederick Engels, *Collected Works*, ed. James Allen, Philip S. Foner, Howard Selsam, Dirk J. Struick, and William Weinstone, trans. Clemens Dutt (New York: International, 1975), 3:302.

25. Susan Stewart, *Poetry and the Fate of the Senses* (Chicago: University of Chicago Press, 2002), 328.

26. Theodor Adorno, "On Lyric Poetry and Society," in *Notes to Literature*, ed. Rold Teidemann, trans. Shierry Weber Nicholsen (New York: Columbia University Press, 1991–92), 1:38, quoted in Stewart, *Poetry and the Fate of the Senses,* 43.

27. Ben Jonson, *Epicoene or the Silent Woman*, ed. R. V. Holdsworth (London and New York: Ernest Benn and Norton,1979); on other aspects of the play, see my "City Talk: Femininity and Commodification in Jonson's *Epicoene*," in *Fashioning Femininity and English Renaissance Drama* (Chicago: University of Chicago Press, 1991).

28. From Pepys's collection in *A Pepysian Garland*, ed. Hyder Rollins (Cambridge: Cambridge University Press, 1922), 31–34.

29. On the sounds of London, and particularly the criers, see Bruce R. Smith, *The Acoustic World of Early Modern England* (Chicago: University of Chicago Press, 1999), 52–71; on music in the streets, see Emily Cockyane, "Cacophony, or Vile Scrapers on Vile Instruments: Bad Music in Early Modern English Towns," *Urban History* 29 (2002): 35–47.

30. Thomas Dekker, *The Non-dramatic Works*, ed. Alexander B. Grossart (New York: Russell and Russell, 1963), 2:50.

31. On bell ringing among young people, see Paul Hentzner's account of his travels in England in 1598, *Travels in England during the Reign of Queen Elizabeth*, ed. Henry

Morley, trans. Richard Bentley (London: Cassell, 1901); Frederic Gerchow, "Diary of the Journey of Philip Juilius, Duke of Stettin-Pomerania, through England in the Year 1602," ed. Gottfried von Bülow, *Transactions of the Royal Historical Society*, n.s., 6 (1892): 7; and Busino, *Journals of Two Travelers*, 169.

32. See Elias, *Civilizing Process*. Recent work on shame is haunted by a binary of inside/outside: commentators approach shame by way of psychoanalytic and developmental theory, on one hand, or by way of the social "context," on the other. On shame, see Thomas J. Scheff, "Shame and the Social Bond: A Sociological Theory," *Sociological Theory* 18 (2000): 84–99.

33. On shame and cultural codes, see Michael J. Casimir and Michael Schnegg, "Shame across Cultures: The Evolution, Ontogeny and Function of a 'Moral Emotion,' " in *Between Culture and Biology: Perspectives on Ontogenetic Development*, ed. Heidi Keller, Ype H. Poortinga, and Axel Schölmerich (Cambridge: Cambridge University Press, 2002), 270–300; and Thomas J. Scheff, "Shame in Social Theory," in *The Widening Scope of Shame*, ed. Melvin R. Lansky and Andrew P. Morrison (Hillsdale, NJ: Analytic Press, 1997), 205–30, and other essays in the collection.

34. *Shame and Its Sisters: A Sylvan Tomkins Reader*, ed. Eve Kosofsky Sedgwick and Adam Frank (Durham, NC: Duke University Press, 1995), 138, 139.

35. Eve Kosofsky Sedgwick, "Shame and Performativity: Henry James's New York Edition Prefaces," in *Henry James's New York Edition: The Construction of Authorship*, ed. David McWhirter (Stanford, CA: Stanford University Press, 1995), 211.

CHAPTER FIVE
COURTSHIP AND CONSUMPTION IN EARLY MODERN PARIS

1. The classic study is L. C. Knights, *Drama and Society in the Age of Jonson* (London: Chatto and Windus, 1937); for the renewed interest in city comedy, see Margot Heinemann, *Puritanism and Theatre: Thomas Middleton and Opposition Drama under the Early Stuarts* (Cambridge: Cambridge University Press, 1980); Susan Wells, "Jacobean City Comedy and the Ideology of the City," *ELH* 48 (1981): 37–60; Gail Kern Paster, *The Idea of the City in the Age of Shakespeare* (Athens: University of Georgia Press, 1985); Theodore Leinwand, *The City Staged: Jacobean City Comedy 1603–1613* (Madison: University of Wisconsin Press, 1986); Mary Beth Rose, *The Expense of Spirit: Love and Sexuality in English Renaissance Drama* (Ithaca, NY: Cornell University Press, 1988); Douglas Bruster, *Drama and the Market in the Age of Shakespeare* (Cambridge: Cambridge University Press, 1992); Jean Howard, *The Stage and Social Struggle in Early Modern England* (London: Routledge, 1994); and Janette Dillon, *Theatre, Court and City, 1595–1610* (Cambridge: Cambridge University Press, 2000).

2. Exceptions include Walter Cohen, *Drama of a Nation: Public Theatre in Renaissance England and Spain* (Ithaca, NY: Cornell University Press, 1985); Roland Greene, *Post-Petrarchism: Origins and Innovations of the Western Lyric Sequence* (Princeton, NJ: Princeton University Press, 1991), and his recent *Unrequited Conquests* (Chicago: University of Chicago Press, 1999); and Nancy Vickers, "Diana Described: Scattered Woman and Scattered Rhyme," *Critical Inquiry* 8 (1981): 265–79; and Vickers, "The Unauthored 1539 Volume in which is Printed the Hecatomphile, The Flowers of French Poetry, and Other Soothing Things," in *Subject and Object in Renaissance*

Culture, ed. Margreta de Grazia, Maureen Quilligan, and Peter Stallybrass (Cambridge: Cambridge University Press, 1996), 166–88.

3. Exceptions are Timothy Reiss, *Toward Dramatic Illusion: Theatrical Technique and Meaning from Hardy to Horace* (New Haven, CT: Yale University Press, 1971); and the fine study of Corneille by Gabriel Conesa, *Pierre Corneille et la naissance du genre comique* (Paris: SEDES, 1989). But see the comments on his comedy in Marc Fumaroli, *Héros et orateurs: Rhétorique et dramaturgie cornélliennes* (Geneva: Droz, 1990); and Thomas Pavel, *L'art de l'éloignement: Essai sur l'imagination classique* (Paris: Gallimard, 1996).

4. See André Stegmann, *L'héroïsme cornélien: Genèse et signification* (Paris: A. Colin, 1968); Georges Couton, *Corneille et la fronde* (Clermont-Ferrand: G. de Bussac, 1951), and *Corneille et la tragédie politique* (Paris: PUF, 1984); Jean-Marie Apostolidès, *Le prince sacrifié* (Paris: Minuit, 1985); and David Clarke, *Pierre Corneille: Poetics and Political Drama under Louis XIII* (Cambridge: Cambridge University Press, 1992); also in English see Timothy Hampton's interesting chapter on Corneille and Shakespeare in *Writing from History: The Rhetoric of Exemplarity in Renaissance Literature* (Ithaca, NY: Cornell University Press, 1990). For a consideration of Corneille's tragedy, traditional categories of the political, and the position of women, see Françoise Lagarde, "Le sacrifice de la femme chez Corneille," *Stanford French Review* 12 (1988): 187–204.

5. A. W. Ward and A. R. Waller, eds., *The Cambridge History of English Literature* (New York: Putnam's, 1910), 4:365. But consider the Caroline "town" comedies of Shirley and Brome.

6. John Brewer and Roy Porter, eds., *Consumption and the World of Goods* (London: Routledge, 1993), 3.

7. Cotgrave's dictionary went through four subsequent editions in England (1632, 1650, 1660, 1673) and was revised and enlarged by James Howell.

8. Historians and cultural commentators debate when to locate what they agree is a revolution in the world of goods. Once located in the nineteenth century and associated with changes in production and distribution linked to the Industrial Revolution, that change in the world of goods has been pushed back to the eighteenth and even the seventeenth centuries. See Lisa Jardine, *Worldly Goods: A New History of the Renaissance* (New York: Talese/Doubleday, 1996); Brewer and Porter, *Consumption and the World of Goods*; Joël Cornette, "La revolution des objets: Le Paris des inventaires après décès (XVIᵉ–XVIIIᵉ)," *Revue d'Histoire Moderne et Contemporaine* 36 (1989): 476–86; Annick Pardailhé-Galabrun, *La naissance de l'intime: 3000 foyers parisiens, XVIIᵉ–XVIIIᵉ siècles* (Paris: Presses Universitaires de France, 1988); Neil McKendrick, John Brewer, and J. H. Plumb, *The Birth of a Consumer Society* (London: Europa, 1982). For a critique of the move to push the revolution in the world of goods back in time, particularly in the English context, see J. C. D. Clark, *English Society, 1688–1832: Ideology, Social Structure, and Political Practice during the Ancien Régime* (Cambridge: Cambridge University Press, 1985).

9. Arjun Appadurai, ed., *The Social Life of Things: Commodities in Cultural Perspective* (Cambridge: Cambridge University Press, 1986); Chandra Mukerji, *From Graven Images: Patterns of Modern Materialism* (New York: Columbia University Press, 1983); Mary Douglas and Baron Isherwood, *The World of Goods: Towards an Anthropology of Consumption* (New York: Norton, 1979); and Jean Baudrillard, *Le système des objets* (Paris: Gallimard, 1968), and *La société de consommation* (Paris: SGPP, 1970).

10. Commentators generally point out that Corneille did not introduce mercantile scenes and characters to the French stage. Always cited are the anonymous *Le mercier inventif,* in which a peddler sells his wares, a similar scene in Coste's *Lizimène,* and a conversation between a butcher and his wife in du Ryer's *Lisandre et Caliste.* See Louis Rivaille, *Les débuts de Pierre Corneille* (Paris: Boivin, 1936), 408; Georges Couton, *Corneille: Oeuvres complètes* (Paris: Gallimard, 1980), 1:1283; and G. J. Mallinson, *The Comedies of Corneille: Experiments in the Comic* (Manchester, UK: Manchester University Press, 1984), 77.

11. Quoted in René Pillorget, *Paris sous les premiers Bourbons, 1594–1661, Nouvelle histoire de Paris* (Paris: Hachette, 1988), 442, trans. mine. Montdory directed the Théâtre du Marais in which Corneille's plays were produced.

12. Couton, *Oeuvres complètes* 1:302, trans. mine. All references are to this edition and are cited by line number in the text.

13. For a detailed social history of the Palais, see Jean-Louis Bourgeon, "L'Île de la cité pendant la Fronde," *Paris et Ile-de-France. Mémoires* 13 (1962): 23–144.

14. *La ville de Paris en vers burlesques contenant toutes les galanteries du Palais, la chicane des plaideurs, les filouteries du Pont Neuf* (Troyes, n.d.); also published under the title "Paris burlesque" and dated 1652. This lame, rhymed translation is mine; I am grateful to Timothy Reiss for the suggested translation of *futre* and for his attentive reading of an earlier version of this chapter.

15. *Galantiser* could be translated "to flirt," but it has an almost technical sense in the play, "to play the gallant," which I have tried to preserve by using the neologism. The verse ends "Ici quelque lingère, à faute de succès / A vendre abondamment, de colère se pique / Contre des chicaneurs, qui, parlant de procès, / Empechent les chalands d'aborder sa boutique" (Here some linen seller failing to sell much gets angry at the shysters talking over some case and preventing customers from reaching her boutique).

16. In the 1648 edition, a scene direction is added at Dorimant's line: "au Libraire, regardant Hippolyte."

17. Nicolas Faret's *L'honnête homme, ou l'art de plaire à la cour* (1630) appeared at the very moment Corneille's first comedies were produced in Paris; his portrayal of his cavaliers Dorimant and Lisandre owes something to the developing conception of *honnêteté.* See, for example, act 2, scene 2, and Hippolite's censure of Lisandre's failure to accompany his *salut* with *un bonjour* (390–93). On *civilité* in early modern France, see Norbert Elias, *The Civilizing Process,* trans. Edmund Jephcott (New York: Pantheon, 1978).

18. Thomas Middleton and Thomas Dekker, *The Roaring Girl,* ed. Andor Gomme (New York: Norton, 1976). All references are to this New Mermaids edition.

19. On Corneille's use of contemporary rhetoric and diction, see Conesa, *Pierre Corneille et la naissance du genre comique,* 51–98.

20. On the Hegelian subject in Corneille, see Serge Doubrovsky, *Corneille et la dialectique du héros* (Paris: Gallimard, 1963).

21. Octave Nadal, *Le sentiment de l'amour dans l'oeuvre de Pierre Corneille* (Paris: Gallimard, 1948), 51.

22. See Gérard Genette, *Figures I* (Paris: Seuil, 1966); and Conesa, *Pierre Corneille et la naissance du genre comique,* 55–82.

23. Cornette, "La revolution des objets," 485.

24. Reiss, *Toward Dramatic Illusion*, 59, 122.

25. *Le menteur: La suite du menteur*, ed. Jean Serroy (Paris: Gallimard, 2000). All references are to this edition.

26. On cultural capital, see the work of Pierre Bourdieu, especially his *Distinction: A Social Critique of the Judgment of Taste*, trans. Richard Nice (Cambridge, MA: Harvard University Press, 1984).

27. *Les lois de la galanterie*, anthologized in Roger Duchêne, *Les Précieuses ou comment l'esprit vint aux femmes* (Paris: Fayard, 2001), 311.

CHAPTER SIX
ARMCHAIR TRAVEL

1. Erica Harth, *Cartesian Women: Versions and Subversions of Rational Discourse in the Old Regime* (Ithaca, NY: Cornell University Press, 1992), 62. On women and exclusion from travel in England, see John Stoye, *English Travellers Abroad 1604–1667: Their Influence on English Society and Politics* (London: Jonathan Cape, 1952, rev. ed. New Haven, CT: Yale University Press, 1989), 38.

2. Jacques Le Goff, *La civilisation de l'occident médiéval* (Paris: Flammarion, 1982), xvii.

3. See, among many recent publications, Mary B. Campbell, *The Witness and the Other World: Exotic European Travel Writing 400–1600* (Ithaca, NY: Cornell University Press, 1988); Stephen Greenblatt, *Marvelous Possessions: The Wonders of the New World* (Chicago: University of Chicago Press, 1991), and the recent collection he edited, *New World Encounters* (Berkeley: University of California Press, 1993); Anthony Pagden, *European Encounters with the New World* (New Haven, CT: Yale University Press, 1993). Recently scholars have begun to consider European travelers to those many geographic locales known as the "East" or the "Orient." On the popularity of the so-called orient in seventeenth-century France, see, for example, Barthèlemy d'Herbelot's compendium entitled *Bibliothèque orientale*, a best seller at its publication in 1697, which went through a number of editions and inspired numerous imitations.

4. Jonathan Dewald, *Aristocratic Experience and the Origins of Modern Culture: France, 1570–1715* (Berkeley: University of California Press, 1993), 87. See also E. S. Bates, *Touring in 1600: A Study of Travel as a Means of Education* (Boston: Houghton Mifflin, 1911); and Stoye, *English Travellers Abroad*. See also Alan Macfarlane, ed., *The Diary of Ralph Josselin 1616–1683* (London: Oxford University Press, 1976).

5. Descartes, *Discours de la méthode* (Paris: Classiques Hachette, 1997), 17. All references are to this edition.

6. See Nathan Edelman "The Mixed Metaphor in Descartes," in *The Eye of the Beholder*, ed. Jules Brody (Baltimore: Johns Hopkins University Press, 1974), 107–20; Sylvie Romanowski, *L'illusion chez Descartes* (Paris: Klincksieck, 1974); Jean-Luc Nancy, *Ego Sum* (Paris: Flammarion, 1979); G. V. Van den Abbeele, "Cartesian Coordinates: Metaphor, Topography and Presupposition in Descartes," in *Voyages: Papers on French Seventeenth-Century Literature*, Biblio 17 (1984): 3–14; and Normand Doiron, "L'art de voyager: Pour une définition du récit de voyage à l'Epoque classique," *Poétique* 73 (1988): 83–108. On travel and the *theatrum mundi* topos in Descartes, see Harth, *Cartesian Women*, 74.

7. Stoye, *English Travellers Abroad*, 38.

8. Ibid., 40.

9. Exceptions include such women as Margaret Cavendish, exiled with the royalist court in France, Hortense Mancini, the so-called vagabond duchess, Queen Christina of Sweden, and Aphra Behn, among others, but such exceptions do not refute the broader claim about women's exclusion from the model of educative travel. See Stoye, *English Travellers Abroad*, 11.

10. James Howell, *Instructions for forreine travell*, ed. Edward Arber for the English Reprint Series (London, 1869). On the frequency and significance of nonforeign travel, see Andrew McRae, "The Peripatetic Muse: Internal Travel and the Cultural Production of Space in Pre-revolutionary England," in *The Country and the City Revisited: England and the Politics of Culture, 1550–1850* (Cambridge: Cambridge University Press, 1999), 41–57.

11. On female literacy in early modern Europe, see Margaret Ferguson, *Dido's Daughters: Literacy, Gender and Empire in Early Modern England and France* (Chicago: University of Chicago Press, 2003); and Jean Mesnard, *Précis de littérature du XVIIe siècle* (Paris: Presses Universitaires de France, 1990).

12. "Les voyages sont venus en crédit . . . dans la Cour et dans la Ville," quoted in Doiron, "L'art de voyager," 84; and by J. Chupeau in his useful essay, "Les récits de voyages aux lisières du roman," *Revue d'Histoire Littéraire de la France* 3–4 (1977): 539.

13. Travel writing is "un divertissement bien plus sage et plus utile que celui des agréables bagatelles qui ont enchanté tous les fainéants et toutes les fainéantes de deça, dont nous voisins italiens, allemands, hollandais ont sucé le venin à leur dommage et à notre honte." Chupeau, "Les récits de voyages aux lisières du roman," 539; on travel writing and its generic models in the period, see Michel Bideaux, "Le voyage littéraire: Genèse d'un genre," *Les modèles du récit de voyage, Littérales* 7 (1990): 179–99.

14. On women, particularly the "riche noblesse de Paris" as readers/consumers of the romance novel, see Maurice Lever, *Le roman français au XVIIe siécle* (Paris: Presses Universitaires, 1981).

15. On the Caroline court and the French salon tradition, see Carol Barash, *English Women's Poetry 1649–1714: Politics, Community and Linguistic Authority* (Oxford: Clarendon Press, 1996), 32.

16. Jacqueline Pearson, "Women Reading, Reading Women," in *Women and Literature in Britain, 1500–1700*, ed. Helen Wilcox (Cambridge: Cambridge University Press, 1996), 92. On women readers and sixteenth-century romance, see Caroline Lucas, *Writing for Women: The Example of Woman as Reader in Elizabethan Romance* (Milton Keynes: Open University Press, 1989).

17. On English women's admiration for Scudéry and seventeenth-century French literary culture, see Barash, *English Women's Poetry*, 34.

18. My translation of the intercalated tale from book 10 of *Artamène, L'histoire de Sapho* appeared under the title *The Story of Sapho* (Chicago: University of Chicago Press, 2003).

19. Lever, *Le roman français au XVIIe siécle*, 11.

20. On the constitution of a reading public, see for England Jonathan Barry's "Literacy and Literature in Popular Culture: Reading and Writing in Historical Per-

spective," in *Popular Culture in England, c. 1500–1850*, ed. Timothy Harris (New York: Saint Martin's Press, 1995). The best overview for France remains Roger Chartier's essay in *Histoire de la vie privée*, ed. Philippe Ariés, Georges Duby, and Henri-Jean Martin, *Livre, pouvoirs et société à Paris au XVIIᵉ* (Geneva: Droz, 1969).

21. See Maurice Lever, who gathers the evidence, particularly from Martin, cited above.

22. See especially René Godenne, *Les romans de Mademoiselle de Scudéry* (Geneva: Droz, 1983), 134; and Joan DeJean, "No Man's Land: The Novel's First Geography," *Yale French Studies* 73 (1987): 175–89.

23. The great promoter of Scudéry as the author of romans à clef is Victor Cousin, who claimed to have discovered a key, now lost, in the Bibliothèque de l'Arsenal that matched *Artamène*'s major characters with well-known persons and events of the Fronde period. See his *La Société française au XVIIᵉ siècle d'après Le grand Cyrus* (Paris: Didier, 1873).

24. On idealism, realism, and the feminine, see Naomi Schor, *George Sand and Idealism* (New York: Columbia University Press, 1993); on Scudéry and idealized spaces, see Elizabeth Goldsmith, *Exclusive Conversations: The Art of Interaction in Seventeenth-Century France* (Philadelphia: University of Pennsylvania Press, 1988).

25. On Aphra Behn and exotica, see Margaret W. Ferguson, "Feathers and Flies: Aphra Behn and the Seventeenth-Century Trade in Exotica," in *Subject and Object in Renaissance Culture*, ed. Margreta de Grazia, Maureen Quilligan, and Peter Stallybrass (Cambridge: Cambridge University Press, 1996), esp. 255; see also Julia Douthwaite, *Exotic Women: Literary Heroines and Cultural Strategies in Ancien Régime France* (Philadelphia: University of Pennsylvania Press, 1992).

26. "Je veux m'instruire par les voyages, je veux m'eprouver dans les occasions, je veux me connaître moi-même"; Madeleine de Scudéry, *Artamène ou le Grand Cyrus* (Paris, 1649–53; Genève: Slatkine Reprints, 1972), 1:152.

27. Madeleine de Scudéry, *Entretiens de morale* (Paris: Jean Anisson, 1692), Qviᵛ.

28. Critics ridiculed the *carte* even before its publication as Scudéry's defensive claims about it reveal in volume 1 of *Clélie*. On its reception, see Claude Filteau, "Le pays de Tendre: L'enjeu d'une carte," *Littérature* 36 (1979): 37–60. On the *carte* generally, see Jean-Michel Pelous, *Amour précieux, amour galant (1654–1675)* (Paris: Klincksieck, 1980). On the gendering of maps and the distinction between chorography and geography in relation to Scudéry's *carte de tendre*, see Eileen Reeves, "Reading Maps," in *So Rich a Tapestry: The Sister Arts and Cultural Studies*, ed. Ann Hurley and Kate Greenspan (London: Associated University Press, 1995), 285–314.

29. Apropos the salon, Alain Viala argues that after 1665, the court comes to monopolize what had been an urban phenomenon; *Naissance de l'écrivain* (Paris: Éditions de Minuit, 1985), 133. On Scudéry's novels and collaboration in the salon, see Joan DeJean, *Tender Geographies: Women and the Origins of the Novel in France* (New York: Columbia University Press, 1991).

30. On the *carte* and territorial and military power, see Alain-Marie Bassy, "Supplement au voyage de Tendre," *Bulletin du Bibliophile* 1 (1982): 13–33.

31. Madeleine de Scudéry, *Clélie: Histoire romaine* (Paris, 1654–60; repr., Geneva: Droz, 1973), 1:391.

32. Ibid., 395.

33. See Bassy, "Supplement au voyage de Tendre."

34. On the salon's relation to a newly developing public interested in literature and letters, see Viala, *Naissance de l'écrivain*.

35. Annick Pardailhé-Galabrun, *La naissance de l'intime: 3000 foyers parisiens XVIIe–XVIIIe siècles* (Paris: Presses Universitaires de France, 1988), 304.

36. Carolyn C. Lougée, *Le Paradis des Femmes* (Princeton, NJ: Princeton University Press, 1976); for a more nuanced perspective on the salon, see Harth, *Cartesian Women*, and particularly her discussion of Habermas and the salon's relation to a developing public sphere. Viala, *Naissance de l'écrivain*, counts forty or more salons in Paris at midcentury. On "Men's Literary Circles in Paris 1610–1660," see Josephine de Boer *PMLA* 53 (1938): 730–86; and Erica Harth, "The Salon Woman Goes Public . . . or Does She?" in *Going Public: Women and Publishing in Early Modern France*, ed. Elizabeth C. Goldsmith and Dena Goodman (Ithaca, NY: Cornell University Press, 1995), 189–92.

37. See Joan DeJean's excellent article on Scudéry and the "Histoire de Sapho," "Amazones et femmes de lettres: Pouvoirs politiques et littéraires à l'âge classique," in *Femmes et pouvoirs sous l'ancien régime*, ed. Danielle Haase-Dubosc and Eliane Viennot (Paris: Rivages, 1991), 153–74, as well as her *Tender Geographies*.

38. Charles Tinker, *The Salon and English Letters: Chapters on the Interrelations of Literature and Society in the Age of Johnson* (New York: Macmillan, 1915), 96. On the Mancini sisters and Hortense's "French" salon in London, see Elizabeth C. Goldsmith, "Publishing the Lives of Hortense and Marie Mancini," in *Going Public*, 20–45. On Katherine Philips, see Barash, *English Women's Poetry*, 66.

39. Pardailhé-Galabrun, *La naissance de l'intime*, 309.

40. Goldsmith, *Exclusive Conversations*, 2.

41. See Filteau, "Le pays de Tendre."

CHAPTER SEVEN
DEATH, NAME, AND NUMBER

1. Medieval London had numerous minor streets and lanes named after individuals, a few of which still survive; they generally commemorate property ownership or association with the street rather than being "named" in honor. See Vanessa Harding, "Space, Property, and Propriety in Urban England," *Journal of Interdisciplinary History* 32 (2002): 549–69.

2. On cognitive mapping and urban space, see Kevin Lynch, *The Image of the City* (Cambridge, MA: MIT Press, 1960; repr., Cambridge, MA: MIT Press, 1986).

3. Robert Hertz's "A Contribution to the Study of the Collective Representation of the Dead," in his *Death and the Right Hand*, trans. Rodney and Claudia Needham (Glencoe, IL: Free Press, 1960), first published in 1907, continues to be widely cited in this regard. More recently, see Richard Huntington and Peter Metcalf, eds., *Celebrations of Death: The Anthropology of Mortuary Ritual* (Cambridge: Cambridge University Press, 1979); S. C. Humphreys and H. King, eds., *Mortality and Immortality: The Anthropology and Archaeology of Death* (London: Academic Press, 1981); and Maurice Bloch and Jonathan Parry, eds., *Death and the Regeneration of Life* (Cambridge: Cambridge University Press, 1982). On the relation of cemeteries and shrines to urban settlement, see Lewis Mumford, *The City in History* (New York: Harcourt Brace Jova-

novich, 1961), 6–10. See also Bruce Gordon and Peter Marshall, eds., *The Place of the Dead: Death and Remembrance in Late Medieval and Early Modern Europe* (Cambridge: Cambridge University Press, 2000). On England, see Ralph A. Houlbrooke, *Death, Religion and the Family in England, 1450–1750* (Oxford: Oxford University Press, 1998). Of particular relevance is Vanessa Harding's important comparative study, *The Dead and the Living in Paris and London 1500–1670* (Cambridge: Cambridge University Press, 2002).

4. Walter Benjamin, *The Arcades Project*, trans. Howard Eiland and Kevin McLaughlin (Cambridge, MA: Harvard University Press, 1999), 522; and McLaughlin's "Virtual Paris: Benjamin's *Arcades Project*," in *Benjamin's Ghosts: Interventions in Contemporary Literary and Cultural Theory*, ed. Gerhard Richter (Stanford, CA: Stanford University Press, 2002), 204–25.

5. On this perceived contradiction and the current preoccupation with memory, see, among many others, Andreas Huyssen, *Twilight Memories: Marking Time in a Culture of Amnesia* (New York: Routledge, 1995).

6. Loosely translated from Pierre Nora, *Les lieux de mémoire* (Paris: Gallimard, 1984), xxiv. On memory and identity politics, see especially Paul Gilroy, *The Black Atlantic* (Cambridge, MA: Harvard University Press, 1993).

7. Jean-Luc Nancy, "*Being With*, concerning not only to be with, but Being with, as a mere 'with,' " Florence Gould Lecture, New York University, April 1996; on the turn to stories and anecdotes in recent literary and cultural theory, see David Simpson, *The Academic Postmodern and the Rule of Literature: A Report on Half-Knowledge* (Chicago: University of Chicago Press, 1995).

8. Francis Bacon, *The Advancement of Learning*, in *Selected Writings of Francis Bacon*, ed. Hugh G. Dick (New York: Random House, 1955), 234.

9. Earliest edition, 1598; all references are to John Stow, *A Survey of London* (London, 1603). For recent treatments of Stow's *Survey*, see the opening chapters of Steven Mullaney, *The Place of the Stage* (Chicago: University of Chicago Press, 1988); Lawrence Manley, *Literature and Culture in Early Modern London* (Cambridge: Cambridge University Press, 1995). In his "Visions of the Urban Community: Antiquarians and the English City before 1800," in *The Pursuit of Urban History*, ed. Derek Fraser and Anthony Sutcliffe (London: Edward Arnold, 1983), 105–24, Peter Clark places Stow in the context of civic annals and antiquarian histories mainly outside London. See also Ian Gadd and Alexandra Gillespie, eds., *John Stow (1525–1605) and the Making of the English Past* (London, 2004).

10. On record keeping and Stow's use of archives, see Piers Cain, "Robert Smith and the Reform of the Archives of the City of London, 1580–1623," *London Journal* 13, no. 1 (1987–88): 3–16.

11. Stow's incorporation of William Fitz Stephen's twelfth-century description of London into the first section of his *Survay* is generally acknowledged. On Stow and Fitz Stephen, see Lawrence Manley, "From Matron to Monster: Tudor-Stuart London and the Languages of Urban Description," in *The Historical Renaissance*, ed. H. Dubrow and R. Strier (Chicago: University of Chicago Press, 1988), 347–74; and both Ian Archer's and Manley's essays on Stow in *The Theatrical City: Culture, Theatre and Politics in London, 1576–1649*, ed. David L. Smith, Richard Strier, and David Bevington (Cambridge: Cambridge University Press, 1995), 17, 36–38.

12. Stow's movement from east to west also traces broadly the processional routes for royal entries and progresses and civic inaugurals and celebrations. On the various monarchic and mayoral routes through early modern London, see Manley, *Literature and Culture in Early Modern London*, 221–74.

13. Mary Carruthers, *The Book of Memory: A Study of Memory in Medieval Culture* (Cambridge: Cambridge University Press, 1990). On London churches and halls as "theatres of memory," see Ian Archer, "The Arts and Acts of Memorialization in Early Modern London," in *Imagining Early Modern London: Perceptions and Portrayals of the City from Stow to Strype 1598–1720* (Cambridge: Cambridge University Press, 2001), 89–113.

14. On Stow's pre-Reformation prejudice for "hospitality" over charitable giving, see Susan Brigden, "Religion and Social Obligation in Early Sixteenth-Century London," *Past & Present* 103 (1984): 67–112; and Ian Archer, *The Pursuit of Stability: Social Relations in Elizabethan London* (Cambridge: Cambridge University Press, 1991), 163–82, and his essay "The Nostalgia of John Stow," in *The Theatrical City*, 27.

15. Quoted in Stanley Rubenstein, *Historians of London* (Hamden, CT: Archon Books, 1968), 31.

16. On the proper name and the humanist epitaph, see Joshua Scodel's fine discussion in *The English Poetic Epitaph* (Ithaca, NY: Cornell University Press, 1991), 48–49.

17. Jacob Burckhardt, *The Civilization of the Renaissance in Italy*, trans. S.G.C. Middlemore (1860; London: Penguin, 1990). The chapter ends with a discussion of memorials that Burckhardt attributes both to the humanist preoccupation with *fama* and to a putative "social equality." Though the humanist turn to history and interest in ruins certainly account in part for the topographic inscription of memory in Renaissance Italy, Burckhardt's claim for "social equality," which I take to be his remarking of the importance of early Italian mercantile republicanism, is of particular interest to my argument here. All over Italy, men and women of the middling sort began to buy, build, create, and endow memorials that witnessed after death their entrepreneurial success in life. On that Italian context, see Samuel Cohn, *The Cult of Remembrance and the Black Death* (Baltimore: Johns Hopkins University Press, 1992). See Max Weber, *The Protestant Ethic and the Spirit of Capitalism*, trans. Talcott Parsons (New York: Scribner's, 1930; repr., New York: Scribner's, 1952), and quoted in Harvey S. Goldman, "Weber's Ascetic Practices of the Self," in *Weber's Protestant Ethic* (Cambridge: Cambridge University Press, 1993), 168.

18. David Simpson, *Situatedness, or Why We Keep Saying Where We're Coming From* (Durham, NC: Duke University Press, 2002).

19. Claire Gittings, *Death, Burial and the Individual in Early Modern England* (London: Crown Helm, 1984), 14, and her "Sacred and Secular: 1558–1660," in *Death in England: An Illustrated History*, ed. Peter C. Jupp and Clare Gittings (Manchester, UK: Manchester University Press, 1999), 147–173.

20. Quoted in Gittings, *Death, Burial, and the Individual in Early Modern England*, 40.

21. W. K. Jordan, *Philanthropy in England 1480–1660* (New York: Russell Sage, 1959), 143; and David Owen, *English Philanthropy 1660–1960* (Cambridge, MA: Harvard University Press, 1964), 1. See also Jordan's book *The Charities of London, 1480–1660: The Aspirations and the Achievements of the Urban Society* (London: Allen and Unwin, 1960).

22. Owen, *English Philanthropy*, 1. For a discussion of Jordan's claims concerning the Reformation and charitable giving, see Archer, *Pursuit of Stability*, 163–82. For a similar debate in the context of funereal sculpture and monuments between assertions of individualism and Reformist ideas about death, see Nigel Llewellyn, "The Royal Body: Monuments to the Dead, for the Living" in *Renaissance Bodies*, ed. Lucy Gent and Nigel Llewellyn (London: Reaktion Books, 1991), 218–40.

23. John Weever, *Ancient Funeral Monuments* (London: Thomas Harper, 1631).

24. Ian Archer shows that the repair and beautification of pre-Reformation sites and monuments was well under way before Laud and traces its performative, even ritual, features; "The Arts and Acts of Memorialization in Early Modern London," 101. See also Eamon Duffy, *The Stripping of the Altars: Traditional Religion in England, 1400–1580* (New Haven, CT: Yale University Press, 1992).

25. Such systematic record keeping only began in Paris in 1670. See Harding, *The Dead and the Living*; and Pierre Chaunu, *La mort à Paris: XVIᵉ, XVIIᵉ, et XVIIIᵉ siécles* (Paris: Fayard, 1978).

26. Thomas R. Forbes, *Chronicle from Aldgate: Life and Death in Shakespeare's London* (New Haven, CT: Yale University Press, 1971), 78–80.

27. Harding, *The Dead and the Living*, 8.

28. On the rise of charitable giving in response to increased urban pauperism, see Brigden, "Religion and Social Obligation in Early Sixteenth-Century London," 67–112. On the diffusion of privilege and relative prosperity of early modern London's inhabitants, see the challenge mounted to the claims of A. L. Beier and others by Valerie Pearl, "Change and Stability in Seventeenth-Century London," in *The Tudor and Stuart Town: A Reader in English Urban History 1530–1688*, ed. Jonathan Barry (London: Longmans, 1990), 139–65; and Archer, *Pursuit of Stability*.

29. Browne's own memorial in the church of Saint Peter Mancroft at Norwich was also subject to the erosion of time. In 1840, workmen digging in the vault accidentally broke the lid of Browne's tomb to discover, in the words of the *DNB*, bones "found to be in good preservation" and "fine auburn hair [that] had not lost its freshness" (3:69). Browne's once hirsute skull now resides in a glass case in the museum collection at Norwich Hospital. See also Ralph Houlbrooke, "Civility and Civil Observances in the Early Modern English Funeral," in *Civil Histories: Essays Presented to Sir Keith Thomas*, ed. Peter Burke, Brian Harrison, and Paul Slack (Oxford: Oxford University Press, 2000), 67–86, who discusses Browne in relation to English funereal practice. On death in the period with emphasis on tragedy, see Michael Neill, *Issues of Death: Mortality and Identity in English Renaissance Tragedy* (Oxford: Clarendon Press, 1997).

30. Quoted from the introduction to R. H. A. Robbins's edition, *Religio Medici, Hydriotaphia and The Garden of Cyrus* (Oxford: Clarendon Press, 1972), xvi.

31. See Leonard Nathanson, *The Strategy of Truth: A Study of Sir Thomas Browne* (Chicago: University of Chicago Press, 1967), 179, 181.

32. Frank J. Warnke, "A Hook for Amphibium: Some Reflections on Fish," in *Approaches to Sir Thomas Browne*, ed. C. A. Patrides (Columbia: University of Missouri Press, 1982), 54; Edmund Gosse, *Sir Thomas Browne* (London: Macmillan, 1924), 205; and Stanley Fish, *Self-Consuming Artifacts* (Berkeley: University of California Press, 1972), 366. See also Anne Drury Hall, *Ceremony and Civility in English Renaissance Prose* (University Park: Pennsylvania State University Press, 1991), who in discussing *Religio Medici* produces Browne's prose as "a space for a rhetoric of private

emotion" for a "liberal pluralistic society" (184, 185), and describes what she terms as his "free imagination of the 'particular devotion' of the individual" (182).

33. *The Works of Sir Thomas Browne*, ed. Geoffrey Keynes (Chicago: University of Chicago Press, 1964), 165. All references are to this edition.

34. See also BM Sloane Ms. 1848, fol. 194: "Large are the treasures of oblivion, and heapes of things in a state next to nothing almost numberlesse; much more is buried in silence than is recorded, and the largest volumes are butt epitomes of what hath been. The account of time beganne with night, and darknesse still attendeth it."

35. On the cumulative rather than the subordinated in Browne's prose style, see Morris Croll's discussion of the curt period in "*Attic" and Baroque Prose Style* (Princeton, NJ: Princeton University Press, 1966; repr., Princeton, NJ: Princeton University Press, 1969), 211–19.

36. In George Williamson, *Milton and Others* (London: Faber and Faber, 1965), 181; first published in *Modern Philology* 62 (1964): 110–17.

37. Charles Taylor, *Sources of the Self* (Cambridge, MA: Harvard University Press, 1989), 202–3.

38. Quoted in Patrizia Lombardo, "The Ephemeral and the Eternal: Reflections on History," in *Rediscovering History*, ed. Michael Roth (Stanford, CA: Stanford University Press, 1994), 391.

39. In the anonymous ballad "Deat[hs] Dance" (fig. 30), the speaker calls on death to "shew his face . . . at many a rich man's place" in the city—"Water side,/Where Merchants purchase golden grains," the Royal Exchange, Westminster, Paul's, at taverns and gaming houses. From Early English Books Online, reproduced from an original in the British Library.

40. Harding, *The Dead and the Living*, 270. On the off-putting effects of death and disease, see Margaret Pelling, "Skirting the City? Disease, Social Change and Divided Households in the Seventeenth Century," in *Londinopolis: Essays in the Cultural and Social History of Early Modern London*, ed. Paul Griffiths and Mark S. R. Jenner (Manchester, UK: Manchester University Press, 2000), 154–75.

41. For a full discussion of Browne's puns in the context of seventeenth-century Neo-Platonism, see Lauren Shohet, "Figuring the Seventeenth Century: Body, Rhetoric, and Knowledge in Masque and Science" (Ph.D. diss., Brown University, 1995).

42. Jacques Derrida, *Of Grammatology*, trans. Gayatri Chakravorty Spivak (Baltimore: Johns Hopkins University Press, 1974), 109.

43. Karl Marx, *Capital: A Critique of Political Economy*, ed. Frederick Engels, trans. Samuel Moore and Edward Aveling (New York: International Publishers, 1967), chap. 1; Jean-Joseph Goux, *Symbolic Economies: After Marx and Freud*, trans. Jennifer Curtiss Gage (1973; Ithaca, NY: Cornell University Press, 1990).

44. In 1950 J. H. Hexter published his influential article, "The Myth of the Middle Class in Tudor England," *Explorations in Entrepreneurial History* 2 (1950), reissued in his *Reappraisals in History* (Evanston, IL: Northwestern University Press, 1961), which became orthodoxy among historians for some decades. Recent scholarship has questioned his claims and demonstrated that there was indeed a rising "middling sort" in England in the sixteenth and seventeenth centuries, particularly in London. See the essays in Jonathan Barry and Christopher Brooks, eds., *The Middling Sort of People: Culture, Society and Politics in England 1550–1800* (New York: St. Martin's Press, 1994). See also Harding, *The Dead and the Living*, who shows that in both London

and Paris there was competitive consumption and "a flourishing tradition of monumental commemoration, that may indeed have reached new heights of elaboration and expense" in the period (275).

45. For recent work on the implications of early modern accounting practices, particularly with reference to gender, see Mary Poovey, *A History of the Modern Fact* (Chicago: University of Chicago Press, 1998), chap. 2. Among the numerous seventeenth-century memorials are those of many London guilds, ambassadorial memorandums, memorials on coinage and credit (William Davenant), and so forth. In the preface to the reader of *Religio Medici*, Browne uses the term "memorial" interestingly in protesting that essay's unauthorized publication: "the intention was not publick: and being a private exercise directed to my selfe, what it delivered therein was rather a memorial unto me then an example or rule unto any other" (Keynes, *Works of Sir Thomas Browne*, 9–10); as so often in Browne, the phrase resonates with the many meanings of "memorial."

46. Nora, *Les lieux de mémoire*, xxvii; see also Carolyn Steedman, *Dust: The Archive and Cultural History* (New Brunswick, NJ: Rutgers University Press, 2002), for a similar argument: "Working-class people, their image, their appurtenances, were used to tell . . . some kind of story of the bourgeois self" (127).

CHAPTER EIGHT
SEX IN THE CITY

1. Jules Michelet, *Mother Death: The Journal of Jules Michelet, 1815–1850*, trans. and ed. Edward K. Kaplan (Amherst: University of Massachusetts Press, 1984), 121–22, quoted in Jacques Rancière, *Les noms d'histoire* (Paris: Seuil, 1992), trans. by Hassan Melehy as *The Names of History: On the Poetics of Knowledge* (Minneapolis: University of Minnesota Press, 1994), 62–63.

2. See Renate Bridenthal and Claudia Koonz, *Becoming Visible: Women in European History* (Boston: Houghton Mifflin, 1977). This chapter began as a paper to address issues raised by a session at the 2000 Shakespeare Association meeting entitled "Feminist Historiography and Shakespeare's London: Rewriting Women's History." The session's charge begins from the assumption that "much recent work on gender has focused on women who have left textual traces of their lives and activities (i.e., letters, books, manuscripts . . .). Yet there were women living in [early modern] London whose lives are not so easily discernible . . . or whose 'told histories' mask a more complex situation. . . . What are the challenges facing feminist historiography as it attempts to 'recover' this history?"

3. See Martin Ingram, *Church Courts, Sex and Marriage in England, 1570–1640* (Cambridge: Cambridge University Press, 1987), 284. See also Ruth Karras, "The Regulating of Brothels in Late Medieval England," in *Sisters and Workers in the Middle Ages*, ed. J. M. Bennett, Elizabeth Clark, Jean F. O'Barr, A. Viden, and S. Westphal-Wihl (Chicago: University of Chicago Press, 1976; repr., Chicago: University of Chicago Press, 1989), 100–134; Leah Lydia Otis, *Prostitution in Medieval Society: The History of an Urban Institution in Languedoc* (Chicago: University of Chicago Press, 1985); and Lawrence Stone, *The Family, Sex and Marriage in England 1150–1800* (New York: Harper, 1979) on what he terms "casual, semi-amateur prostitution" prac-

ticed by both single and married women who, according to Stone in a remarkable locution, had sex in the field "partly to earn money, and partly, it would seem, for mere pleasure" (391). On the fluid patterns of sexual behavior and definitions of prostitution in London, see Faramerz Dabhoiwala, "The Pattern of Sexual Immorality in Seventeenth and Eighteenth-Century London," in *Londinopolis: Essays in the Cultural and Social History of Early Modern London*, ed. Paul Griffiths and Mark S. R. Jenner (Manchester, UK: Manchester University Press, 2000), 86–106.

4. On commercial sex and its vocabulary, particularly in the context of the work of Thomas Dekker, see John Twyning, *London Dispossessed: Literature and Social Space in the Early Modern City* (New York: St Martin's Press, 1998).

5. Ian Archer, *The Pursuit of Stability: Social Relations in Elizabethan London* (Cambridge: Cambridge University Press, 1991); and Paul Griffiths, "The Structure of Prostitution in Elizabethan London," *Continuity and Change* 8 (1993): 39–63. See also Robert Shoemaker, *Prosecution and Punishment: Petty Crime and the Law in London and Rural Middlesex 1660–1725* (Cambridge: Cambridge University Press, 1991).

6. Thomas Dekker, *News from Hell* (1606), sig. Bii. Commentators have claimed that in the nineteenth century, "as a result of women's revised relation to space, her new ability to 'wander' (and hence to 'err'). Most significantly, the prostitute ostentatiously exhibited the commodification of the human body." Early modern prostitution gives the lie to the putative newness of this relation to urban space. See Mary Ann Doane, *Femmes Fatales: Feminism, Film Theory, Psychoanalysis* (New York: Routledge, 1991), 263.

7. Archer, *Pursuit of Stability*, 211. On male reputation and sexuality, see Bernard Capp, "The Double Standard Revisited: Plebian Women and Male Sexual Reputation in Early Modern England," *Past & Present* 162 (1999): 70–100.

8. Griffiths disputes this claim on the basis of the Bridewell courtbooks; "The Structure of Prostitution in Elizabethan London," 48.

9. Vol. 1, 1559–62; 2, 1574–76; 3, 1576–79; 4, 1597–1604; 5, 1604–10; 6, 1634–42.

10. On the founding of Bridewell, its powers, and jurisdiction, see Griffiths, "The Structure of Prostitution in Elizabethan London," 41–43. For an excellent discussion of Bridewell in a literary context, see William Carroll, *Fat King, Lean Beggar: Representations of Poverty in the Age of Shakespeare* (Ithaca, NY: Cornell University Press, 1996).

11. On the difficulties of ascertaining an average fee, see Griffiths, "The Structure of Prostitution in Elizabethan London," 47.

12. See Archer, *Pursuit of Stability*, 211–15.

13. Griffiths, "The Structure of Prostitution in Elizabethan London," 55.

14. Ibid., 49.

15. See Carolyn Steedman, *Dust: The Archive and Cultural History* (New Brunswick, NJ: Rutgers University Press, 2002). 47.

16. Griffiths, "The Structure of Prostitution in Elizabethan London," 41, 53.

17. Ibid., 40. Plays, poems and pamphlets often corroborate the evidence of the courtbooks about the organization and practice of prostitution in early modern London: as the prostitute Luce boasts in *Westward Ho!* of the Inns of Court men who are her clients: "I will suffer one to keepe me in diet, another in apparel; another in Phisic; another to pay my house rent" (4.1.71–73). One problem with Griffiths's account, which is attentive to the discrepancies between the so-called literary texts and historical documents, is that he looks at courtbooks only between 1559 and 1610, but at literary

texts dating mainly from the 1590s through the seventeenth century, and well into the eighteenth, a broad swath he would never cut with archives. There are courtbooks, in fact, for as late as 1642.

18. Laura Gowing, *Domestic Dangers: Women, Words and Sex in Early Modern London* (Oxford: Clarendon Press, 1996), 59.

19. Ronald B. McKerrow, ed., *The Works of Thomas Nashe*, 5 vols., reprinted from original 1904 edition with additions by F. P. Wilson (Oxford: Blackwell, 1966). All references are to Wilson's updated edition.

20. On Ovid and ovidianism in the late sixteenth century in England, see William Keach, *Elizabethan Erotic Narratives* (New Brunswick, NJ: Rutgers University Press, 1977).

21. See Ian Moulton, "Transmuted into a Woman or Worse: Masculine Gender Identity and Thomas Nashe's 'Choice of Valentines,'" *ELR*, 27 (1997): 57–88; M. L. Stapleton, "Nashe and the Poetics of Obscenity: 'The Choise of Valentines,'" *Classical and Modern Literature: A Quarterly* 12 (1991): 29–48; and recently Katherine Duncan-Jones, "City Limits: Nashe's *Choise of Valentines* and Jonson's *Famous Voyage*," *Review of English Studies* 56 (2005): 247–62. An exception is Jonathan Crewe's *Unredeemed Rhetoric: Thomas Nashe and the Scandal of Authorship* (Baltimore: Johns Hopkins University Press, 1982).

22. There are six known extant copies in miscellanies dating from the first quarter of the seventeenth century, only three of which were known when the text was added to McKerrow. Wilson based his text on the Petyt MS 538, vol. 43 (Inner Temple Library) written in a remarkably clear and beautiful italic hand and still considered the preferred text. It appears among a varied group of literary sundries, all in the same hand, in a larger miscellany. Immediately preceding it are short verses against tobacco and three dramatic monologues in response to a prince's request for advice from his counselors; a dialogue between constancy and inconstancy said to have been spoken before Queen Elizabeth at Woodstock follows it. Also among the poetic materials in the group are several of the Countess of Pembroke's translations of the Psalms and Petrarch's *Trionfi*.

23. Thomas Nashe, *The Choise of Valentines*, ed. John S. Farmer (London: 1899).

24. "It seems always to have been supposed that the Earl of Southampton is meant, but surely Lord Strange is a much more likely person. The dedicatee was, as we learn from the sonnet which follows, a 'sweete flower of matchless Poetrie' and the 'fairest bud the red rose ever bare' i.e., I suppose, a connexion of the royal family. Lord Strange was known as a poet, and was, by his mother, descended from Henry VII"; McKerrow/Wilson, *Works of Thomas Nashe*, 4:141.

25. Ibid., 3:481; and J. B. Steane, *The Unfortunate Traveller and Other Works* (New York: Penguin, 1972).

26. On "betterment" migration, see chapter 1; Twyning, *London Dispossessed*, 55, discusses this passage from Dekker and the practice of preying on new immigrants.

27. Thomas Nashe, *Christs Teares over Jerusalem* (London, 1593; repr., London: Scholar Press, 1970), S2ʳ; as do many of his contemporaries, Nashe argues *in utramque partem*.

28. Thomas Cranley, *Amanda: or the Reformed Whore* (London, 1635), K2ᵛ.

29. Bridewell Hospital Records, Guildhall Library, BCB 4 (microfilm), fols. 64, 46ᵛ, printed in Patricia Crawford and Laura Gowing, *Women's Worlds in Seventeenth-*

Century England (London: Routledge, 2000). Cristine M. Varholy reads this case and others based on her work with the courtbooks in "On Their Backs: Clothing and the Early Modern London Sex Trade" (unpublished manuscript). A longer version of this paper is forthcoming in the *Journal of Popular Culture*.

30. Bridewell Courtbooks, book 3, 279ᵛ, and book 3, 280; I am grateful to Paul Griffiths for this reference and transcription.

31. See Joan Rivière's "Womanliness as Masquerade," in *Psychoanalysis and Female Sexuality*, ed. Hendrik M. Ruitenbeek (New Haven, CT: Yale University Press, 1966).

32. Both Wilson and Steane gloss "lyning" as "leman"; Farmer as "Ladye," but "lyning" is an archaic form of the word "linen" and the speaker is clearly addressing Francis's smock, asking leave to raise it.

33. Moulton, "Transmuted into a Woman or Worse," 81.

34. On Murano glass in England, see Hugh Tait, *The Golden Age of Venetian Glass* (London: British Museum, 1979); Luigi Zecchin, *Vetro e vetrai di Murano*, 3 vols. (Venice: Arsenale, 1987); and W. Patrick McCray, *Glassmaking in Renaissance Venice: The Fragile Craft* (Aldershot: Ashgate, 1999).

35. On the trade in exotic drugs, see Jonathan Gil Harris, " 'I am sailing to my port, uh! uh! uh!': The Pathologies of Transmigration in *Volpone*," *Literature and Medicine* 20 (2001): 109–32.

36. Nashe, *Christs Teares*, W1ʳ.

37. On the international character of prostitution, see the early printed book *Le miroir des plus Belles Courtisanes de ce Temps* (1631), the title page of which claims it appeared as well in Dutch and German, and the first engraving of which shows a man smoking before the fire being shown a picture of a courtesan while another stands nearby looking at portraits in a gallery. The remainder of the book details the women available from all over Europe with portraits in which their costume and headdresses, and so forth, signal their national origins; it includes brief verses on a variety of topics.

38. Crewe, *Unredeemed Rhetoric*, 51–54; Crewe argues that "the poem stages a radical dislocation and consequent loss of ontological security, not only for its speaker, but for love poetry as such."

39. See Moulton, "Transmuted into a Woman or Worse," 71–86.

40. In an excellent study of the poem, Helga Duncan, "Body of Ideology: The Image of the Prostitute in Thomas Nashe's *The Choise of Valentines*," argues that the poet "uses" Francis's body, which performs "on cue for the reader" and is thus disciplined by discourse and poetic operations (unpublished paper).

41. Moulton points out that the only one of the six extant manuscripts of the poem known to have belonged to a woman, British Library Add. MS 10309 [fols. 135ᵛ–139ᵛ] omits all reference to the dildo and ends instead with Francis's sexual frustration; the dildo ending is also missing from two others, Dyce No. 44 and a manuscript in the Rosenbach collection in Philadelphia. Moulton interprets this omission as "a step toward the reductive and perversely utopian male fantasies characteristic of the later genre of pornography"—at once the removal of "the emblem of male anxiety" and the erasure of "a source of female pleasure" ("Transmuted into a Woman or Worse," 87–88).

42. Henri Sauval, *Histoire et recherches des antiquites de la ville de Paris*, 3 vols. (Geneva: Minkoff, 1973), 511–16.

43. The notion of the sturdy beggar "miraculously" healed was also widespread in England and perhaps most famously represented in the Simon Simpcox plot of *2 Henry VI*, in which Simpcox, who pretends to be both blind and lame, is exposed when he is whipped and jumps over a stool and runs away. Stage directions call for "follow and cry, 'A miracle! A miracle!' " On the sturdy beggar, see particularly Carroll, *Fat King, Lean Beggar*.

44. On the relation between charity, urban crime, and the elite, see the work of Craig Dionne and his essay, "Fashioning Outlaws, the Early Modern Rogue and Urban Culture," in *Rogues and Early Modern English Culture*, ed. Craig Dionne and Steve Mentz (Ann Arbor: University of Michigan Press, 2004).

45. M-Françoise Christout, *Le ballet de cour de Louis XIV (1643–1672)* (Paris: Picard, 1967).

46. Pierre de l'Estoile, *Mémoires-journaux* (Paris: Librairie des Bibliophiles, 1880; repr., Paris: Tallandier, 1982), vol. 8, 208.

47. See Susan Bernstein, "Freud's Couch" (unpublished manuscript).

EPILOGUE
PAPERWORK

1. Michael Fischer, "The New Criticism in the New Historicism: The Recent Work of Jerome J. McGann," in *The Cultural Politics of the New Criticism* (Cambridge: Cambridge University Press, 1993), 323. On footnotes, see Anthony Grafton, *The Footnote: A Curious History* (Cambridge, MA: Harvard University Press, 1997).

2. Natalie Zemon Davis, *Fiction in the Archives: Pardon Tales and Their Tellers in Sixteenth-Century France* (Stanford, CA: Polity Press, 1987), 5.

3. John Twyning, "The Literature of the Metropolis," in *A Companion to English Renaissance Literature and Culture*, ed. Michael Hattaway (Oxford: Blackwell, 2000), 119–32.

4. Ibid., 120.

5. See chapter 1, note 22, for a brief bibliography.

6. See Lawrence Manley's *Literature and Culture in Early Modern London* (Cambridge: Cambridge University Press, 1995) for a detailed and encyclopedic survey of urban writing. For a fine, carefully delimited study of London theater, see Janette Dillon, *Theatre, Court and City 1595–1610: Drama and Social Space in London* (Cambridge: Cambridge University Press, 2000).

7. For the most comprehensive review of these debates, see Linda Woodbridge, *Vagrancy, Homelessness, and English Renaissance Literature* (Urbana: University of Illinois Press, 2001).

8. Mark Jancovich, *The Cultural Politics of the New Criticism* (Cambridge: Cambridge University Press, 1993), 142.

9. Jacques Rancière, *Les noms d'histoire* (Paris: Seuil, 1992), translated by Hassan Melehy as *The Names of History: On the Poetics of Knowledge* (Minneapolis: University of Minnesota Press, 1994). Rancière's book is a polemical assault on the claims of the *annales* school. For a survey of *annales* history and the arguments it has provoked among historians, though he does not include Rancière, see Peter Burke, *The French Historical Revolution: The Annales School 1929–89* (Cambridge: Polity Press, 1990).

10. Jules Michelet, *Mother Death: The Journal of Jules Michelet, 1815–1850*, ed. and trans. Edward K. Kaplan (Amherst: University of Massachusetts Press, 1984), 121–22, quoted in Rancière, *Les noms d'histoire*, 62–63.

11. Jacques Derrida, *Mal d'archive* (Paris: Galilee, 1995).

12. See Carolyn Steedman's brilliant "materialist" reading of Derrida's *Archive Fever* in *Dust: The Archive and Cultural History* (New Brunswick, NJ: Rutgers University Press, 2002), 1–37.